Working with Neglected Children and their Families

Safeguarding Children Across Services
Series editors: Carolyn Davies and Harriet Ward

Safeguarding children from abuse is of paramount importance. This series communicates messages for practice from an extensive government-funded research programme designed to improve early recognition of child abuse as well as service responses and interventions. The series addresses a range of forms of abuse, including emotional and physical abuse and neglect, and outlines strategies for effective interagency collaboration, successful intervention and best practice. Titles in the series will be essential reading for practitioners with responsibility for safeguarding children.

Carolyn Davies is Research Advisor at the Thomas Coram Research Unit at the Institute of Education, University of London.

Harriet Ward is Director of the Centre for Child and Family Research and Research Professor at Loughborough University.

Safeguarding Children
Across Services

Effective Working with Neglected Children and their Families

Linking Interventions to Long-term Outcomes

Elaine Farmer and Eleanor Lutman

Jessica Kingsley *Publishers*
London and Philadelphia

First published in 2012
by Jessica Kingsley Publishers
116 Pentonville Road
London N1 9JB, UK
and
400 Market Street, Suite 400
Philadelphia, PA 19106, USA

www.jkp.com

Library of Congress Cataloging in Publication Data
A CIP catalog record for this book is available from the Library of Congress

British Library Cataloguing in Publication Data
Farmer, Elaine, 1949-
 Effective working with neglected children and their families : linking interventions to long-term outcomes / Elaine Farmer and Eleanor Lutman.
   p. cm. -- (Safeguarding children across services)
 Includes bibliographical references and index.
 ISBN 978-1-84905-288-7 (alk. paper)
 1. Social work with children. 2. Family social work. I. Lutman, Eleanor. II. Title.
 HV713.F265 2012
 362.76'53--dc23
                          2012008215

ISBN 978 1 84905 288 7
eISBN 978 0 85700 609 7

Printed and bound in Great Britain

Contents

List of Tables, Figures and Boxes

Acknowledgements

The Department for Children, Schools and Families (now the Department for Education) funded this study as part of the Safeguarding Research Initiative. We are very grateful for this assistance and would particularly like to thank our Research Liaison Officer, Dr Carolyn Davies for her invaluable assistance.

We are extremely grateful to the seven local authorities that allowed us access and introduced us to children and their parents. In particular, their administrative staff made our lives considerably easier by being well organized and extremely efficient. Team managers and social workers made us welcome, facilitated the work and were interested in what we were doing. We are also indebted to the children, young people, their parents, social workers and team managers who talked to us at length and shared their experiences with us.

Regular meetings with our Research Advisory Group were valuable and we would like to thank Jenny Gray from the Department for Education, Olive Stevenson, Harriet Ward, Mike Stein, Judith Harwin, Viv Prior, Lorraine Radford, Jenny Robson from the Who Cares? Trust and Cathy Ashley from the Family Rights Group for giving their valuable time to help us with this work.

We would also like to thank Julie Selwyn for her generous help and advice on the analysis of the children's outcomes, Carol Marks who provided an extremely efficient, fast and accurate transcription of the interview recordings and Melanie Turner who so ably entered the Statistical Package for the Social Sciences (SPSS) data. Lorna Henry and Lynne Harne also carried out some of the interviews for us and we would like to thank them for their assistance.

We have tried to represent accurately the different experiences and views of neglect in this report and also convey some of the complexity of the issues. However, if there are any errors they are solely our responsibility.

1

Introduction

What We Know

At various times in our history, child neglect has been a major focus of public concern, before dropping off the public radar, partly as a result of shifts in the priority accorded to other forms of maltreatment (Parker in Farmer and Owen 1995). In recent years, the number of children registered (or subject to a protection plan) on the grounds of neglect in the UK has shown a steady increase from 39 per cent in 2002 to 44 per cent in 2010 (Department of Education (DFE) 2010a; Department of Health (DH) 2002). Moreover, Radford and her colleagues' study (2011) shows that in the UK neglect is the most prevalent type of family maltreatment for children of all ages. Five per cent of children under 11, 13 per cent of 11–17-year-olds and 16 per cent of 10–24-year-olds had been neglected at some point in their childhoods. In addition, children who have experienced neglect often also feature in serious case reviews (e.g. Brandon *et al* 2008b; Brandon *et al* 2011; Rose and Barnes 2008).

Yet, in spite of the extent of neglect, until recently there had been relatively little research on this subject in the UK (e.g. Bifulco and Moran 1998; Browne and Lynch 1998; Jones and Gupta 1998). Studies from the DfE research programme on Safeguarding have begun to fill this gap, with two relevant research reviews, one on identifying neglected children (Daniel, Taylor and Scott 2011) and the other on neglected adolescents (Rees *et al* 2011).

What has been missing has been research evidence for practitioners about how best to help neglected children in their day to day work and information about children's outcomes some years later. This study addresses these issues by answering the questions: Once neglected children have been identified, do professionals intervene effectively and are children then kept safe? What are the outcomes for children when viewed over a five-year period?

Defining neglect

Definitions of neglect usually point to a child's needs not being met, generally through acts of omission and resulting in harm or impairment (DePanfilis 1999; Dubowitz *et al.* 1993). Researchers argue that the focus of definitions of neglect should be primarily on the experiences of the child rather than the culpability of the parents (Dubowitz *et al.* 2005). *Working Together to Safeguard Children* defines neglect as:

> the persistent failure to meet a child's basic physical and/or psychological needs, likely to result in the serious impairment of the child's health or development. Neglect may occur during pregnancy as a result of maternal substance abuse. Once a child is born, neglect may involve a parent or carer failing to:
>
> o provide adequate food, clothing and shelter (including exclusion from home or abandonment);
>
> o protect a child from physical and emotional harm or danger;
>
> o ensure adequate supervision (including the use of inadequate care givers); or
>
> o ensure access to appropriate medical care or treatment.
>
> It may also include neglect of, or unresponsiveness to, a child's basic emotional needs. (Department for Children, Schools and Families 2010b, p.39)

As indicated by this definition, neglect does not take a single form. Rather it is a heterogeneous category which includes various types of neglect. A number of researchers have attempted to categorize neglect by type (e.g. Minty and Pattinson 1994; Sullivan 2000), resulting in several generally agreed categories of neglect. Physical neglect is likely to be the most familiar and includes deficiencies in the areas of hygiene, warmth, clothing, food and eating (Minty and Pattinson 1994). More specifically, medical neglect concerns the failure to provide or access medical care for the child or delay in doing so (DePanfilis 2006). Emotional neglect involves a lack of responsiveness to the child's needs; carers may be psychologically unavailable and the child's sense of self-worth and positive identity is not promoted (Horwath 2007a; Iwaniec 1995; Minty and Pattinson 1994). Educational or cognitive neglect includes lack of school attendance and lack of stimulation or encouragement of intellectual development (DePanfilis 2006; Horwath 2005a). Finally, supervisory neglect can be defined as failing to ensure that the child is engaged in safe activities in a safe area or failing to provide either adequate supervision or adequate substitute care in the caregiver's absence (DePanfilis 2006; Dubowitz *et al.* 2005; Horwath 2005a, 2007a). These types of neglect are, of course, not mutually exclusive. Minty and Pattinson (1994) consider that physical neglect includes an element of emotional neglect, while the reverse is not always true (see also Cawson *et al.* 2000).

Neglect also varies by severity and chronicity (Dubowitz *et al.* 1993). Chronic neglect is pervasive and ongoing, whereas episodic neglect occurs at intervals, generally at times of crisis (Horwath 2007a). Dubowitz and his colleagues (1993, 2005) suggest that neglect exists on a continuum ranging from the child's needs being fully met (optimal) to not being met at all (grossly inadequate).

The impact on the child

Neglect can have serious long-term effects on children's cognitive, socio-emotional, and behavioural development (Hildyard and Wolfe 2002). The effects appear to be cumulative (Hildyard and Wolfe 2002) and pervasive damage has been shown to children's health (Drotar *et al.* 1990). Neglect has significant neurodevelopmental consequences for young children (De Bellis 2005; Perry 2000) and may potentially affect the development of older children and adolescents (De Bellis 2005). Neglect affects the child's brain development through elevated levels of stress chemicals and negative environmental circumstances such as lack of stimulation, which in turn can affect the child's functioning if development does not take place during 'critical periods' (De Bellis 2005). Neglectful parenting can also affect the essential processes of early attachment and subsequent development. Children who receive care which is unpredictable, rejecting or insensitive are more likely to develop attachments that are less secure (Howe, Dooley and Hinings 2000).

Children's educational achievement and cognitive development can be particularly affected by neglect. Research has shown that neglected children have lower levels of functioning in this area than other groups of children (Eckenrode, Laird and Doris 1993; Erickson, Egeland and Pianta 1989; Kendall-Tackett and Eckenrode 1996; Kurtz *et al.* 1993; Perez and Widom 1994). In addition, younger children with a history of neglect can have poor speech and language problems (Gaudin 1999; Hildyard and Wolfe 2002).

Neglected children have poorer emotional knowledge and are less able to discriminate between different kinds of emotions (Pollak *et al.* 2000; Shipman *et al.* 2005; Sullivan *et al.* 2008). There is also evidence of lower self-esteem (Egeland, Sroufe and Erickson 1983) and higher levels of emotional problems (Erickson *et al.* 1989). Adolescents who have experienced neglect have also shown higher ratings on measures of depression and hopelessness and are more prone to suicide (Arata *et al.* 2007). Neglect also impacts on children's social development with evidence that neglected children are more withdrawn and socially isolated and less socially competent (Crittenden 1992; Dubowitz *et al.* 1993; Erickson *et al.* 1989; Herrenkohl *et al.* 1991).

Studies have shown that neglected children tend to be more aggressive than non-neglected children (Erickson *et al.* 1989; George and Main 1979; Herrenkohl *et al.* 1991; Knutson *et al.* 2005; Kotch *et al.* 2008) and are also more unco-operative and non-compliant (Egeland *et al.* 1983; Erickson *et al.* 1989). Neglect has also been linked with later delinquency, offending and violent behaviour (Smith, Ireland and Thornberry 2005; Thornberry, Ireland and Smith 2001).

Fatalities appear to result from neglect at similar rates to those from physical abuse (Margolin 1990; see also Bridge Child Care Consultancy Service 1995; Laming 2003). In addition, neglect is particularly associated with a high risk of co-occurrence with other kinds of maltreatment and is most likely to reoccur (Farmer and Owen 1995; Farmer *et al.* 2011; Hindley, Ramchandani and Jones 2006).

Disability and neglect

Research from the US (Sullivan and Knutson 2000) has shown that disabled children are 3.4 times more likely than others to suffer maltreatment and 3.8 times more likely to be neglected. They are also more likely to experience multiple forms of maltreatment and multiple episodes. Disabled children are judged to be more vulnerable to maltreatment (Westcott 1993) because they may experience greater physical and social isolation, a lack of control over their lives and bodies, greater dependency on others which can be exploited (Sobsey and Doe 1991) and problems in communication (including a lack of vocabulary to describe abuse in some alternative communication systems). Disabled children are also more likely than others to experience respite care or go to residential schools (Abbott, Morris and Ward 2001) where they may be isolated and vulnerable to abuse from adults (Morris 1998a, 1998b; Paul and Cawson 2002; Stuart and Baines 2004a, 2004b; Sullivan, Vernon and Scanlon 1987; Utting *et al.* 1997) and peers (Paul, Cawson and Paton 2004) or may suffer harsh regimes (Howlin and Clements 1994; Smith 1992), with little attention from local education and children's services (Abbott *et al.* 2001; NSPCC 2003). Disabled children may also experience additional types of abuse, such as over-medication (Kennedy 1995; Westcott and Cross 1996).

Causes and contributing factors

Much of the research on neglect (principally from the US) has focused on its causes and consequences. For example, Gaudin (1993) and Crittenden (1999) suggest that child neglect occurs as a result of a complex interaction between a range of psychosocial and environmental factors, which impair parenting and parent–child relationships, including poverty, domestic violence, low self-esteem, social isolation, mental health problems and substance misuse (see also Bifulco and Moran 1998; Christensen *et al.* 1994; Cleaver, Unell and Aldgate 2011; Ethier, Lacharite and Couture 1995; Farmer and Owen 1995; Stone 1998).

While most poor families do not neglect their children, the majority of neglectful families which come to the attention of children's services, partly because they seek assistance (Burke *et al.* 1998), are poor (Bifulco and Moran 1998; Stevenson 2007). Cawson's study (2002) supports the association between neglect and lower socio-economic class and Dubowitz (1994) suggests that some forms of physical neglect may be directly attributable to poverty. However, while poverty may be associated with an increased likelihood of neglect, it does not predetermine neglect and McSherry (2004) suggests the relationship between the two should be viewed as circular and interdependent.

Neglecting parents report less informal support and see their neighbourhoods as less helpful than others (Gaudin 1993; Hartley 1989; McGlone, Park and Roberts 1996; Polansky *et al.* 1985; Thoburn, Wilding and Watson 2000) and some are excluded from local networks. However, increased informal support for these families may not be the solution as negative interactions with critical relatives are not helpful (Gaudin 1993).

There is some research that provides support for a link between the parent's childhood experiences and maltreatment of their own children. Jinseok (2009) found that parents who reported having been neglected or physically abused in their childhood were more likely to report their own neglectful or physically abusive parenting behaviour than those who had not. However, others caution that the nature of these relationships is somewhat uncertain and a less deterministic view should be taken which recognizes other important influences (Gaudin 1993; Stevenson 2007).

The experience of witnessing domestic violence is potentially very damaging to children (Hester *et al.* 2007; Radford and Hester 2006). It has been found to be present for almost half of children suffering or likely to suffer significant harm (Thoburn and Lewis 1996) and in over half (52%) of children on the child protection register (Farmer and Owen 1995). Domestic violence features fairly frequently in cases of child neglect. Wilding and Thoburn (1997) and Horwath and Bishop (2001) found the presence of domestic violence in around a fifth of cases where neglect was also present, while Antle and colleagues (2007) and McGuigan and Pratt (2001) found higher occurrence rates (29% and 40% respectively). Interestingly, Antle and colleagues also found that domestic violence was associated with more severe neglect and a limited social support network for the family. However, domestic violence was not systematically addressed in child welfare case plans (Antle *et al.* 2007).

Parental mental health problems can lead to a deterioration in parenting capacity and the failure to meet the child's physical and emotional needs (Minty 2005). Child maltreatment has been shown to be associated with parental mental health problems and more specifically depression (Kotch *et al.* 1995; Sheppard 1997). Studies have found a link between these difficulties and physical neglect (Carter and Myers 2007) and child neglect more generally (Ethier *et al.* 1995).

An estimated 250,000 to 350,000 children in the UK have parents who are problematic drug users, which is about one child for every drug user (Advisory Council on the Misuse of Drugs (ACMD) 2003). Harm to children through parental drugs misuse can begin before the child is born and there is substantial evidence of the impact of drugs on unborn children (ACMD 2003; Chasnof and Lowder 1999; Walker and Glasgow 2005), resulting in withdrawal symptoms and distressed behaviour when the child is born. In relation to alcohol problems, around 1.3 million children live with parents who are thought to misuse alcohol (Prime Minister's Strategy Unit 2004). As with drugs misuse, the mother's alcohol intake can impact on the child in utero (Cleaver *et al.* 2011) and, at the extreme end, can cause foetal alcohol syndrome.

Parental substance misuse is prevalent among families who come to the attention of children's services. The ACMD (2003) reports that, on average, parental substance misuse featured in 25 per cent of cases of children on the child protection register. Other studies that investigated the prevalence of substance misuse in families known to children's services report figures ranging from 20 per cent to 70 per cent, depending on the sample size and point of contact with children's services (Cleaver *et al.* 2011; Farmer *et al.* 2011; Forrester 2000; Harwin *et al.* 2003; Ryan,

Harwin and Chamberlain 2006). Research by Forrester and Harwin (2006) suggests that more serious child welfare concerns arise in cases that involve parental substance misuse. Sadly, parental substance misuse problems also feature in serious case reviews (Brandon *et al.* 2008b; Reder and Duncan 1999; Reder, Duncan and Gray 1993), highlighting that these difficulties can put children at serious risk of harm or death.

Parental substance misuse can impact on parenting capacity as the parent is unable to focus consistently on the needs of the child. This can result in neglect, and studies have shown an association between parental substance misuse and neglect (Chaffin, Kelleher and Hollenberg 1996; Kelleher *et al.* 1994). Older children report the significant impact of parental substance misuse on their lives and can often end up caring for themselves and their parents (Bancroft *et al.* 2004).

The presence of parental learning disability is associated with neglect through omission (Tymchuk 1992; Tymchuk and Andron 1990) and concerns about neglect are the most common form of concern raised about children cared for by parents with learning difficulties, compared to other forms of abuse (McConnell and Llewellyn 2002). Neglect is more likely if the mother's resources, knowledge, skills and experiences are insufficient to meet the needs of her child (Tymchuk 1992). It is thought that parents with learning difficulties are more likely than others to have their children removed from their care (Emerson *et al.* 2005; McConnell and Llewellyn 2002; Tarleton, Ward and Horwath 2006). However, there is a high prevalence of psychiatric problems, deprivation and social disadvantage in the population of parents with learning difficulties (McConnell and Llewellyn 2002), so intellectual disability may not be the only factor contributing to the parents' difficulties.

Black and minority ethnic (BME) families may have different experiences to those of white families and circumstances may impact on them in different ways. For example, BME families are more likely than white families to live in poverty (Department of Health 2000) and this is likely to increase the stressors on these families. In some families, difficulties may be compounded by the impact of migration and trauma. BME children also have different experiences of the care and child protection systems compared to white children. Barn (2006) suggests that BME children are more likely to be subject to a child protection plan than white children. However, Thoburn and colleagues (2000) found that BME children were less likely to be the subject of a child protection enquiry (section 47) and more likely to be provided with an assessment of need. In relation to neglect, the same study found that BME children were less likely to be referred for neglect compared with white children and that emotional neglect was more likely to be recorded as emotional abuse in BME families than others (Thoburn *et al.* 2000).

The gender of the parents is another significant issue to consider in relation to child neglect. Neglect has been found generally to be conceived in terms of the absence of maternal care even when fathers were present (Farmer and Owen 1995; see also Tanner and Turney 2003). Work often then focuses on mothers and bypasses father figures, even when they present risks to the children, often because of domestic violence (Farmer and Owen 1998). Dubowitz and colleagues (2000) found that when fathers were more involved, had a longer duration of involvement and felt that they were more effective parents, there was less neglect.

However, a recent review of the literature on helping and noticing the neglected child emphasizes that no one factor predicts neglect (Daniel *et al.* 2011). Rather the ecological model, which encompasses a constellation of factors, is a powerful framework for helping to understand which children might be at greater risk of neglect (Daniel *et al.* 2011).

Case management

While the existing literature shows the multiple contributors to neglect and its negative impact on children, much less is known about the practice issues for professionals involved in working with neglect or about case management in relation to neglect.

The decision to refer concerns about neglect is a complex task and Horwath (2007b) suggests that other factors may influence a practitioner's decision to refer in cases of neglect, in addition to the nature of the concerns. These factors include the practitioner's perception of what comprises neglect, their interpretation of their role and the views of their colleagues and manager, the perception of social work services and of the benefits of referral, and their own personal feelings such as fear, guilt and anxiety. Using vignettes, Stone (1998) found that there was relatively little relationship between how dangerous practitioners felt situations were, and whether they would make a referral.

Once cases are known to children's services, it can be difficult to decide when compulsory intervention is necessary to safeguarded children (Allsop and Stevenson 1995; Gardner 2008; Minty and Pattinson 1994), where improvements are not forthcoming within the children's timescales (Farmer and Moyers 2008; Farmer and Owen 1995; Farmer *et al.* 2011; Ward *et al.* 2003) or where parents sabotage work (Crittenden 1999). Lack of co-operation from parents can make intervention difficult (Farmer *et al.* 2011; Henry 2008; Stone 1998), for example Farmer and Owen (1998) found that when children were registered, parents often hotly disputed the view that they were neglectful. Problems can be compounded in long-term cases by not tackling hostile and unco-operative families which in turn can compromise children's safety and well-being (Brandon *et al.* 2005; Stanley and Goddard 2002).

There is also some evidence that neglect cases may be treated differently to those involving other types of maltreatment when they come to the attention of children's services. For example, referrals for neglect and emotional abuse have been found to be less often investigated or subject to a child protection conference than other referrals (Gibbons, Conroy and Bell 1995). The main recent UK study on neglect and emotional abuse by Thoburn and her colleagues (2000) has provided useful information on the sifting of *referred* cases prior to the introduction of the assessment framework. This study found that a quarter of all referrals to children's services were for neglect, with many leading to little or no intervention. Thoburn and her colleagues (2000) also found that when initial assessments were undertaken with families of children referred because of concerns about emotional abuse and neglect, they tended to be low key and to concentrate on 'risks' rather than on the needs of the children.

Other difficulties in working with child neglect include: establishing appropriate thresholds for intervention in the absence of a 'trigger' event and the view that neglect is hard to establish in court (Dingwall, Eekelaar and Murray 1983; Farmer and Owen 1995; Tanner and Turney 2003). The often long-term nature of neglect cases brings associated case management difficulties due to the difficulties in working with neglect in a clear, systematic way (Gardner 2008). Families where there are concerns about neglect can become 'revolving door' cases where they are opened in response to a specific concern, limited or no work is done with the family and the case is closed only to be reopened after further concerns are raised (Department of Health 1995; Parton and Mathews 2001; Thoburn *et al.* 2000). Social work teams under pressure due to high workloads may take an approach towards child neglect which 'underwhelms' rather than 'overwhelms' workers and focus on immediate safety issues rather than ongoing concerns (Horwath 2005b). In an analysis of serious case reviews, Brandon and colleagues noted that many of the cases where neglect had been an issue had been known to children's services for many years but 'agencies appeared to avoid or rebuff parents through closing the case, re-assessing, referring on, or through offering a succession of workers' (Brandon *et al.* 2008b, p.324).

It can be difficult to maintain an accurate perspective on the extent of difficulties because of the habituation associated with long-term work (Farmer and Parker 1991), and in some cases parents' feelings of hopelessness can affect workers (Stevenson 2005). Social workers may deal with these feeling of hopelessness by focusing on the present and putting aside knowledge from the past, termed the 'start again syndrome' by Brandon and colleagues (2008b). Consequently, pieces of information may be treated discretely, which together present a more worrying picture (Reder *et al.* 1993). Workers may also apply the 'rule of optimism' (Dingwall *et al.* 1983) in which, in a liberal society, workers use considerations of cultural relativism and parents' natural love to offset and excuse adverse parental behaviour. Reluctance to jeopardize an established relationship with a parent may also affect how cases of neglect are managed (see also Corby 1987). In this way a worker's approach to the case may be influenced by a 'fixed view' or 'pervasive belief' about the case which leads to selective interpretation of information and difficulty in acknowledging contrary information (Haringey Local Safeguarding Children Board 2009; Reder *et al.* 1993). For all these reasons social workers require effective supervision (Howe *et al.* 1999).

Intervention

Many of the studies of intervention in cases of neglect are from the US or draw on small samples in the UK. These studies contain some general messages. For example, it is clear that the multiple nature of parents' problems require varied interventions, often long-term (Gaudin 1993; Stevenson 2007; Thoburn *et al.* 2000) and tailored to individual needs, including services directed at specific parental problems such as substance misuse (DePanfilis 1999; Dubowitz *et al.* 1993; Macdonald 2005). Some US research has suggested that cognitive-behavioural interventions including parent training, social skills training and stress management may be effective with parents who neglect their children (DePanfilis 1999) and widening social support for parents is considered important (Daro 1988). Research from the US has also indicated that multi-dimensional programmes which include home-based intervention may be useful (DePanfilis and Dubowitz 2005; Ethier *et al.* 2000). In the UK, intensive family support based on sustained professional relationships has been found to be particularly effective in cases of neglect (Tunstill, Blewett and Meadows 2009). The Nurse-Family Partnership programme (Olds 2006) which involves intensive home visiting for vulnerable, first time, young parents was piloted in the UK, found to be successful (Barnes *et al.* 2008, 2011) and has now been expanded. Iwaniec and McSherry (2002) highlight the importance of addressing parent–child interaction patterns to prevent longer-term attachment problems for the child. In addition, neglected children also need direct services to help them to overcome cognitive, academic and social deficits (DePanfilis 1999). A recent systematic review into treatment for child neglect found that very few studies met the criteria for inclusion and only five were rated as having good or fair internal validity (Allin, Wathen and MacMillan 2005). Four of these studies evaluated treatments for victims of child neglect, such as play therapy and a day treatment programme, and one further study evaluated multisystemic therapy. These treatments varied in their efficacy. Two of the play therapy programmes showed sustained gains on several measures such as peer interaction and co-operation but another did not result in lasting improvement for neglected children. Multisystemic therapy appeared to result in fewer negative parent–child interactions, while the comparison group who received parent training showed a reduction in social problems. However, in practice there are few specialist interventions in the UK for neglected children and their parents, and little information about which combinations of routine interventions provided through children's services departments are most effective.

In the absence of evaluations of interventions for neglect in the UK, commentators have contributed ideas about case management, many of which need to be tested. It has been suggested that comprehensive assessments (Department of Health 2000; Department of Health, Department for Education and Employment and Home Office 2000) require observations of parent–child relationships (Tanner and Turney 2003), attempts to involve fathers (DePanfilis 1999) and interviews with children about their perceptions of family life (Bridge Child Care Consultancy Service 1995; Stevenson 2007), while the assessment of neglect requires attention to information from a range of agencies, as each may hold separate pieces that together show the whole picture (Munro 1999; Sanders, Colton and Roberts 1999). Because such assessments may take time, there is the risk that practitioners will be influenced more by their initial impressions than by new information (Farmer 1999; Harran 2002; Munro 1999). In addition, social work tools such as the Signs of Safety approach (Turnell and Edwards 1997) and the Graded Care Profile (Srivastava, Stewart and Ayres 2005) may prove useful aids to the assessment process.

The value of a therapeutic helping alliance with the social worker has also been emphasized (Dore and Alexander 1996; Gaudin 1993; Jones 1996), allowing for a 'managed dependency' with the parent(s) (Daniel 1998). However, much less attention has been paid to the balance between control and support that would optimize intervention (Farmer and Parker

1991) or how risks are reassessed over time (Farmer 1999; Farmer and Owen 1995).

Relevant research on reunification

Much of the research on reunification does not distinguish between children who are looked after for reasons relating to neglect and those looked after for other reasons, but a few studies do make specific reference to the influence of neglect on patterns of return and outcome.

Factors associated with the likelihood of reunification

Most studies that have examined the impact of maltreatment on patterns of reunification have found that children placed as a result of neglect are reunified more slowly than those placed for other reasons (Courtney, Piliavin and Wright 1997; Courtney and Wong 1996; Davis, Landsverk and Newton 1997; Glisson, Bailey and Post 2000; Harris and Courtney 2003). Davis and her colleagues (1997) found that those placed as a result of neglect were likely to remain in care five times longer than children who were in care for other reasons, while one study (Glisson *et al.* 2000) found that pre-adolescent children placed because of neglect were more likely to return home than neglected adolescents. More specifically, some studies have found that children placed for neglect are likely to remain in care for longer than those placed because of physical abuse (Farmer and Parker 1991; Wells and Guo 1999) or sexual abuse (Courtney 1994) or either of these (Grogan-Taylor 2001). However, two studies have contrary findings, with children placed because of physical abuse being reunified more slowly than those who were in care for neglect (Goerge 1990; Lewandowski and Pierce 2002).

Factors associated with return breakdown

Neglect as the presenting problem and limited parental skills have been shown in three American studies to be associated with disrupted returns (Courtney 1995; Davis, English and Landsverk 1993; Hess, Folaron and Jefferson 1992). However, although in our reunification study neglect was not found to be associated with either return disruption or the quality of the reunions, returns were more likely to disrupt and to be or poor quality when there was evidence of poor parenting skills prior to the return (Farmer *et al.* 2011). A number of other factors which are often also associated with child neglect have been found to be associated with the breakdown of reunification. For example, in the US, social and environmental variables have been shown to be associated with return breakdown, including poverty, exposure to drugs and inadequate housing (Courtney 1994, 1995; Jones 1998; Schuerman, Rzepnicki and Johnson 1994). Reunification disruption has also been shown to occur more often with single parent families, where isolation and poverty may lower parental effectiveness (Schuerman *et al.* 1994), and is associated with social isolation and lack of support from the extended family, friends and neighbours (Farmer *et al.* 2011; Festinger 1994; Terling 1999), as well as with the number and/or severity of parental problems (Hess *et al.* 1992; Jones 1998). Packman and Hall in the UK (1998) found that breakdown of return for accommodated children was more likely when the initial separation was because of parental mental illness, alcohol or drugs misuse (see also Hess *et al.* 1992). However, none of these parental difficulties were significant predictors of return breakdown in our reunification study, although lack of parental alcohol and drug misuse was associated with better return quality (Farmer *et al.* 2011). Since many of these factors are associated with child neglect, it may be that returns are less successful when children are looked after for reasons of neglect than for other reasons, or that some aspects of neglect do predict poorer outcomes, while others do not.

Gaps in knowledge

It can therefore be seen that there is a lack of research that focuses specifically on neglect and a tendency for research studies to fail to distinguish between neglect and other forms of maltreatment. However, the evidence that is available indicates that the effects of neglect on children can be highly deleterious. In particular, there is little UK evidence on the management of cases of neglect or on interventions specifically for neglected children and their families, with much of the available information drawn from practice ideas rather than research. There is even less research on the outcomes over time of neglected children known to children's services.

Not only has there been very little research in the UK on how children's services departments and other professionals deal with children where the major concern is neglect, but there is even less information on neglect that has been considered sufficiently serious to necessitate children being looked after for a period, before they can be returned to their parent(s). This study therefore aims to fill these gaps in our knowledge by examining the management and outcomes of a cohort of neglected children longitudinally (all of whom have been returned to a parent from care). This is important since children who have been neglected and their parents often require long-term work, and many of the consequences of neglect and of earlier decisions and case management will only become evident as time goes on.

2

Study Aims and Methods

Aims of this book

This book is based on a major study which followed up a cohort of neglected children who had been looked after and reunified with a parent. It had three broad aims:

1. To examine the case management, interventions and outcomes of a consecutive sample of neglected children (who had been looked after and were all returned home during a set year), from the point of first referral to children's services departments until five years from their return home.

2. To investigate which factors (e.g. child or family factors, case management, services or informal supports) are related to outcomes for children at the five-year follow-up point.

3. To explore through in-depth interviews with social workers how far parents and children engage with professional interventions and whether there are particular issues in cases of neglect which make the work more complex or demanding.

Design of the study

The research builds on data collected for a study on reunification carried out by the first author (Farmer *et al.* 2011). This study followed up a consecutive sample of 180 children, aged 0 to 14, who were all returned home to a parent or parent figure (stepparent/parent's partner or adoptive parent) from care in six local authorities during a one-year period.[1] The cases had then been followed up for two years. Of these 180 children, 121 had experienced some form of neglect before returning home. The current study employed a catch-up prospective design whereby this subsample of neglected children were followed up for a further three years, which was *five years* from the original return.

Families were contacted to inform them about the study using the same procedures that were used in the reunification study and their consent to access the case files was sought. We were unable to follow up 11 of the 121 children because either access was denied (4) or closed files could not be located (7).

This subsample of 110 children was then supplemented with an additional sample of 28 children from one new local authority (and from further cases identified in two of the six original authorities), using exactly the same sampling frame as had been used in the reunification study. This made a full sample of 138 children.

However, for 13 cases in the sample we were unable to view the files a second time but were able to collect some key information about the case from social worker interviews or we could use the outcome data from the reunification study because the case had been closed since our previous follow-up. There will therefore be occasions where these cases will be excluded from the analysis.

Data on the full sample of 138 children were collected by a review of their case files five years from the original return and by means of semi-structured interviews with social work practitioners in the current or recently closed cases, together with a small number of interviews with parents and children.

The study therefore focuses on neglected children who had been returned home from care and who may therefore be at the more serious end of the spectrum.

The sample of 138 children was drawn from seven local authorities: one London borough, two metropolitan districts, one unitary authority

---

1   The first or only return during that period was selected as the return we focused on and was defined as:

Return home to a parent or parent figure (stepparent/parent's partner or adoptive parent) when the child was either discharged from care or placed with parents under a supervision, interim or care order.

The following children were excluded from the sample:

- children aged 15 or over at the time of the return
- children who had only been looked after for six weeks or less, *unless* they re-entered care within one year
- children who were looked after only as an agreed respite arrangement.

and three county shire authorities. Authorities were located in London, the Midlands, the South East and the South West and three of them had a substantial proportion of black and minority ethnic (BME) children.

The 138 children (19% of whom were BME) came from 104 families. Eighty-one children had no siblings in the study but there were 24 sibling groups in the sample. The children returned home at an average age of eight years old. A quarter of the children (26%) returned home under the age of five, 28 per cent were aged between five and nine and the remaining 46 per cent were aged 10 to 14. There was little difference between the local authorities in the average age at return.

Interview sample

Thirty-six professionals from six local authority areas were interviewed in cases that were open or had recently been closed. Of these, three were team managers, four were senior practitioners, 18 were social workers, one was a family support worker and the remaining ten were leaving care workers or young people's advisors. They provided information on 50 children in the sample.

Twenty-seven of the interviewees were women and nine men, with the majority (53%) in the 41-plus age group. Sixteen per cent were younger than 30 and 31 per cent were between 30 and 40. Twenty-eight (78%) held a social work qualification and of these, 43 per cent had more than 10 years post-qualification experience, 14 per cent had between six and ten years, 32 per cent had three to five years' experience and the remaining 11 per cent had worked as social workers for two years or less.

There were difficulties in making contact with parents and children for the purpose of interviewing them. Given the length of time of the follow-up, we found that families had often moved from where they had been living, and/or changed their telephone number (especially mobile phone numbers), or simply never answered any calls. If the case was open and we had managed to interview the allocated worker, we asked for their help in contacting the families, but since many of the cases (52%) were open to leaving care workers, they were not in touch with the parents and often had difficulties in engaging the young people themselves. Once spoken to, families were often keen to participate in the research, but because of the tremendous difficulties in contacting families, the numbers eventually interviewed were considerably fewer than had originally been planned.

Interviews were conducted with six parents. Three interviews were held with mothers, one with a father, one with a mother and her partner, and one with a father and the child's grandmother. Six interviews were conducted with young people, three of whose parents we had also interviewed. At the time of the interviews, the young people were aged between 11 and 19 years old. Three were boys and three were girls.

Prior to the interviews, details of the study were explained again and the researcher clarified the confidentiality agreement, explaining that it did not extend to any new or current child protection concerns. Written consent to conduct the interview was then obtained. It was made clear to parents and children that they could take a break or stop the interview at any time and that they could 'pass' on any questions they did not want to answer. Interviews were then coded directly onto the interview schedules and were also digitally recorded or taped (with consent). Children received a £10 gift voucher and a certificate as a thank-you for their time, while parents received a £10 gift voucher and £10 to cover any expenses they had incurred. Following the interviews, researcher ratings were completed and the digital/tape recordings of the interviews were transcribed.

SUPPORTING PARENTS AND CHILDREN
The interviews could be emotive and provision was made for parents, children and researchers to access support if they desired. Separate 'help and advice lines' sheets were compiled for parents and children, which listed national websites and helpline numbers and their hours of operation. These were given to all the parents and children at the conclusion of the interviews.

Measures
CASE FILE REVIEW SCHEDULE AND CASE SUMMARIES
The case files of the 138 children were reviewed using a structured schedule. This included details of the neglect the child had experienced before returning home, data on the final three-year period and on the management of the case from the first referral to the five-year follow-up point.

The schedule included some researcher ratings, including those related to children's outcomes in terms of the child's overall well-being at the five-year follow-up point (or the point at which the case was closed if earlier) (see Chapter 9). These ratings were informed by all the information on file relating to children's educational, health and emotional and behavioural development, combined with information from the summaries. Extensive discussion informed the definition of the categories. The same field researcher undertook all the initial ratings and the few areas of uncertainty were discussed with the other researcher until agreement was reached.

A detailed narrative summary was also written for each child, including an analysis of the management of the case as a whole. This was in addition to the detailed case summaries of each child's history that we had from the reunification study, which covered events before the original return and up to the two-year follow-up point.

LIMITATIONS

Case file information has some limitations. Some of these relate to data that are not routinely recorded on files (for example receipt of benefits) and others to information that is found on some but not other files, so that there may be missing data on particular issues. In addition, case records are by definition the social workers' constructions of events. Nonetheless, we found them to be a rich source of information about the children, parents and returns and they allow access to the whole range of the population under study, which is not possible with interviews. This study aimed to capitalize on the strengths of these two sources of information.

In total, 102 of the 138 (74%) cases in the study had been open at some point during the final three-year period, so we had the most information about children receiving long-term services and somewhat less for closed cases, which had sometimes been more successful.

INTERVIEW SCHEDULES

Semi-structured interviews were developed using open questions to yield qualitative data with the addition of a small number of quantitative variables.

SOCIAL WORKER INTERVIEW

The main focus of this interview was to elicit information on how the child was currently faring and the social worker's involvement in the case. Social workers were asked about the child's current placement or return, services that had been provided, their work with the parents and their general views of neglect.

Because it was very rare for a child to have the same social worker throughout the whole of the five-year follow-up period, these interviews do not relate to the same time periods as the case file reviews and are analysed separately.

PARENT INTERVIEW

The parents were asked about the current return if children were at home, or their current placement if living elsewhere, and any other recent returns. Details of any assistance from children's services were sought, including which services were seen as helpful. Their views of the sorts of parental behaviour that they would consider to be neglectful were also gained.

CHILD/YOUNG PERSON INTERVIEW

As a number of the young people had already moved to independent living, two interview schedules were developed, which were to be used depending on whether the young person was living at home, with another caregiver or was living independently.

The interviews with children and young people living at home or with another caregiver focused on: their family; their current living situation; the last time they were with a parent, if they were not at home; and assistance from children's services and other professionals, including which services were seen as helpful. They were also asked to reflect back on things that had happened in their lives and for their views about neglect.

The interviews with young people living independently had broadly the same structure but also included questions on employment and training, financial issues, psychological health and girlfriend/boyfriend/partner relationships.

REFERENCE GROUPS

The development of the parent and child interview schedules was informed by two separate reference groups, one with parents and the other with young people. We also piloted the interview schedules and measures with these groups.

Procedures

SETTING UP THE STUDY

Approval for the study was obtained from the Ethics Committee at the School for Policy Studies, University of Bristol and from the Association of Directors of Children's Services. The researchers were also subject to enhanced Criminal Records Bureau checks and a Privileged Access Agreement was obtained from the Department of Constitutional Affairs so that court papers held on file could be read.

ANALYSING THE DATA

In the analyses small variations in sample size across tables are not commented on unless the reasons for the missing data are important to the analysis. Relationships were considered to be statistically significant where $p<.05$, that is any association described as significant indicates a relationship beyond the 5 per cent level of probability, although a more stringent test of $p<.02$ was used in the analysis of factors relating to outcomes. All statistical analyses were undertaken using the Statistical Package for the Social Sciences (SPSS).

In what follows, the names and some of the details of the individuals who are described have been changed in order to preserve confidentiality.

Terminology

To aid the reader, the following are a list of terms that will be used in the book and their definitions.

Return – return home to a parent or parent figure (stepparent/parent's partner or adoptive parent) when the child was either discharged from care or placed with parents under a supervision, interim or care order.

The original return – the first return to either parent that occurred during the period when we selected the cases.

The two-year follow-up – exactly two years from the start date of the original return (whether or not it had ended before that point).

The final three-year period – from the date of the end of the two-year follow-up to exactly five years after the start date of the original return.

The five-year follow-up – the period of five years from the start date of the original return, which included both the two-year follow-up and the final three-year period.

Now that the aims and methods used in the study have been outlined, we begin by considering the early experiences of the children in the study.

3

The Children's Early Experiences

This chapter describes the characteristics of the children in the case file sample and their experiences before returning home, including previous periods in care. It covers their parents' difficulties and details of the neglect that the children had experienced to provide a deeper context for later consideration of their outcomes.

The sample

The characteristics of the children in the sample are shown in Table 3.1.

As can be seen, 59 per cent of the children were boys and 19 per cent were from a black or minority ethnic background, with the majority of these children of mixed ethnicity (19 of 26). Fifty-seven children had siblings in the sample and the children came from 104 families.

The parents' histories

The childhoods of the children's parents had often been troubled and almost half (49%) of the 104 birth mothers had experienced abuse or neglect when they were growing up, while more than a quarter (26%) had been in care themselves. Information about the 112 birth fathers was too sparse to be reliable.

Three-fifths of the mothers (59%) had their first child while they were still teenagers and a quarter (27%) had already had children taken into care or adopted (with 15% permanently removed) before a file was opened for the child in the study. A further third (36%) of the families had been involved with children's services (although had not had children removed) before concerns arose about the child. Thus, almost two-thirds (63%) of the families were closely involved with children's social care before the children in the study were referred.

Table 3.1 Characteristics of the case file sample

No. of children	138 from 104 families
Gender	82 boys (59%); 56 girls (41%)
Age at the start of the return	26% aged 0–4 years; 28% aged 5–9 years; 46% aged 10–14 years Range 0 –14 years, Mean 8.07 years (sd 4.56)
Age at five-year follow-up point	26% aged 5–9 years; 28% aged 10–14 years; 46% aged 15–19 years Range 5–19 years, mean 13.07 years (sd 4.56)
Ethnicity	112 White (81%); 19 Mixed Ethnicity (14%); 7 Black African/Black Caribbean/Asian/South American (5%)
Nationality	136 British (99%); 2 other (1%)*
Disability	17 children had a physical disability (12%)
Special educational needs	26 children had a statement of special educational needs (23% of children aged 4+ at the start of the return)
Siblings	57 children had siblings in the sample (42%)

* Of which one was asylum seeking.

By the time they entered care before the return on which we focused, most children (89%) had experienced poor parenting, characterized by inconsistent discipline, aggressive or unresponsive parenting, a lack of stimulation or low levels of warmth and affection. Domestic violence, substance misuse or 'concerning sexual activity' (such as prostitution, open use of pornography or having multiple partners) featured in a high proportion of the families (87%), as shown in Table 3.2. These behaviours often co-existed and there was evidence of two or more of them in over two-thirds (70%) of the families (which was considerably higher than the 50% occurrence of two or more such behaviours in the reunification study (Farmer *et al.* 2011)). Domestic violence and substance misuse were especially likely to occur together (40%).

Table 3.2 Parental behaviours

Behaviour	Percentage of families (n=104)
Domestic violence	**74**
Domestic violence only	17
Domestic violence and substance misuse	40
Domestic violence and concerning sexual activity	3
Domestic violence, substance misuse and concerning sexual activity	14
Substance misuse (alcohol or drugs misuse)	**66**
Substance misuse only (alcohol only 4%, drugs only 4%, both 2%)	10
Substance misuse and domestic violence	*40*
Substance misuse and concerning sexual activity	2
Substance misuse, domestic violence and concerning sexual activity	*14*
Concerning sexual activity	**19**
Concerning sexual activity only	1
Concerning sexual activity and domestic violence	*2*
Concerning sexual activity and substance misuse	*2*
Concerning sexual activity, domestic violence and substance misuse	*14*

In 44 per cent of the families a parent had mental health problems. (This figure is an underestimate as it only includes children who had lived with a parent with mental health difficulties before entry to care and who had returned to the same parent.)

Parental relationships were often unstable and by the time they entered care few children had been living with both birth parents (13% of families); a fifth (19%) had been with one parent and their partner, almost two-thirds (63%) had lived in single-parent families (usually with lone mothers), while a small number of families (5%) included grandparents or other relatives.

History of children's services involvement

Professional concerns about the children usually began early. Over half (56%) of the children were first referred to children's services before the age of two, with almost a third (32%) referred before or immediately after their birth, due to concerns about their mother's mental health or parenting ability.

Concerns about the care of the children continued into their pre-school years and three-quarters (76%) had been referred to children's services before they started school (see Figure 3.1). Two years nine months was the average age at first referral.

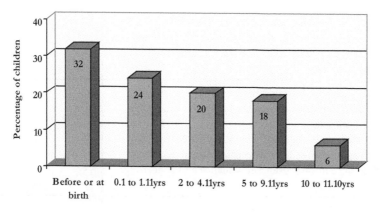

Figure 3.1 Age at which children first referred to children's services (n=136)

Three-fifths of the children (58%) were subject to a child protection plan when they entered care (then called child protection registration) or had been previously. In addition, child protection concerns had been raised about most (78%) of the 58 children who had not been on plans, often leading to child protection investigations and child protection conferences.

A fifth (22%) of the children had already been subject to a care, interim or supervision order at some point. Not surprisingly, concerns about their siblings had been raised in most cases (91%).

The children's early experiences in care

When tensions in the home had got to breaking point or children were considered to be at risk of significant harm, they often entered care. Half of the children (51%) had been looked after once or more before the care period immediately before the return (including a fifth who had been in care or accommodation twice or more already) and a few (13%) had been in respite care. As many as half (52%) of the children had first entered care before the age of five. A fifth of the children had already spent between one and five years in the care system.

Neglect and other maltreatment

All of the children in the study had been neglected before going into care. Indeed, almost a fifth (17%) had been neglected before they were born, that is to say their mothers had misused alcohol or drugs during pregnancy, had failed to seek ante-natal care or in other ways put the unborn baby at risk.

Neglect is a heterogeneous category that varies by type, severity and chronicity. We therefore noted in detail the different types of neglect that the children had experienced (see Table 3.3).

Table 3.3 Types of neglect

Type of neglect	Number	Percentage
Supervisory neglect (n=131)	106	81
Physical neglect (including nutritional and pre-natal neglect) (n=133)	107	81
Emotional neglect (n=130)	101	78
Educational or cognitive neglect (n=122)	60	49
Medical neglect (including neglect of mental health needs) (n=123)	42	34

Note: The sample sizes vary in this table due to missing data in some cases.

Supervisory neglect, which included lack of supervision or leaving the child alone or with inappropriate carers, occurred frequently (81%). Over three-quarters of the children (76%) lacked supervision, commonly through being left at home or outside alone, or being in the care of a parent who was intoxicated. A further third of them (37%) were inappropriately supervised (including being left with under-age carers or those who had offended against children or had learning difficulties). In a few cases (17%) problems had arisen because teenagers or unsuitable adults were frequent visitors to the household.

It was just as common (81%) for children to be physically neglected where there was a failure to meet their needs for physical care, food, clothing, cleanliness and safety. The details of such neglect can be seen in Table 3.4 and it is interesting to note that 'failure to thrive' was not common (14%).

Table 3.4 Physical neglect

Neglect	Number	Percentage
Hygiene standards in the home (n=126)	55	44
Insufficient food or inadequate nutrition (n=128)	55	43
Inadequate or dirty clothing for child (n=124)	47	38
Cleanliness of child (n=121)	40	33
Housing hazards (lack of safety features, dangerous objects/situations) (n=123)	28	23
'Shuttling' of child (repeatedly left in the care of others) (n=124)	21	17
Failure to thrive (n=125)	17	14
Home cold or poorly heated (n=121)	17	14
Abandonment of child for 6 hours + (n=127)	11	9
Child thrown out/excluded from household (n=129)	10	8

Note: The sample sizes vary in this table due to missing data in some cases.

Just over-three quarters of the children (78%) experienced emotional neglect (see Table 3.5), which included witnessing domestic violence, lacking adequate warmth or emotional support, rejection alone (see Quinton *et al.* 1998) or with siblings, and restrictions, such as having no access to parts of the house or being prevented from socializing with peers.

Educational or cognitive neglect and was experienced by almost half of the children (see Table 3.6). This included problems with the child's school or nursery attendance (with one child's attendance recorded as 17%), and school exclusion. Other children lacked crucial stimulation, with some ending up with poor speech and language skills.

Table 3.5 Emotional neglect

Neglect	Number	Percentage
Child witness to domestic violence (n=125)	66	53
Child denied adequate warmth or emotional support (n=125)	61	49
Child witness to marital/domestic rows (n=120)	44	37
Child rejected (n=123)	32	26
Child singled out for rejection (n=123)	22	18
Child unnecessarily restricted or isolated (n=126)	21	17
Child a 'parenting' child (n=120)	17	14
Child has to care for parent (n=123)	14	11

Note: The sample sizes vary in this table due to missing data in some cases.

Table 3.6 Educational or cognitive neglect

Neglect	Number	Percentage
Lack of nursery/school attendance (n=113)	54	48
Child excluded or suspended from school (n=103)	23	22
Lack of stimulation (n=122)	23	19
Child passive, withdrawn or isolated (n=122)	20	16
Child has poor language skills (n=120)	13	11

Note: The sample sizes vary in this table due to missing data in some cases.

The medical needs of a third of the children were neglected, as can be seen in Table 3.7, with one child having to have 11 teeth removed and his brother 13 due to lack of dental care.

Table 3.7 Medical neglect

Neglect	Number	Percentage
Medical/dental appointments not kept (n=120)	32	27
Medical/dental treatment not received (n=121)	24	20
Mental health appointments not kept (n=130)	3	3
Refusal or delay to provide mental health care (n=130)	1	1

Note: The sample sizes vary in this table due to missing data in some cases.

An analysis was undertaken to ascertain how far the types of neglect outlined in Table 3.3 correlated with each other and formed part of the same factor(s). Since medical and physical neglect both loaded highly on the same factor we combined these types of neglect to form one overall physical neglect variable as can be seen in Table 3.8.

Table 3.8 Final types of neglect

Type of neglect	Number	Percentage
Supervisory neglect	106	86
Physical neglect (including medical and ante-natal neglect)	110	83
Emotional neglect	101	78
Educational or cognitive neglect	60	49

These different types of neglect were usually experienced in combination, with nearly a third (30%) of the children experiencing two types, 37 per cent exposed to three kinds and 23 per cent all four. Older children were more likely to have experienced multiple types of neglect (Pearson's r $(136)=0.44$, $p<.05$).

Interestingly, there were only a few significant relationships between the specific types of neglect and parental difficulties. This may be due to the fact that the neglect may not have been occurring at the same time as the parental difficulties. Alcohol misuse and domestic violence were significantly related to supervisory neglect, domestic violence was significantly related to educational neglect, and parental mental health problems to physical neglect.

In addition, a quarter of the children (24%) lived in chaotic homes, a few were exposed to anti-social behaviour models in the family (3%) or were disabled but their needs were not being met (3%). A tenth of the children (11%) were injured as a result of neglect, with most requiring hospital treatment, while a fifth (22%) were not protected from physical abuse from the other parent or another adult. For each child a count was undertaken of the number of types of neglectful situations to which they had been exposed. The average number of neglect experiences was 7.54 (range 1–24; sd 4.16). Over a third of the children (36%) had experienced five or fewer such kinds, while two-fifths had experienced six to ten and the remainder (24%) 11 or more (see Figure 3.2).

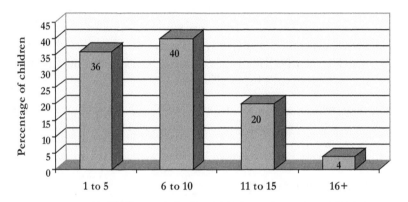

Figure 3.2 Number of types of neglect experiences

Exposure to higher numbers of types of neglectful experiences was significantly associated with more severe neglect (F (2, 135)=24.06, p<.05) and with more chronic neglect (t (54.79)=4.02, p=.001), an issue to which we now turn.

Severity and chronicity of the neglect

We used researcher ratings to assess both the severity and chronicity of the neglect for each child. There is some debate in the literature as to whether severity should be assessed in terms of parental action/inaction or the impact of such action/inaction on the child. We have attempted to combine the two in this categorization. The severity of the neglect was rated as follows:

- **Minor** – low-level neglect that the child experienced without the likelihood of significant harm. There were usually a small number of incidents or low levels of concern in one or two areas. The neglect was not pervasive or a long-standing problem.

- **Moderately severe** – care of the child has fallen considerably below that which would normally be expected. There are multiple examples of neglect and there are often sustained or repeated concerns. Alternatively there may be isolated incidents which put the child at risk of harm. There may be some evidence of the impact of the neglect on the child and the neglect was moderately severe.

- **Very severe** – care of the child has fallen significantly below that which would normally be expected. There are multiple examples of neglect and there are often sustained or repeated concerns. Alternatively there may be isolated incidents which put the child at risk of harm. The neglect was very severe (as opposed to moderately severe) when there was evidence of *significant* risk or actual harm to the child or where the neglect was so pervasive that all aspects of the child's life were being affected.

Using these ratings, a tenth of the children (9%) had experienced minor neglect, for half (54%) it was moderately severe and for a third (37%) very severe (see Table 3.9).

Table 3.9 Severity of neglect

Neglect	Number	Percentage
Minor neglect	13	9
Moderately severe neglect	74	54
Very severe neglect	51	37

Box 3.1 Case example – Minor neglect

Vicky was the youngest of three children. When she was almost a year old there was a referral from the emergency duty team after an incident of domestic violence between her parents. It was also reported that the family had no money to feed the children. Six months later children's services received a fax from the police stating that the children had been found near a busy road and had to be returned home. Later that year the children witnessed a violent incident between their parents during which their father threatened their mother with a knife.

Box 3.2 Case example – Moderately severe neglect

Abdullah's parents' early relationship was characterized by violence and as a result a care order was obtained but was later discharged after an apparently successful return home. Abdullah's parents then separated and his mother was left caring for him and his younger sister Falzah. However, there were allegations of shouting and abusive language. Abdullah and Falzah's school attendance was also poor and their mother was said to have had several new partners in the house without regard for the children's safety. There were reports from neighbours that the children were often locked out in the garden without an adult or played in the street unsupervised. Abdullah had become withdrawn, was missing his father and had begun stealing food and making himself sick. Both parents appeared to be using him as a go-between.

Box 3.3 Case example – Very severe neglect

When he was aged four Harrison sustained serious burns to his body. He had been trying to pour boiling water from a kettle while unsupervised and had slipped. Harrison's mother did not take him to hospital for several hours because she was worried that he would be taken away from her.

The chronicity of the neglect was defined as follows:

- **Episodic neglect** – the case was characterized by substantial periods of adequate care or the neglect consisted of infrequent or isolated incidents. This could have been because the child was very young when he or she started to be looked after or the child had spent periods with another parent or carer who provided a better level of care.

- **Chronic neglect** – the child had received low levels of care over a sustained period of time.

Four-fifths of the children (80%) experienced neglect which was chronic, with the remaining fifth (20%) experiencing more episodic neglect.

Box 3.4 Case example – Episodic neglect

Cheryl spent her first ten years living with her mother, Susan. At first there were concerns about Susan's ability to protect Cheryl and her siblings from her violent partner. Susan then separated from him and there was a later incident when Cheryl (aged three) and her siblings were left unattended in a café while Susan went shoplifting. There was then an unsubstantiated allegation that Susan had been leaving the children alone.

No further concerns were recorded until Susan became involved with a new partner and Cheryl, at the age of eight, witnessed a violent incident between Susan and her new partner.

Cheryl later (aged 10) moved to live with her father. Cheryl then alleged that she was treated differently to the other children, locked in her room and had her belongings taken away. She was then accommodated.

Box 3.5 Case example – Chronic neglect

There were long-standing concerns about neglect in the Brentwood family dating back to before Bryony was born. Two older siblings experienced neglect arising from poor hygiene at home and also inadequate supervision, missed health appointments and failure to protect the children from the risks posed by other adults. As a result, Bryony was placed on a child protection plan at birth under the category of neglect. For the next ten years Bryony (and her younger siblings once they were born) experienced neglect involving frequent accidents due to lack of supervision, very dirty conditions in the home and failure to provide adequate medical care, including a complete lack of dental care. These concerns then resulted in the children being looked after.

Severity and chronicity were significantly associated with each other (χ^2 (2)=34.31, p=.001). Minor neglect was more likely to be episodic, while moderately and very severe neglect were more likely to be chronic.

Children who lived with a parent who misused alcohol had an increased likelihood of experiencing very severe neglect, while children who grew up with domestic violence or parental mental health problems more often than others were subject to moderately severe neglect (Table 3.10).

Table 3.10 Relationship between parental difficulties and severity/chronicity of neglect (n=138)

	Domestic violence	Alcohol misuse	Drug misuse	Inappropriate sexual activity	Mental health problems
Severity of neglect	p<.05	p<.05	NS	NS	p<.05
Chronicity of neglect	NS	NS	NS	NS	NS

NS = not significant.

Severity was also significantly associated with the child's age (F (2, 135)=9.93, p<.05), with linear contrasts revealing that the children who experienced very severe neglect were significantly older than others.

Other maltreatment

Most children (84%) were abused as well as neglected, with only 16 per cent experiencing neglect alone (see Table 3.11). Children most often experienced emotional (65%) and physical abuse (61%) as well as neglect, and least often were subject to sexual abuse (27%). However, as many as 17 per cent of the children had experienced neglect and all the other types of abuse.

Table 3.11 Neglect and other maltreatment

Maltreatment	Percentage of children (n=138)
Neglect	**100**
Neglect only	16
Neglect and physical abuse	13
Neglect and sexual abuse	3
Neglect and emotional abuse	16
Neglect, physical and sexual abuse	3
Neglect, physical and emotional abuse	28
Neglect, sexual and emotional abuse	4
Neglect, physical, sexual and emotional abuse	17
Overall prevalence	
Emotional abuse	65
Physical abuse	61
Sexual abuse	27

Number of adversities

A measure of the total number of adversities experienced, other than neglect, before entry to care, was constructed by counting the number of problematic parental behaviours the children had been exposed to (domestic violence, drug misuse, alcohol misuse, inappropriate sexual activity and poor parenting skills), the number of forms of abuse they had suffered or been at risk of (physical abuse, emotional abuse, sexual abuse or exposure to adults with convictions against children) and whether they had experienced the death of a parent or primary carer. Only four children (3%) had experienced none or one of these adversities, while 70 per cent had experienced between four and nine (see Figure 3.3). The average number of adversities for the children was 4.4 (sd 1.8).

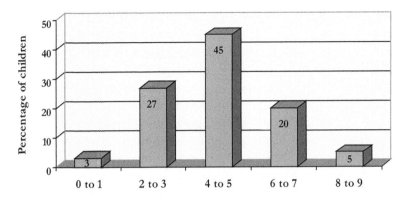

Figure 3.3 Number of adversities experienced

The impact on children of neglect, abuse and poor parenting

We collected details of the children and their families from the first referral about them to five years after the original return, and used these to provide a picture of the variety of ways in which children presented over the whole period.

Many of the children had clear difficulties, some of which were attributable to the neglect or other types of parenting deficits that they had experienced. The impact of neglect and poor parenting was sometimes evident when children did not reach their developmental milestones. For example, there were concerns that Joel at the age of two had no speech and would only grunt as a result of a lack of stimulation. Ethan was not properly toilet trained at the age of five and had to wear nappies, while Tony had mild to moderate developmental delay as well as speech and language delay, which were attributed to the neglect he had experienced. Ella lost the hearing in one ear due to lack of treatment and Jayden only gained four pounds in weight in three years because he was not fed properly.

In other cases, too, the impact of neglect or violent parenting was clear. For example, care proceedings were started in respect of Jarvis when he was aged 12 because of the number of domestic incidents that had been reported, his mother's severe alcohol use and his consequent neglect. Reports for care proceedings stated that Jarvis had been emotionally harmed by observing his mother being drunk and by the responsibility he felt for her welfare. Levi, too, began to display behavioural problems from the age of two and he became violent and self-harming. His behaviour deteriorated at the age of seven and he became a frequent offender. His poor behaviour started at the time that his abusive and violent stepfather joined the family and diminished during periods of relative safety and stability.

A number of children were over-responsible for their parents or for siblings who were also being neglected by their parents, to the extent that one child would seek out her siblings during breaks between classes to ensure that they were all right, while others would leave school or not attend in order to look after drinking or drug-using parents.

The children's neglect was often reflected in their poor school attendance. This could result in poor progress at school and a number of children were several years behind with their schoolwork and literacy skills. At the age of six, Nadine had only attended school for half the expected time and so her reading age was two years below her chronological age. Joe was destructive and aggressive towards his teachers and was permanently excluded at the age of seven. For a year he received one hour a day tuition and he then began shoplifting and taking part in burglaries with his father after his father's release from prison.

Emotional problems were also common among the children. These included anxiety, distress, low self-esteem, psychological problems, being withdrawn, wetting, soiling, eating problems, head banging, self-harming and suicide attempts. For example, Leila at the age of four had frequent emotional outbursts, was aggressive, stole food and said she wanted to kill herself.

It was common for children, as they grew older, to display behaviours such as violence, aggression, offending and drug and alcohol use. For example, Ben returned home to his mother after he absconded from foster care at the age of 13. While at home his offending increased and he was charged with numerous offences, including assault, criminal damage, breach of the peace, racially aggravated assault, arson and theft.

This chapter shows the extensive neglect that children had often experienced and suggests the impact that it had on them. In the next chapter we consider the services that were provided to assist them and their parents.

4

Services and Interventions

This chapter describes the services and interventions provided for both parents and children during the final three-year follow-up period. In addition, the qualitative analysis of the case summaries, which covered the period from the first referral until the five-year follow-up point, provided further information.

Services for parents during the final three-year period

We considered the services and interventions provided for parents only where the case was open for at least three months during the final three-year period and where the child had been at home for at least a month. This excluded cases where there was little opportunity to provide any assistance. Of the 77 families (102 children) whose cases were open at any point during the final three-year period, there were 52 families (68 children) where the case had been open for at least three months and the child had been home for at least a month during this time. The analysis focuses on these 52 families.

Support for mental health problems (50%) and financial help (45%) were most often provided for parents, with help from disability or other specialist social workers or assistance with their own difficulties, such as domestic violence, least common (see Table 4.1). Support for parents was mainly provided while the child was living at home but was sometimes given when children were living elsewhere, perhaps as part of preparation for a return home or assistance for parents in overcoming their difficulties so that a later reunification might be possible. Help for drug and alcohol problems was far from universal, with only 38 per cent of parents who misused drugs and 16 per cent who misused alcohol receiving help during the final three-year period.

Table 4.1 Types of support received by parents (n=52)

Support	Overall provision (%)	Provided only while child at home (%)	Provided only while child not at home (%)	Both (%)
Respite	12	12	N/A	N/A
Day care or activity group	16	16	N/A	N/A
Transport	22	22	N/A	N/A
Financial support	45	41	2	2
Material support	16	14	0	2
Assistance with housing	10	–	–	–
Family support worker (or similar)	18	18	0	0
Family centre	4	–	–	–
Disability/other specialist worker	2	0	2	0
Parenting programme/ other help with parenting skills	18	14	2	2
Work on parent–child relationship	4	4	0	0
Help with parental difficulties, e.g. domestic violence	2	2	0	0
Support for drug problems for parents with this difficulty (n=8)	38	13	13	13
Support for alcohol problems for parents with this difficulty (n=19)	16	11	0	5
Support for mental health problems for parents with this difficulty (n=16)	50	13	13	25
Work on budgeting	4	4	0	0
Assistance with literacy skills	6	6	0	0

N/A = not applicable.

Most of the support provided for parents was short-term (70%), with a fifth of parents (21%) receiving longer-term support (more than six months) and a tenth (9%) receiving a mixture of long- and short-term support. This was not related to whether or not the children were subject to orders or were on child protection plans.

Three-quarters of the parents received some kind of specific help, but a quarter (23%) did not, although they all had social workers who may have provided support. Two-fifths of the parents (46%) received one or two types of support and a quarter (23%) three or four (see Figure 4.1). Eight per cent of the parents received five or more kinds of assistance, with the maximum of ten being provided to one family with little sustained improvement. Interestingly, the level and type of assistance for parents did not differ significantly according to whether or not children were subject to care or supervision orders or were subject to child protection plans.

On the other hand, the child's age was significantly associated with the level of parental support received, with the number of types of support being much lower for the parents of older children (Pearson's r (50)= -0.37, p=.008). This ties in with the findings of the reunification study, where adolescents and their parents received lower levels of services and intervention than younger children (Farmer *et al.* 2011). It may be that the focus of support moves away from parents and onto the adolescents themselves, and later towards supporting them into independence and leaving care.

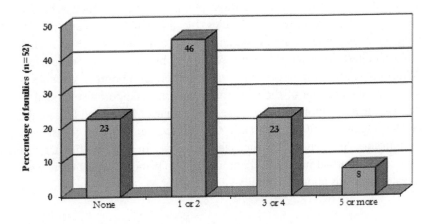

Figure 4.1 Number of different types of support for parents provided during the final three-year period

A fifth (22%) of the parents were referred to specialist support services during the final three-year period but did not receive a service because they failed to turn up for appointments.

For two-fifths of the parents (38%) we judged that the services they received were sufficient. The remaining three-fifths (62%) of parents were considered to need more help. We recorded the three key areas where we judged that parents had required more support. Help with the child's behaviour was most needed (27%), followed by assistance with alcohol problems (23%) and parenting skills (13%) (see Table 4.2). The children tended to be older in cases where the parents were considered to need more support, although this difference was not statistically significant (see Chapter 9).

For the 40 families where the parents had received support, it was considered that in only a quarter of cases the services provided had fully addressed the underlying problems relating to neglect. In a further two-fifths of cases (41%) their problems had been partially addressed and in a third (34%) not at all addressed. There was inadequate intervention in 62 per cent of cases where parents misused drugs, and in as many as 84 per cent of cases where parental alcohol misuse was an issue. Interventions were also inadequate in 80 per cent of cases where parents had mental health difficulties, in 63 per cent of those with severe financial problems, in a third where parents had learning difficulties and in a quarter of cases where parenting difficulties or domestic violence predominated.

Information on the informal support received by parents was scant. Informal support during the final three-year period was recorded as having been provided to only 14 families by the children's grandparents (four families), other relatives (six families) or other adults such as friends (two families). Two families were supported by more than one person. While the relationship between informal and formal support was not clear-cut, parents in receipt of the most forms of formal support also tended to receive the most informal support (see also Farmer, Moyers and Lipscombe 2004; Quinton 2004), although this difference was not statistically significant. This may reflect their ability to ask for help or the fact that sources of informal support were more likely to be noted where there were greater concerns about the family.

Table 4.2 Types of support needed by parents (n=52)

Support	Number	Percentage
More/some help with behaviour/child management	14	27
More/some support for alcohol problems	12	23
More/some parenting skills training/ parenting programme	7	13
More/some health/mental health support	4	8
More/some help with own adversity	4	8
More/some support for drug problems	4	8
More/some work on protecting child from harm	2	4
More/some social work assessment	1	2
More/some respite care	1	2

Note: Some parents with drug, alcohol or mental health problems who were not receiving help were not coded as needing help as either the child was at home for a short period or the problems were not severe (mental health problems).

Services for children during the final three-year period

We had information on the services provided to 93 of the 102 children whose cases were open for at least three months during the final three-year period. Almost half (47%) of the young people with drugs misuse difficulties received help but only 8 per cent of young people with alcohol misuse problems did so. Over a quarter (28%) of the young people were provided with assistance with independent living skills/living independently, while work on sibling relationships, on parent–child relationships or on self-esteem were rarely provided (see Table 4.3). Slightly more services were provided when children were in care than when they were at home.

Most of the support provided for children was short-term (77%), with a fifth (18%) receiving longer-term support (more than six months) and 5 per cent receiving a mixed picture of both.

Almost a third of the children (31%) did not receive any support during the final three-year period. However, all but two of these children did have an allocated social worker at some point during these three years, so other work may have been provided. A further third (33%) received one kind of support, 15 per cent received two and 21 per cent received three or more types of assistance (see Figure 4.2).

Table 4.3 Types of support received by children during the final three-year period

Support	Overall provision (%)	Provided only whilst child living at home (%)	Provided only whilst child living away from home (%)	Provided at both stages (%)
Mental health provision (incl. counselling)	26	9	17	0
Work on school attendance/ issues	18	8	9	0
Help with dealing with past adversities	13	3	10	0
Mentor or befriender	10	2	8	0
Other help (e.g. sports project, specialist health support)	9	3	3	3
Help with behaviour	8	1	6	1
Work on staying safe	8	3	3	1
Life story work	8	0	8	0
Work on anger management	6	1	3	1
Work on self-esteem	4	1	2	1
Work on parent-child relationship	3	1	1	1
Work on sibling relationships	1	1	0	0
Help with drugs misuse for young people with this problem (n=17)	47	0	47	0
Specific help with independent living skills/living independently (n=50)	28	8	20	0
Help with alcohol misuse for young people with this problem (n=13)	8	0	8	0

n=93 unless otherwise stated.

The number of different kinds of support provided was significantly higher for older children (Pearson's r (91)=-0.22, p<.05). This may be linked to the decrease in support for their parents and increasing help as young people approach adulthood, or be a response to the range of challenges presented by some of the young people. The level of support received was also associated with the three stability outcome groups (which are explained in detail in Chapter 10). Children in the at home group at the five-year follow-up received fewer types of support than those who were by then placed stably away from home, who again received fewer types of support than those in the unstable category (F (2, 90)=6.08, p<.05). This relationship is partly explained by the differences in the children's ages between the three stability outcome categories (see Chapter 10) and the fact that the cases of children at home were more likely to be closed, thus giving less time in which services could be provided.

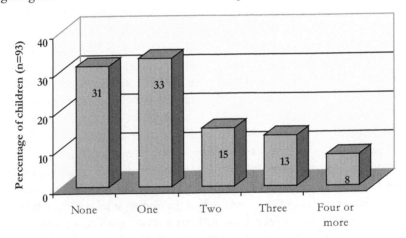

Figure 4.2 Number of different types of support for children provided during the final three-year period

In addition to such services, half of the children (53%) received additional support with their schooling either in mainstream schools (25%) or via specialist help, such as home tuition or transfer to a pupil referral unit or special school (28%). Schools were highly supportive to a third (34%) of the children and occasionally (6%) to both children and their parents.

Referrals were made to specialist support services for 16 per cent of the children during the final three-year period, but these services were not received because either the child failed to turn up for the appointment (11%) or the service was not available (5%).

Three-fifths of the children (61%) had an allocated social worker throughout the whole of the final three years. A further third of children (34%) had periods when they had no worker, while there was no allocated social worker for a few children (5%) throughout the three years (probably because these four cases were only open for short periods of time). Only a fifth of children (22%) had the same social worker throughout the three years, while the remainder had an average of 1.7 changes of worker (range 1–5, sd 1.34). Social work visits took place regularly (18%) or fairly regularly (42%) for most children, although for a third visits were infrequent and for a few (6%) very variable. In a quarter of cases the social work provided to children and parents had been exceptionally good, that is the workers had been consistent and purposeful, had monitored children's progress to ensure that they were safe when at home and had worked proactively towards another type of placement when this was appropriate.

Most (80%) of the eligible young people received support from leaving care teams. However, the level of support provided by them varied, with over half of the young people receiving a very high (25%) or high (29%) level and the remainder receiving adequate (38%) or low (8%) levels of assistance. Youth offending teams were involved in 28 per cent of cases, with the supervision of young people on orders being their main focus.

For two-fifths of the children (42%) the support that they had received was judged to be sufficient. For the remaining three-fifths of children (58%) we recorded the three key areas where, in the researchers' view, the child needed more support (see Table 4.4). Alcohol and drugs support were most needed (85% and 53% respectively), and help with living independently was often required (32%), as was help with finding a job (27%). Children who were thought to need more assistance were significantly older than those with sufficient support (t (87)=8.35, p<.001), again perhaps because these children were experiencing greater levels of difficulty. Children in the unstable outcome group (see Chapter 10) were much more likely to need further support than others (χ^2 (2)=19.76, p<.001).

Although children's views about the usefulness of these services were rarely recorded on file, for 23 per cent there was evidence that a service had been especially helpful. These services included psychological help for sexually abusive behaviour for one boy and NSPCC support and life story work for two others, with several children benefiting from the one-to-one support provided by mentors, outreach workers and community support workers.

In terms of informal support, there was evidence on file that 38 per cent of the children had a particularly supportive relative, friend or other adult. This information was not recorded consistently and so may be an underestimate.

Table 4.4 Types of support needed by child during the final three-year period

Support	Number	Percentage
No more support needed	37	42
More/some individual support, e.g. mentoring	19	21
More/some work on child's history	12	13
More/some help with behaviour/anger management	11	12
More/some health or mental health support	7	8
More/some social work assessment	5	6
More/some family relationship help (e.g. parent-child, sibling)	4	4
More/some specialist social work (e.g. disability)	2	2
More/some work on sexualized behaviour	1	1
More/some work on keeping safe	1	1
More/some help with boundaries/social interactions	1	1
More/some support with alcohol problems (for those with this difficulty n=13)	11	85
More/some support with drug problems (for those with this difficulty n=17)	9	53
More/some help with living independently (for those who had lived independently n=19)	6	32
More/some help with finding or keeping a job (for those over 16 years and no longer in education n=26)	7	27
More/some education support (for those of school age n=86)	7	8
More/some help with offending behaviour (for those over 10 years n=43)	3	7
More/some children's clubs/after-school activities (for those of school age n=86)	2	2

n=89 unless otherwise stated.

Services for both parents and children

Local authority specialist teams undertook short-term, intensive work with a few families (12%) at times of crisis. In addition, over half of the cases (54%) involved intervention from other agencies. Co-operation between agencies appeared to be high, with agencies co-ordinating their services and working together very well in most cases (59%), quite well in a third (36%) and not very well in only 5 per cent.

Although most cases, where children were at home for at least a month during the final three-year period, received some kind of professional input (96%), it appeared that in only a minority of cases (8%) had intensive professional intervention itself enabled the child to remain at home or prevented the child from returning to care.

How far support was matched to identified needs

Overall, the researchers considered that two-fifths (42%) of the cases received an appropriate level of support, as the match between the needs of the case and the support provided was good, or they were receiving little or no support but did not need it. Conversely, 58 per cent of the cases were not receiving sufficient support as the match between the needs of the case and the support provided was fair or poor. The following two case examples illustrate these differences.

Box 4.1 Case example – Appropriate level of support provided

Toby aged 5 and his brother Miller, 3, were removed from their mother Rita's care because of concerns about neglect. While Toby and Miller were in foster care Rita began attending appointments at a drugs project and underwent a detoxification programme prior to starting a residential assessment with the boys. This assessment was not successful and the care plan for Toby was changed to permanence via adoption. Life story work was undertaken with Toby and he received support from CAMHS to help him with the transition to his adoptive placement. Toby was identified as having developmental delay and was receiving additional support in school in relation to these difficulties.

Box 4.2 Case example – Insufficient support provided

At the start of the final three-year period Alex, who was aged 14, was living with his 16-year-old sister Louise. At this point he was not being cared for by an adult over the age of 18. On at least two occasions Alex spent short episodes with his father after being forcibly taken back to live with him. Alex was scared of his father's violence and was hit by him but no action was taken to protect him. When the case was closed, Alex was still living with Louise, who had just turned 18 years old. He was still not in education and had not been for the previous year, with a lack of action on the part of any agency to resolve this problem.

The existence of court orders or child protection plans was not related to how far services matched the needs of the family. This could be because by this later stage many of the children had been on orders or plans for quite some time, supervision orders might have expired and a number of children were by then looked after. In contrast, court orders (although not child protection plans) had been related to service provision at the time of the original return (Farmer *et al.* 2011).

On the other hand, children's age did make a difference. Families with younger children significantly more often received appropriate levels of support (t (87)=8.35, p<.001) than others. This could be because it was harder to meet the many needs of older children (see Chapter 9), they were more able to opt out of services or because children's services departments did not prioritize adolescents (see also Farmer *et al.* 2011). Again, children in the unstable outcome group were much more likely than others to lack appropriate levels of support (χ^2 (2)=19.76, p<.001), partly no doubt because of their older age.

In conclusion, the support provided for parents and children was variable. Specific additional needs for assistance were identified for a substantial minority of parents and children. Most support was short term and tended not to address the underlying problems relating to neglect. While the parents of older children received less support, the older children themselves received more than younger children, probably because of their increasing levels of behavioural difficulties. In spite of this, for most adolescents the support they received was inadequate.

Services and support for parents and children from first referral to the end of the five-year follow-up

As we have seen, the case files showed that during the final three-year period 77 per cent of parents and 69 per cent of children received some specialist services in addition to social work assistance. Qualitative analysis of the case summaries, which covers the longer period from the first referral until the five-year follow-up point, showed that 90 per cent of families received some kind of additional service during this longer period, aimed at the parent or child or whole family. Such services included help with parental mental health problems, with parental substance misuse, assistance from family centres, CAMHS or parenting programmes, from family support workers, respite care, counselling, life story work, play therapy, mentors and befrienders, play schemes, 'keep safe' work and help from the youth offending team.

The qualitative analysis indicated that further support was needed by a considerable proportion of families, including services for parental drug and alcohol misuse, assistance with children's behaviour problems, work on parenting, services to address the child's offending behaviour and young people's drug and alcohol problems, respite care, material support and help with children's education. A particular gap was in the provision of direct help with children's behavioural problems and advice on behavioural management for their parents. In addition, children's therapeutic needs were often not met. For example, Sian was placed at a residential school due to exclusions from school and behaviour problems which her mother was unable to manage. Sian initially did well at this school for the first year but she then began showing challenging behaviour and was soiling twice a day. It emerged that Sian had been visiting the flat of a local man and had been sexually abused by him. Sian continued to be looked after in various residential units and foster placements and had been in care for over five years when she returned home to her mother after refusing to return to her foster placement. During all this period of children's services' involvement, specialist services were never provided for Sian's behavioural and emotional difficulties or for the sexual abuse she experienced.

In a few families some support was provided but this appeared to be inadequate given the presenting problems. For example, as we have seen, Levi at two years old had behavioural problems and from three was violent and self-harming. Family support was provided but his behaviour deteriorated and by the age of seven he had started a fire and was party to a burglary. He continued to offend frequently and was eventually remanded to the care of children's services at the age of 14. Levi's severe behavioural problems were evident at a very early age but the specialist input, which included an educational psychologist, family support work and additional educational support, did not succeed in addressing the severity of his problems, probably because of the continuing adversities he experienced while living with his parents.

As we will see in Chapter 6, some families lacked important services because they refused to engage with them. For example, Mrs Jennings did not take up offers of therapeutic help for her three children when they returned home to her, despite these being strongly recommended. She said that this would unsettle the children and that they themselves did not want to attend. In addition to the lack of services, there were a few families who lacked basic social work support. This could be in the form of a lack of visiting or a 'hands off' approach to managing the case.

Now that we have considered the services provided to children and parents during the final three-year period, we turn to look at how the cases were managed overall.

5

Case Management
Responding to Risk and Working with Safeguarding Procedures and the Courts

We analysed in more depth how the cases of the 138 children in the study were managed by undertaking a qualitative analysis of the original detailed in-depth case summaries from the reunification research, supplemented by the additional information from this study. We aimed to consider how the cases were managed over their whole course, that is from the children's birth (or the earliest referral about them) until the five-year follow-up after their original return home. In doing so, we were often considering the management of the 104 families, as on the whole, case management did not vary substantially by child, although at other times we refer to issues in relation to the 138 children. In addition, we include some of the quantitative data from the case files.

The impact of neglect as a presenting problem
How far was neglect the focus of concern?
All of the children in the study were neglected before entering care and, as we have seen, most (84%) experienced other forms of maltreatment. Where other forms of abuse were present, we considered that neglect was the dominant issue in case management in two-fifths (40%). For a third of cases, there appeared to be even attention to neglect and to other maltreatment, while for the remaining quarter (24%) the emphasis was on other types of maltreatment. Where the emphasis was on other types of

maltreatment at the expense of neglect (27 children), generally (78%) this was appropriate given the circumstances of the case. However, in a few cases (6) other types of maltreatment had dominated case management such that neglect had been inappropriately marginalized.

It was not uncommon (47%, 65 cases) for issues other than maltreatment to dominate case management at the expense of neglect. Where this occurred, it generally (60%) involved parental drug and alcohol misuse or mental health difficulties. The child's behaviour was the issue which received most emphasis in other (27%) cases, while for a few it was the children's school attendance or their health or mental health difficulties. Again, we considered that in most cases (72%) this emphasis on other issues had been appropriate, although in a minority (28%) it had not.

Overall, this meant that for 15 per cent of children (21) the neglect to them had been marginalized and there had been an overemphasis on other types of maltreatment or on other issues. For example, Denise had been neglected by her mother, who misused alcohol and drugs and was involved in prostitution, so that Denise became the subject of a care order at the age of ten. However, domestic violence by her mother's partner dominated the way in which this case was subsequently seen, so that at a family support conference the chair said that as far as she could remember: 'Social services had not expressed any concerns about mum's care of Denise but that the problems focused on mum's partner.'

It is clear then that in a few cases the central focus of case management moved away from neglect, which was not then given due attention.

Triggers for intervention

In many cases the neglect children experienced was noted and sometimes led to the provision of services, but often more decisive action for these children (or even simply reopening the case) did not occur until they had experienced an incident of physical or sexual abuse or there had been a particularly serious incident of domestic violence (Cleaver and Walker 2004; Department of Health 1995; Horwath 2002; Jowitt 2003; Stone 1998). Indeed, we judged that in a third of cases a specific incident had been the trigger for child protection procedures or the use of care proceedings (see e.g. Dickens 2007; Horwath 2005a, 2005b; Masson et al. 2007; Masson et al. 2008b; Stevenson 2005; Tanner and Turney 2003). For example, because of concerns about Alan's older siblings, he was subject to a child protection plan at birth and a supervision order was made. A year later the case was closed when Alan was aged two. Further concerns were then raised over a seven-year period about lack of supervision, neglect and violence towards Alan from both parents and because his mother was not coping with his behaviour. A number of child protection investigations were undertaken because of injuries to Alan but he was only finally removed under police protection when he was found with extremely severe bruising.

Other incidents which triggered intervention to protect children were when a parent was found drunk in charge of a young child, threatened or actually took an overdose or attempted suicide, when there were parental mental health problems, some of which involved the parent being hospitalized, or when parents were imprisoned. Of course, children might also enter care if their parents were unable to control them, they showed sexually abusing behaviour or were violent, the parent went into hospital or as a result of being remanded to care. A number of admissions occurred at the request of a parent who was not coping with the children, occasionally accompanied by a social work note on file that there had been no food in the house. Sometimes the police were instrumental in arranging for children to go into care, such as when they attended a domestic incident and became concerned at the state of the accommodation or were called out to children who had been left on their own. Indeed, the one type of neglect which led to intervention was when children were abandoned or left unsupervised or the parents refused to have them back home (Masson 2002; Masson *et al.* 2007).

Although such specific incidents were usually the trigger for intervention, neglect was occasionally responded to when it was combined with other issues, so that there was a serious accumulation of concerns (see also Daniel *et al.* 2011; Farmer and Owen 1995; Sanders *et al.* 1999; Stone 1998). For example, in one case four children (aged between one and thirteen) were removed and placed in care because of the regular presence in the home of a convicted sex offender who had physically abused Evan (aged 13) and Matt (aged 9) and the deteriorating behaviour and attendance of both boys at school. The three older children were all exhibiting emotional and behavioural problems at that time, with Evan showing defiance and physically fighting his mother, Rose at 11 being enuretic and Matt being aggressive and verbally abusive to his mother and disruptive at school. There had also been serious concerns about the health of both boys and the state of the home. This combination of difficulties led children's services to believe that they had sufficient evidence to take further action.

In the absence of a trigger event, there was often no intervention to safeguard children, even when they experienced severe and often chronic neglect over long periods, including lack of stimulation, missed medical appointments, non-attendance or even at times no enrolment in school, children being left alone, not having appropriate clothes or regular meals, losing weight or failing to put on weight, children who were dirty and unwashed in school so that their peers avoided them, extremely unhygienic home conditions, lack of bedding and the use of inappropriate carers.

Often the situations which constituted neglect were not referred to as neglect in the case files and no cumulative picture of the extent of neglect and its sequelae was built up, even though some children were noted as being developmentally delayed or years behind with their schoolwork. Indeed, even though the provision of regular high quality information on the physical development of children has been seen as essential (Stone 1998) and a number of inquiries into child deaths (Bridge Child Care Consultancy Service 1995; London Borough of Brent 1985; London Borough of Greenwich 1987) criticized social work failure to recognize serious neglect through ensuring that regular monitoring of children's weight or height took place, this kind of evidence was rarely found in the files. As these children grew older, as we have noted, children's services focused on their presenting behaviours, such as aggression, sexualized behaviour, absconding and offending, without reference to their antecedents in the previous neglect to them and often also prior exposure to domestic violence (see also Farmer et al. 2004; Smith 1995).

Assessment
Types of assessment
Assessment is key to understanding children's situations and determining what work should be undertaken (Turney et al. 2011). Initial and core assessments of the parents by social workers were most commonly undertaken, with some specialist and residential assessments. The few assessments of children were undertaken for those who had particularly severe problems. For example, one sexually abusing boy was assessed by a psychiatrist as a persistent offender with conduct and attachment disorders, an expressive language disorder and some autistic spectrum functioning. Another boy was assessed as having a reading age of 5 when he was aged 11.

Timing of assessments
After children's services had received a referral, social work assessments were completed on nearly half (46%) of the families (48 of the 104 families). When children were the subject of care proceedings, social work assessments were undertaken, while assessments by psychologists,

psychiatrists and other therapists were almost as common. In addition, 7 of the 11 residential assessments occurred during care proceedings. Parenting assessments were completed on four families during care proceedings but there was only one case where a report by an addictions specialist was commissioned. This is surprising given that substance misuse was common among parents (see Chapter 3) and one might question whether other assessments really got to grips with the nature of these addictions (see Masson *et al.* 2008b). Nonetheless, assessments within care proceedings, were often helpful to the management of the case as they assisted in making clear plans about whether the children should return home or should be placed permanently elsewhere. Sometimes this was the only time in the case when there was clarity of planning for the child.

In a third (36%) of the families (37 of 104 families) social work assessments were carried out while children were looked after but were not subject to care proceedings. The focus of these assessments tended to be on either the possibility of reunification or decision-making in relation to alternative permanence plans. Specialist assessments were rarely completed while children were accommodated.

There were very few instances (9) where assessments were undertaken *after* the child had returned home from care. These were completed either shortly after the start of the return to assess reunification progress or some time into the return after concerns had been identified.

The impact of social work assessments

Social work assessments then could have a major influence on decision-making about children. For example, a small number of children were removed from home or accommodated after an assessment highlighted concerns about the child or difficulties within the family. In contrast, in a few cases, children remained at home following the completion of an assessment showing that the home situation was satisfactory.

A child protection conference could be convened or care proceedings started as a consequence of an assessment which raised concerns. In addition, while some assessments led to support being provided to children or their parents, others did not. However, as we will see, when cases lacked assessment, services were often lacking.

Specialist assessments

Specialist assessments by experts were completed for over a third of the families (38%), generally as part of care proceedings, and as we have seen, were particularly influential in relation to decisions about whether children should return home or not. Most children either returned home following a specialist assessment or alternative permanence plans were made for them, so that specialist assessments were often key in progressing the management of a case. It was clear that in some cases there had been little progress towards securing a stable environment for the child until care proceedings were started and a specialist assessment was sought. For example, once Ollie's second return home broke down when he was aged 11 and his grandparents were unable to care for him any longer, care proceedings were started. The psychiatric assessment of Ollie's mother during the care proceedings was not positive as it was felt that she would need years of therapy to become stable. Therefore, the plan for Ollie was changed to permanence away from his birth family and he was placed in a long-term placement with foster carers.

In other cases, children were returned home on the basis of expert reports by professionals. For example, during care proceedings work was completed with the Lesley family by a family centre while Spencer and Lisa were in care. The programme was for an intensive period of work with the whole family and involved a team of child psychologists, psychiatrists, psychotherapists and social workers. Mrs Lesley made very good progress during the assessment and halfway through was allowed unsupervised contact with the children. The recommendation of the family centre upon completion of the assessment was for reunification of the children with their mother. The return home was successful, supervision orders were made and after they expired the case was closed.

The local authority was in agreement with (or was unable to oppose) the majority of the expert assessments that were carried out (see also Iwaniec, Donaldson and Allweis 2004). However, in two cases the local authority ignored an expert assessment. In one, Holly was assessed by psychiatrists on two occasions because of her difficult behaviour, the first when she was aged seven. Both assessments recommended that she should be accommodated, but this did not occur as the local authority decided that she should remain with her parents. In another case, a psychiatric report in care proceedings found that ten-year-old Anna was suffering from psychological problems as a result of exposure to domestic violence and her father's alcohol problems. The report recommended long-term foster care, but this advice was ignored and the plan was later changed to return her to her parents.

Lack of assessment

Few cases lacked assessment completely, and some had had timely assessments at particular points in time. However, given that many of the older children had long histories of children's services involvement, assessments were found fairly infrequently overall. In just over a quarter of the families it was clear that an assessment had been needed – either because of the level of needs of the child or parents or because children were returning to households where they had experienced abuse or neglect – but no assessment had been conducted.

Lack of assessment often led to children being returned home to, or remaining in, circumstances that were not suitable or were detrimental, and was also linked to a lack of services. Some children experienced further maltreatment after being returned home to situations that had not been assessed.

Moreover, when children were returned to parents who had not been assessed, these returns often broke down, sometimes quite quickly. A number of children and young people continued to display difficult behaviour (including offending and drug use) or this behaviour increased while they remained in, or were returned to, family situations that had not been assessed. For example, there were concerns about Fran when she was aged 13 because she appeared to have been left alone for several days by her mother and was thought to be using drugs. She was therefore accommodated for a short period until she informed the local authority that she would be staying with her mother, having absconded home from a residential unit. This return was not assessed and was unsuccessful due to Fran's spiralling drug use and increasing offending.

A few families and children had a clear need for support but did not receive any service because an assessment had not been carried out. For example, as we have seen, Alex had numerous placements in care after a return to his mother broke down and from the age of 14 he was cared for by his older sister. There was no assessment of his needs, little work was carried out and Alex had no educational provision, even though he wanted to learn basic literacy and numeracy skills.

How adequately were concerns about the children followed up?

In as many as three-fifths of the families referrals expressing concerns about risks to the children, mostly about maltreatment, were not adequately followed up or appropriate action was not taken after the referrals were received (see e.g. Munro 1996, 1999). These referrals were generally from other professionals, neighbours or relatives, although sometimes risks to children had been identified by social work staff. Indeed, after the children had gone to live with their parents for the original return, referrals about their safety and welfare were made about as many as 73 per cent of them. In some cases no action at all was taken after a referral was received and in others only a minimal response was made, which did not appear to reflect the seriousness of the risks, and cases were sometimes closed shortly afterwards.

For example, a neighbouring children's services department made a referral stating that Keira's mother took her to a local pub every other night where she drank to excess. Staff at the pub had heard three-and-a-half-year-old Keira saying to her mother, 'Don't beat me up. Don't chain me up' and had seen Keira running around the car park. There were further referrals about alcohol-fuelled incidents, leading to an overnight stay in care. Two months later, after Keira's mother abandoned her when she was drunk, police protection was used for the third time, and at the age of four Keira was placed with foster carers for a sustained period. However, until this point Keira had remained at home despite referrals about her care and her mother's continued drinking.

There are many possible explanations for why more action was not taken in response to these referrals. It was noticeable that referrals from neighbours or relatives were often discounted or ignored (Farmer and Owen 1995; Munro 1996, 1999). Moreover, in some cases each concern appeared to have been viewed in isolation and not as part of a bigger picture, alongside other concerns and in the light of the whole history of the case (Daniel et al. 2011; Farmer and Owen 1995; Horwath 2007a; Iwaniec et al. 2004; Munro 1998, 1999, 2005b; Sanders et al. 1999; Secretary of State for Social Services 1974). Thus, sufficient action might not have been taken in response to a single referral as on its own it might not have appeared particularly serious; but when viewed in conjunction with others, it was clear that more action should have been taken.

For this reason, children's services departments need to ensure that up-to-date chronologies are maintained on all children, that these record all referrals about risks and that they are reviewed when a new referral is received. Research has also shown that the assessment of neglect requires attention to information from a range of agencies, as each may hold separate pieces that together show the whole picture (Munro 1999; Sanders et al. 1999), and it was not uncommon for other agencies, especially schools and health visitors, to have major concerns about these children.

In a few instances parents denied the allegations against them and, as a result, they were not pursued futher. For example, a number of concerns were reported about Ailsa (aged two and a half) and her siblings who were aged five and two months. The health visitor stated that the family had frequently missed appointments with her. There were also two referrals from neighbours alleging that Ailsa's mother left the children locked in the house alone for two to three hours at a time. Enquiries were made but when Ailsa's mother denied the allegations the case was closed.

In a small number of cases there were internal delays or staffing problems within children's services which resulted in a lack of action following the receipt of referrals. For example, Phillip's school raised concerns about the bruising they had observed on him when he was aged six. His mother was offered an office appointment but did not attend. A home visit by a duty officer was planned but did not take place. Shortly afterwards a member of staff from the hostel to which the family had moved reported concerns that Phillip and his younger siblings were being cared for by older men while their mother and her partner were out. These referrals were not followed up and the team manager later noted with concern on file that if further issues were raised, they needed to be followed up in a speedier and more efficient manner. Some of these cases were being treated as Section 17 children in need cases which may have meant that social workers were not seeing them as cases where abuse and neglect were key issues (Laming 2003).

Another explanation for lack of action is that workers were applying the 'rule of optimism' (Dingwall *et al.* 1983) in which, in a liberal society, workers use considerations of cultural relativism and assumptions about parents' 'natural' love to offset and excuse adverse parental behaviour. In a similar way, Corby (1987) found that social workers were reluctant to action child protection procedures in cases of moderate injury to children in families with whom they were already working, either from concern about departmental overreaction or because of not wanting to believe that people with whom they had formed a relationship could have perpetrated the injuries. Workers may also be anxious to avoid damaging the relationships they have made with families and wish to avoid stigmatizing parents who they see as already disadvantaged by, for example, living in poverty. More generally, there may have been an overidentification with the parents at the expense of the children (Haringey Local Safeguarding Children Board 2009; Stevenson 2007).

In addition, it can be difficult to maintain an accurate perspective on the extent of children's difficulties because of the habituation associated with long-term work (Farmer and Parker 1991). In this situation, workers can become desensitized or inured to maltreatment or poor standards of care (Daniel *et al.* 2011; Reder *et al.* 1993; Stevenson 2007) and the threshold for action may be set too high. At the same time, some workers (and team managers) may be very anxious to avoid children entering care, partly because of a perception of the poor outcomes of looked after children (see e.g. Baxter 1989; Berridge and Cleaver 1987; Triseliotis *et al.* 1995) – although subsequent research has shown that looked after children's outcomes are better than those of children returned to their parents (Davies and Ward 2011; Wade *et al.* 2011; Ward, Brown and Westlake 2011). In addition, local authorities may be keen to keep the numbers of children in care down, both for reasons of cost and to keep their numbers in line with those of other authorities. While we found that, in general, action was taken more expeditiously when young children (under six) were at risk rather than with those who were older, a surprisingly large number of young children were left in high risk situations.

Overall, as a result of referrals not being adequately followed up, children were often left insufficiently protected.

Important problems not addressed

Given the multiple problems that many neglectful parents face, their needs can often dominate at the expense of those of their children (Jones and Gupta 1998; Miller and Fisher 1992). We found that in half of the cases a clear focus on the key issues in the case had not been consistently maintained by children's services. We also found that the number and range of child and family problems made working with the families particularly difficult in a tenth of cases.

More specifically, in over a third of the families (36%) there were key problems that had not been addressed by children's services. Generally, these problems were parental difficulties, including alcohol or drugs misuse, domestic violence, mental health problems and lack of parenting skills. In one typical example, after returning home, Mollie witnessed a number of serious incidents of domestic violence between her parents but was not removed from home despite domestic violence being one of the reasons why she had initially been looked after as a baby. We found that alcohol misuse was the issue that was most often not addressed (see also Farmer *et al.* 2011; Harwin and Forrester 2002), with few examples of parents entering treatment, so that children returned time and time again to mothers and fathers whose parenting was impaired by their drinking. Because of the lack of action addressing parental difficulties, children experienced many adversities as a result of living with parents with such problems.

In addition, children's difficult and disturbed behaviours were sometimes not addressed and therapeutic help was often not provided for them at all or not in a sufficiently timely way. In a severe example, Will was accommodated because his mother could not cope with his sexually abusive behaviour to his sibling, and it was made clear that Will would need long-term therapeutic help. Work focusing specifically on this behaviour was not started until almost a year after he had come to the attention of children's services. In the meantime, he had had four unsuccessful returns home during which he continued to sexually abuse his sister. Moreover, parents were often not given assistance to help them deal with their children's behaviour.

It was noticeable that children whose behavioural problems or risky behaviours were not addressed often went on to have poor outcomes as their behaviour deteriorated, and some became increasingly involved in offending or drugs use. For example, Jade's involvement with drugs and alcohol was apparent early on in her involvement with children's services, when she was aged 12. However, this was not addressed at an early stage and Jade became a persistent absconder from care and her drugs use and offending behaviour increased significantly. Her problems were only stemmed temporarily by periods in secure units or young offender institutions and her drug use was never successfully addressed.

Failure to safeguard children

In exactly half the families there was clear evidence of a failure to protect children. These were cases where children's services were involved but where the children had gone on to experience further maltreatment or harm, which might have been prevented had different actions been taken.

Child protection plans/court orders

It was a surprise to find that at the time that these children were not protected, most (71%) had been on child protection plans or care or supervision orders but that this had not kept them safe, an issue to which we will return.

Safeguarding the child while at home

In a fifth of families, children were not safe at the point of returning home. This was because they returned home to situations that were unchanged from when they began to be looked after, they returned to parents where other problems were clearly apparent or they returned to situations that were relatively unknown since there had been no assessment.

In addition, children were not protected while at home in almost two-fifths (39%, 41) of the families. In these cases, children were not removed following concerns being raised or they were left too long in damaging circumstances. For example, Craig returned home to his mother following a period in care due to domestic violence between his parents and the physical abuse of his brother. In spite of an initial positive assessment, during the 19 months Craig was at home, there was a catalogue of referrals and concerns about his mother's drug use, risky adults visiting the home, lack of supervision and possible physical abuse. Children's services took no action and Craig was only removed from the situation when his father took him and his brothers to stay with him because of his grave concerns about their mother's care.

Unsuitable returns

In some cases children returned home to completely unsuitable situations, sometimes with children services' agreement. For example, a witness saw Harmony's mother knock her to the floor, kick her, drag her to her feet and punch her on the chin because she had stolen money from her mother's purse during a contact visit at home. However, return remained the plan and Harmony went home at the age of 11.

Sometimes unsuitable returns occurred because children refused to return from their family to their foster home or residential unit and the social worker agreed to the return; or one of the parents simply took the child to live with them from their placement or from school or the child absconded home and this new arrangement was agreed to, even though, as in three of the cases, the father figures were known to be either violent or drug dealers. At other times such returns were occasioned by a lack of suitable placements in care or more rarely a new social worker was prepared to give the parent yet another chance.

It was also clear that when children had been accommodated, social workers did not consider that there was much they could do to stop such returns. Sometimes young people were by then out of control, but a very unsuitable return could, as we have seen, also confirm them in extremely anti-social behaviour, spiralling offending or substance misuse. In addition, a few children had spent a long period of their early life away from parents (such as one boy who had been brought up by his stepmother until the age of 13 when she could no longer cope) and there appeared to be no bonding with their parents, which made subsequent returns vulnerable to breakdown. Over and above this, as we will see, some unsuccessful returns were made during care proceedings.

Repeated attempts to return children home

Over a third (38%) of the children experienced two or more failed returns home. In some of these cases it appeared that the children were being repeatedly returned home to circumstances that remained essentially unchanged. For example, Leah was cared for by her mother who had learning difficulties and drank to excess. While at home Leah experienced neglect and two incidents of sexual abuse, the first when she was only three and a half. She was accommodated for relatively short periods and returned home to her mother and stepfather on three occasions with no attempt to address their parenting deficits or the mother's drinking.

Variability in effective safeguarding over time

In a third (33%) of the relevant families (17 of the 52 non-safeguarded families) the children were not effectively protected at any point during children's services' involvement. Darren's case, which is described in detail in Chapter 6, is one such case. He experienced severe physical abuse, cruelty, sexual abuse, neglect and emotional abuse, yet this led to only one period on a child protection plan and one serious consideration of care proceedings, which were not pursued.

In 27 per cent of the cases where safeguarding was ineffective (14 of the 52 non-safeguarded families) children were protected at some times but not at others. For example, as previously noted, due his parents' difficulties, Alan was made subject to a child protection plan at birth and care proceedings started (safeguarding). Alan was only removed from home for a short period, a supervision order was made and when it expired the case was closed. Numerous concerns were then raised about Alan over a number of years and there were several child protection investigations because of physical abuse, but no child protection plan (lack of safeguarding). Alan was only removed after bruising was observed on his face (safeguarding), but he was quickly returned home to his father (who was the likely perpetrator of the physical abuse) without an assessment, after he absconded from care (lack of safeguarding).

The children in one in five (19%) of the relevant families (10 of the 52 non-safeguarded families) were better protected at earlier points during their history than was the case later on. For example, after concerns about neglect and emotional abuse Naomi was accommodated at the age of five and care proceedings were started a month later, due to escalating concerns about her siblings who remained at home. Naomi was returned home at the age of six, following recommendations from the children's guardian and psychiatrist. A supervision order was made but the return was not a success, with a series of concerns being raised about neglect, drug use, inappropriate visitors to the household and sexual abuse. Thus, although early action had been taken to safeguard Naomi, after she was returned home she was further maltreated before any action was taken again.

The children in another fifth (21%) of the families (11 of the 52 non-safeguarded families) were better protected as time went on than was the case earlier. These were cases where it took a long time for children's services to recognize the seriousness of the issues and intervene at the appropriate level. For example, there were numerous referrals about Dean from the age of three that he was subject to neglect and physical and emotional abuse. However, little was done and the case was frequently closed. Dean was then accommodated for the first time at the age of 11 at his mother's request. However, after less than two months in care Dean's mother took him home but this unsatisfactory return only lasted overnight. A care order was then obtained with a plan for long-term fostering.

In summary, children were quite often not effectively protected while they were at home and this casts doubt on some of the decision-making for returns, in some cases even when on child protection plans or court orders.

The effectiveness of child protection plans

Child protection plans (which replaced the child protection register) are intended to keep children safe, primarily by marshalling resources and providing services and monitoring (Farmer and Owen 1995; Gibbons *et al.* 1995). In addition, it puts parents on notice that their parenting has been abusive or neglectful and will therefore be subject to scrutiny. By implication it is the first step on a tariff where the next step might be care proceedings if things do not improve. Farmer and Owen (1995) found that parents often hotly disputed that they were neglectful parents when the registration category had been neglect.

Nearly three-quarters (72%) of the children were subject to a child protection plan at some point between the first referral and the five-year follow-up point. The researchers judged that the plans were helpful to case management in three-fifths of these cases (58%), that is to say they brought about positive changes or encouraged parental co-operation. In the remaining two-fifths of cases they had not been so effective.

Lack of child protection plans left children at risk

In a fifth of the families, the researchers considered that a plan should have been made to protect the children when it had not been. For example, Jason was exposed to domestic violence, neglect and physical and sexual abuse, and was known to children's services from the age of three, yet interventions never went beyond holding an initial child protection conference.

It was unclear why child protection plans were not used to protect these children who were clearly at risk, but we did note that this applied to a higher proportion of children in some authorities (42% in one) than in others (none in two authorities). Thus it appears that the threshold for making children the subject of plans in some local authorities was set too high or was perceived to be so, and thus no initial child protection conference was called. This accords with the findings of Masson and her colleagues (2008b) that the use of child protection plans prior to care proceedings varied widely by local authority.

Moreover, it has been found that a child's plight may be underestimated in line with a general reduction in expectations to fit what is perceived as the norm for a given family (Miller and Fisher 1992). In addition, it appeared that workers in these cases had developed a fixed view and were not open to contrary views or observations suggesting that the children were at considerable risk (Farmer 1999; Munro 1996, 1999, 2005a; Reder and Duncan 1999; Reder *et al.* 1993). This raises the question of whether team managers had adopted the same views or whether supervision had not uncovered what was happening in these cases.

Child protection plans not used early enough
Sometimes children had experienced maltreatment over long periods before a child protection plan was made, as in the case of a brother and sister who were the subject of a great deal of concern over four years (including bite marks, drastic weight loss and many missed medical appointments) before a plan was made when they were aged five and six. In a similar way, ten-year-old Isobel was the subject of two child protection enquiries relating to sexual abuse and to being made to deliver and use drugs, neither of which led to a plan. A child protection plan was finally made after Isobel found her mother unconscious from an overdose. This again suggests that at times the threshold is set too high for holding an initial conference and that it is sometimes only crossed after a particularly dramatic trigger event occurs.

Child protection plans which were ineffective
There were a surprising number of cases (42% of the plans) where the use of child protection plans was considered by the researchers to have been ineffective, that is they had not adequately safeguarded children. While they were on plans, children had remained at risk or subject to

abuse and neglect for some period and action was not taken to protect them soon enough or at all. In such situations children on plans were neglected or emotionally or physically abused while living with their parents, sometimes over long periods. This is surprising given that these cases would have been subject to child protection review meetings at regular intervals. However, research has reported on the under-evaluation of risks at child protection conferences (Corby and Mills 1986) and the difficult interpersonal dynamics that can affect them (see e.g. Hallett and Stevenson 1980; Hallett 1995). Moreover, child protection reviews can be subject to process weaknesses, so that they may not question the original construction of risk, which can then have an enduring influence on the way in which later risks to children are interpreted. This means that new information which challenges this view may be ignored (Farmer 1999; Haringey Local Safeguarding Children Board 2008; Munro 1996; Sinclair and Bullock 2002).

In quite a number of cases it was clear that the social worker was hoping that the child protection plan would provide an incentive for a parent to stop drinking or using drugs or that domestic violence would diminish, but all too often their expectations were disappointed. Quite often the plan did not assist in engaging the parents or it produced insufficient impetus to effect change in the parents, or any change that occurred was short-lived. One social worker wrote honestly on file: 'In respect of registration, I do not feel that this makes a difference to the level of co-operation given by mum.'

Some parents did not comply with the child protection plan and in one case it was noted on file that the mother failed to appreciate why the children were on plans in the first place When neglect was the primary category there would often have been no child protection enquiry, so this part of the process, which can have a major impact on parents and persuade them of the seriousness with which the children's services department views concerns (Brandon *et al.* 1999; Department of Health 1995; Farmer 1993) was lacking. Sometimes there were continuing referrals about abuse and neglect to children subject to plans and these did not reach the threshold for more coercive action or even, on occasion, were not investigated.

There were a number of reports that child protection plans were discontinued at a stage when the parents were still not coping or when the perpetrator of the abuse remained unknown. Whilst assistance was often forthcoming, parents were not always engaged or willing to take up services and in one case, although 'keep safe' sessions for an abused girl had been recommended at two separate reviews, they had not been taken up, as her mother was obstructive, clearly fearing what might be revealed.

Some authorities might add to the categories of the plan as concerns continued, such as adding physical or emotional abuse to the original category of neglect. Other children were subject to plans on two, three or even four occasions, which did indicate that the authority was endeavouring to be proactive in response to concerns about the children (see also Stone 1998). Sometimes it was during a second or third plan that care proceedings were instigated, at times as the result of an incident which lifted the case over the threshold for more coercive intervention, such as a mother's threat to kill her child. Occasionally, a child protection plan might have appeared to be the only way to try to safeguard a child, such as, for example, when attempts to obtain a care order or make an adoptive placement had been thwarted by the opposing views of the children's guardian and/or an expert opinion, an issue to which we will return.

Although a number of children were made subject to child protection plans, either before birth or immediately afterwards, this did not always protect them when they stayed with or returned to parents who maltreated them. While, as we have seen, there was a greater tendency for continued neglect to attract less intervention than physical or sexual abuse, a number of children suffered continuing physical abuse, which social workers had come to view as 'acceptable' in some way. This was even on occasions true of sexual abuse. For example, in one case, it was known that the mother often associated with convicted sex offenders who had sexually abused her children, yet the children remained with these parents for many years.

Child protection plans for adolescents

The use of child protection plans declines steadily with age, although neglect remains the most common category of registration even among the 10–15-year-old age group (Rees et al. 2011; Rixon and Turney 2007). In this study, too, we found that child protection plans were much less often used for older children, even when they were putting themselves at risk, and they did not appear to be a very effective vehicle for change in these situations (see also Gibbons et al. 1995). For example, Shayla was put on a plan at the age of 14 because of her drugs misuse, offending behaviour and possible involvement in prostitution. The plan was discontinued five months later even though there had been no improvement.

Child protection plans that were effective

Of course, in quite a number of cases (58% of children on plans) child protection plans had been used to good effect. Sometimes plans were effective because they served to focus attention on the difficulties in the case and this led to appropriate action to protect children, such as tailored services or entry to care. For example, after it emerged that Ethan and Luke were being neglected, medical appointments were being missed and Ethan was not properly toilet trained at the age of five, the children were made subject to a plan. The next day a home visit was made and the house was found to be in a very poor state. The stairs were dirty with clothing and bits of food, the landing had unclean clothes everywhere, Ethan's bedclothes were dirty and the kitchen sink was overflowing with unwashed plates and mouldy food. The social worker spoke to Ethan and he said lots of people lived in the house and sometimes he slept in the bath. Because of concerns about their safety, the children were accommodated with foster carers the same day.

The effectiveness of care proceedings

In two-thirds (67%) of cases, care proceedings were used at some point between the first referral and the five-year follow-up point. However, about two-thirds of the plans made during care proceedings and as a result of specialist assessments were not successful or were not realized. This compares with half in Hunt and Macleod's study (1999). We now turn to investigate what part care proceedings played in the management of the children's cases.

Lack of care proceedings

In at least 15 families, care proceedings were not taken in spite of children living in a highly unsatisfactory situation; and the researchers judged that proceedings had been needed, a situation dubbed 'professional paralysis' by Iwaniec and her colleagues (2004). Certainly, it can be difficult to decide when compulsory intervention is necessary in neglect cases to safeguard children (Allsop and Stevenson 1995; Minty and Pattinson 1994), where improvements are not forthcoming within the children's timescales. For example, Ken's mother had long-term mental health problems and suffered domestic violence from his father for seven years, so that the family moved between refuges and bed and breakfast accommodation. Ken missed a lot of school and when he entered foster care at the age of 11 he was five years behind in his reading. A report by an educational psychologist stated that he had been damaged by his mother's mental health problems, was confused as to why he was in care and felt rejected by his extended family who were unwilling to care for him. The social worker considered care proceedings but instead, for reasons unknown, Ken returned to his mother at the age of 13, after which he rarely attended school.

Insufficient evidence for care proceedings

In four of these fifteen cases it was clearly stated on file that it was thought that there was insufficient evidence for care proceedings, an issue which is a particular hurdle in cases of neglect (see e.g. Dingwall *et al.* 1983; Farmer and Owen 1995; Stevenson 2007; Tanner and Turney 2003). The view that there is insufficient evidence may be one held by the social worker, sometimes influenced by the team manager, or in some cases it is contained in the advice of the legal department, as was true in the Baby Peter Connelly case (Haringey Local Safeguarding Children Board 2008, 2009). Dickens (2007) has shown that local authority lawyers want to find a 'catapult' in order to take action in cases of neglect and much less often act on the basis of an accumulation of concerns. Indeed, it was clear that some local authority legal departments gave excessively cautious advice and that sometimes managers had felt unable to challenge such advice. For example, in the case of Petra, when she was aged eight, a meeting was held to consider the multiple maltreatment she had experienced. However, a move to care proceedings was not made, since the legal advice was that there was insufficient evidence to proceed. It is worth noting that such advice is sometimes influenced by the legal department's experience of their local court.

The test for granting an interim care order to remove a child from their parents is that 'the child's safety requires interim protection' (Re K and H (2007)). However, there has been some uncertainty about what this means, particularly in cases of long-term neglect where children have experienced poor care for months or years. The issue of removal became more complicated when the High Court added a further test for removal under an interim care order of 'an imminent risk of really serious harm that is whether the risk to the child's safety demands immediate separation' (Re L (2007)). Subsequently, the Court of Appeal rejected Ryder J's approach on the basis that he had not intended to change the law (Re L-A (2009)). Howe (2009) has also commented that to justify removal of a child from a home where domestic violence is a feature, the local authority needs to demonstrate that the risk of harm has become acute; a chronic situation is not enough. This is thought to apply to all long-term neglect cases. Uncertainty in the courts about the threshold for removal at the interim stage provokes disputes in proceedings (Pearce, Masson and Bader 2011). Moreover, a very strict approach to removal from neglectful homes during proceedings is particularly problematic because these proceedings continue, on average, for more than a year (Family Justice Review 2011).

Care proceedings left too late

In other cases, although care proceedings were eventually taken, the children were left for too long in damaging circumstances before proceedings were initiated (see also Farmer and Moyers 2008; Selwyn *et al.* 2006; Ward, Munro and Dearden 2006). The researchers judged that, in relation to the care episode before the original return, 28 per cent of children had been left too long before being removed from their parents. Of the children (33) who experienced further episodes of care during the final three-year follow-up period, 30 per cent appeared to have been left too long before being removed. For example, there was a catalogue of referrals from a range of agencies about Melissa and Bradley being neglected from when they were small until they went into care when they were aged 8 and 11 and care proceedings started. Most of the time there was little response to these referrals and the case was frequently closed (see Re E (2000)). Each referral seemed to have been viewed in isolation and not in the context of previous concerns. In a later disruption meeting after Bradley's foster placement had broken down, the chair stated that the children had been left for too long with their mother and that it would have been much better for them if they had been removed far sooner.

In such cases, children suffered prolonged and often chronic neglect and not infrequently also other forms of abuse, but the usual response was one of family support, and incidents were not always fully investigated. A few children seemed simply not to attract the kind of concern that would usually be generated by frequent referrals of maltreatment and certainly, once such a pattern of non-response was established, it could become entrenched. This again is what Reder and his colleagues (1993) call the maintenance of a fixed view about a case in a closed professional system (which does not let in discrepant views or observations) and is an example of the phenomenon by which new information is selected and interpreted as confirmation of a previous hypothesis (Moore 1985; Munro 1999; Sheldon 1987). Certainly, the extent of harm to the children was insufficiently well recognized and the incidents were often viewed one by one, rather than their cumulative impact recognized (Farmer 1999).

Unsafe returns to parents made when children were on care orders

In a fifth of the families (21 families affecting 28 children), although care proceedings were initiated and care orders made, children were left with or were returned to parents who were unable to care for them adequately or keep them safe. This accords with Hunt and Macleod's findings (1999) that testing return in the course of care proceedings does not protect against breakdown. Indeed, in only 16 per cent of the families where care orders were made and children were returned to parents (4/25 families or 4/32 children) were they effective. It is a matter of concern that in some of these cases children were returned several times while on a care order to parents who were unable to look after them adequately. Occasionally, the returns occurred because the parents were managing a younger sibling and so it was thought (erroneously) that they might cope with their older children.

Sometimes, when the returns were going badly, the children were made subject to child protection plans in cases where it would have been more appropriate to remove them. In a few cases in this group, by the time that reunification with parents was finally seen as not viable, children were unable to settle or be contained in care and were moved from placement to placement. In all these cases, either the return to a parent on a care order broke down or the children's behaviour worsened so markedly that disruption was highly likely. But when these returns in care proceedings failed, local authorities rarely either moved to plan for children's long-term care or, if the order had been discharged, initiated care proceedings a second time (see also Iwaniec et al. 2004). Harwin and her colleagues (2003) have suggested that returns on care orders require careful tracking by reviewing officers, so that if a review identifies difficulties, a re-evaluation of progress with the help of a CAFCASS officer might result in the case being returned to court.

To give one example, Mollie and her sister were taken into police protection when Mollie was one month old and after a positive residential assessment she and her sister were returned to their parents on care orders 11 months later. However, in spite of the many difficulties during the return – including neglect, serious domestic violence, the father's substance misuse and the parents not engaging with services, making it difficult to monitor the situation – both girls remained at home for four years until the mother, while drunk, assaulted a police officer who had arrived to deal with a domestic dispute. This and other cases in this group also suggests that there needs to be more clarity about the standards expected during reunification (Trotter 2002), about the consequences if these standards are not maintained and also what action will be taken if these expectations are not met (Biehal 2006; Davies and Ward 2011; Farmer 2009; Farmer et al. 2011). Without this, children may remain for long periods in unsatisfactory situations until, if they are lucky, a trigger event propels them into care.

Specialist and children's guardians' assessments which were problematic

Expert assessments were not always right and a number of the returns recommended by experts or children's guardians in care proceedings subsequently broke down or were detrimental to the children. This accords with Hunt and Macleod's finding (1999) of unwarranted over-optimism on the part of courts and the professionals advising them. For example, after Sasha's seventh return home and her mother's clear inability to give up drinking or to care for her, children's services initiated care proceedings when she was aged 12. However, they were unable to get the care order that they requested because an addictions specialist believed that her mother had abstained from drinking since Sasha was last accommodated. On the basis of this expert opinion, shared care was recommended, supported by a supervision order. In fact, Sasha's mother never engaged with any service for her drinking and she misused alcohol throughout. Shared care was detrimental for Sasha because of her mother's continued influence and by follow-up she was using drugs and alcohol and her future looked bleak.

In another example, a psychological assessment completed during care proceedings concluded that Mrs Bray, the mother of Cathy (aged 11), Gus (aged seven) and their three younger siblings, would always struggle because of her learning difficulties and that the chance of effecting change was low, but might be improved with a smaller family. As a result, the care plan became adoption for the youngest three children, but for Cathy and Gus to remain at home on supervision orders. This was despite the children already having been the subject of a previous set of care proceedings that ended in supervision orders which were not effective and the parents having been given numerous chances to improve over the years (which they only did sporadically with enormous inputs from children's services). Cathy and Gus continued to experience high levels of neglect (and in Cathy's case sexual abuse) in a return that was detrimental to them.

Clearly, it is crucial that expert opinions and those of children's guardians are carefully weighed and tested in court, especially as it has been found that lack of self-confidence on the part of social workers in their own expertise and that of their legal departments means that they are wary of challenging children's guardians (Iwaniec *et al.* 2004). Yet this can mean that long experience of lack of change by parents in a case is cast aside in favour of a recent and one-off assessment which ignores this history (Stevenson 2007). This would suggest that the system would be improved if the judge or magistrate reviewed all cases (or at least those which end in supervision orders or returns on care orders) every six months after they have been decided, in order to assess whether the disposition has safeguarded children and ensured that they have a secure and permanent base. Alternatively – although this would be less effective – it would be useful if the medium-term outcomes of decisions made on the basis of expert assessment and children's guardians' recommendations could be fed back to them and to the courts to enable professionals, judges and magistrates to get feedback on the efficacy of their recommendations. Magistrates and judges might also benefit from information about the 'rule of optimism' and the risks of relying on short-term assessments, even by highly qualified experts.

Supervision orders ineffective

For 15 per cent of the families (16 families affecting 21 children) care proceedings ended up with supervision orders being made but these proved ineffective (see also Hunt and Macleod 1999; Hunt, Macleod and Thomas 1999). In most of these cases children's services departments had wanted care orders and believed (rightly) that a supervision order would not be a strong enough order. With a supervision order, the local authority has no right of entry to the child's home, no right to remove the child and there is no direct way of enforcing the order (Masson, Bailey-Harris and Probert 2008a). In all of these cases the supervision orders did not provide adequate protection for the children or sufficient motivation to ensure that parents maintained any improvements evident before the orders were made. Some of the cases again showed that children's guardians, and sometimes expert assessors, had been over-optimistic and too anxious to give parents the benefit of having another chance, even though a deeper reading of the history might clearly have shown that this was not advisable. These are examples of the 'start again' or clean sheet syndrome, described by Brandon and her colleagues (2008b) in their analysis of serious case reviews, where knowledge of the past is put aside in favour of a focus on the present, and in these examples was a feature of expert opinion, not of social work practice. It is clearly very important that children's guardians and experts pay full attention to the entire prior history in such cases.

For example, Leon was made subject to a child protection plan at birth because of concerns about his siblings. However, although the local authority wished to remove Leon from his parents, they were unable to do so when a supervision rather than a care order was made in care proceedings. While he was at home there were a number of child protection investigations which did not lead to new child protection plans, although it was clear that Leon was being hit by both parents, and on one visit by a social worker Leon passed her a piece of paper with 'Help me' written on it. It was not until Leon was aged 11 that he was placed in a residential unit. When he was later returned to his mother it did not work out and he ended up homeless.

Moreover, in several of these cases, particularly where a parent was addicted to substances, especially alcohol, it was clear that more coercion was needed to prevent parents relapsing (see also Farmer *et al.* 2011). For example, Rose and John were accommodated at their mother's request when Rose was aged eight and John three because of their mother's drinking and drugs use. Care proceedings were initiated and family support was provided for the children and their mother. The court made supervision orders on the recommendation of the children's guardian and the children stayed at home. However, the children's mother resumed drinking and when she started a fire in the house the children were looked after. The children returned twice more to her after this without any improvement in their care and without any further attempts on the part of the local authority to achieve long-term stability for them.

Indeed, for only six families in the study affecting 13 children had supervision orders been successful, that is in only 27 per cent of the families where supervision orders were made (6 out of 22 families, 13 out of 34 children, 38%). (This is considerably worse than Hunt and Macleod's finding (1999) that a third of the returns made under supervision orders failed). It seemed that social workers were unsure how to use supervision orders to improve children's circumstances and so such orders meant very little. Indeed, it appeared that having once initiated care proceedings and not succeeded in gaining care orders, supervision orders provided an appearance of some intervention without having much substance. They very rarely if ever quickly led to a renewed application for a care order even when this was clearly needed (see also Hunt and Macleod 1999; Iwaniec *et al.* 2004). More often moves were made to close cases once the orders expired. One issue here is that the local authority has to start fresh care proceedings and re-prove the grounds for an order where a supervision order has failed. While it might not be justifiable in terms of the European Convention on Human Rights Articles 6 and 8 to convert a supervision order to a care order without any proceedings – the current situation involving the need for the whole panoply of court proceedings lasting many months to begin again from scratch appears to place the barrier to securing adequate protection for children too high in such cases.

Lack of action when returns in care proceedings were unsuccessful

For over half of the children where care proceedings were involved, the child was returned home during or after the care proceedings and was not kept safe.

When supervision orders were made they succeeded for 38 per cent of children but failed for 62 per cent (21), since the situation at home broke down and the children returned to care. Care proceedings were initiated a second time for 9 of the 21 children where supervision orders had failed, although by that time the children were older, so their options for long-term permanence were more limited. (For two children a second supervision order was made and a third child remained at home when the plan for his adoption did not work out.) No further legal action was taken in relation to the other 12 children.

Care orders with plans to return children to a parent were made on 32 children. These only succeeded for four (13%) and failed for 28 (87%). For three children, after the care orders were discharged, care proceedings were initiated on a second occasion and these three children were adopted. Clearly, the decisions made during care proceedings are crucial, since it appears that local authorities may be reluctant to initiate care proceedings a second time, once a return made during care proceedings fails. Moreover, despite the fact that the local authority has parental responsibility under a care order and a duty to exercise this to safeguard and promote the welfare of the child, the courts have imposed additional procedures on local authorities who decide to remove from home children subject to care orders (G v. NCC (2009)). This too may inhibit local authorities from taking action in such cases. There needs to be a much stronger mechanism in place so that if a decision in care proceedings to return children to their parents does not work out, proactive planning does take place which ensures that permanence plans are made and put into action. In a few cases fresh care proceedings may need to be initiated. Independent reviewing officers have a key role to play to ensure this happens and post-order reviews of cases by the courts should be considered (Harwin *et al.* 2003).

We investigated what happened to the 25 other children for whom the returns to parents on care orders failed (and where there were no further care proceedings to secure their future). Twelve of these children returned to parents again on one or more occasions (but this succeeded for only two children). Ten children ended up in care (for only two of whom this was planned to be long-term), one child moved to relatives, while two went to prison. This shows that few of these children later achieved stability at home or in a permanent placement.

Care orders with plans for permanence outside the family were made on 21 children. These succeeded for most (76%) of the children, although five (24%) did not achieve a stable permanent placement. Overall, the plans made in care proceedings did not work out in 62 per cent of cases.

Case planning and plans for permanence
Plans for permanence

For half of the children the decision was made at some point that they should be cared for away from home permanently in either long-term foster care (58% of these plans), kinship (14%) or adoptive homes (28%). However, these plans had not always been achieved by the end of the five-year follow-up. Nearly half of the children (45%) had been placed permanently or progress had been made towards permanent placement, while for 19 per cent a permanent placement had not been found or had broken down. However, for the other third (36%) of these children their plans for permanence had been abandoned or changed and most were then returned home.

Appropriate planning

In many cases, planning for children was appropriate and timely. For example, as we have seen, children's services became involved with Ollie during periods of crisis when his mother was admitted to the local psychiatric hospital. Once Ollie's second return home broke down, care proceedings were started so that planning for his future could take place. He was placed with long-term foster carers at the age of 11 and did well there. He received good services, including help from CAMHS and life story work, and received extra help at school, funded by children's services, so that he could aim for five A–C grades at GCSE.

Shortcomings in case planning

We considered that for over a third (36%) of the children (50) case planning had shortcomings. There was a particular concentration of these difficulties in one local authority where this applied to four-fifths (81%) of its cases, whereas this was true for between 12 per cent and 36 per cent of children's cases in the other local authorities.

The most common situation, affecting 17 per cent of the children, was when plans were made to return children to parents who were unable to look after them adequately. As we have seen, in a considerable number of cases such plans were made and implemented during care proceedings involving children returning to their parents on care or supervision orders. Once children were unsuccessfully returned in care proceedings there were generally no further attempts to make long-term plans for these children away from their parents. In some other cases there had been no assessment of the parents before return and in one case the mother was actually homeless. Sometimes, once the original unsuitable return had taken place, children oscillated between their parents and care.

In other cases in this group, plans were made for long-term care but these later changed to return home, either because the child absconded home because of difficulties in finding a suitable placement, or the parents applied to discharge the care order, or more rarely because the care placement broke down and this led to a reappraisal of the possibilities of return.

A few children had been placed in a residential school for several years, but this was seen as so successful that it was ended by the authority even though they had not tested out the parents' capacity to care, or children absconded home. The benefits of this schooling were rapidly lost if the parents had not changed and the original problems returned.

In a few cases while effective permanence planning did take place, it was considerably delayed, so that either children were by that time too disturbed to be placed for adoption or were placed, but at an older age than had been necessary. Another small group of cases involved young people where plans to consider their future were so severely delayed that their behaviour had become so challenging that no placement could hold them. These young people moved rapidly from one placement to another, sometimes interspersed with unsuccessful returns home. This illustrates the danger of practice which involves 'trying again' with parents, where many returns are attempted without setting timescales or planning for permanence (Biehal 2006; Farmer 2009; Farmer et al. 2011; Harwin et al. 2003).

In ten cases there was very little planning of any sort. In this vacuum, children were returned again and again to parents who could not manage them, where they experienced continued abuse, neglect, domestic violence and lived with parents with alcohol and drug misuse problems. Many oscillated between home and care. Such extreme instability and adversity boded poorly for their futures and some were noted to be many years behind with their schoolwork.

Now that we have examined how cases were managed under child protection procedures and in court proceedings, we look in the next chapter at other issues in working with neglected children and their parents and how their cases were managed overall.

6

Case Management

Working with Parents and Children and Overall Patterns of Case Management

Lack of parental engagement

In a considerable number of families it was difficult to work with the parents of the neglected children because they were hard to engage (see also Crittenden 1999; Farmer *et al.* 2011; Henry 2008; Stone 1998). Only a third of the mothers (31%) were considered to have been very or quite well engaged with their social workers. A further two-fifths were not, while a tenth were actively resistant or hostile. (Engagement levels for the remaining 15 per cent of mothers varied at different times). Thus, there were difficulties in working with 69 per cent of the mothers and with over half (54%) of the father figures, about whom there was less information (Farmer and Owen 1995, 1998; O'Hagan and Dillenburger 1995; Scourfield 2006; Tanner and Turney 2003). In addition, parents attempted to sabotage work in two-fifths of the cases (39%) (see also Crittenden 1999).

While a quarter of the parents did engage with another worker, on the whole parents who were not well engaged with the social worker also tended to have poor engagement with other practitioners.

Avoidance and resistance

Difficulties in working with parents could take a variety of forms, with parental avoidance the most common. Appointments would frequently be missed, parents would be out when professionals visited the home or they would be difficult to contact. For example, professionals tried to work with the Richmond family for eight months but were only able to carry out three successful social work visits to 13-year-old Kelly and her stepfather, whilst there were six unsuccessful social work visits and two unsuccessful police visits.

Some parents directly refused offers of services, advice or support. For example, one child's mother, even after her children were removed, refused to attend treatment for her alcohol misuse or to attend Alcoholics Anonymous. Other parents were restrictive about the times when professionals could visit and one mother was selectively mute, completely refusing to communicate with professionals. Not surprisingly, when parents engaged poorly, their children could be at high risk of abuse or neglect. Such resistance sometimes succeeded in shaking off social workers. Indeed, in a fifth of families where there were problems working with the parents, the case was closed at some point for this reason (see Re E (2000)).

In two-fifths of the cases where there were difficulties in working with the parents, steps were taken to try to protect the children or to engage the parents. Some children were removed or accommodated because of concerns about parental engagement, while others remained looked after for this reason. A number of children were made or remained subject to a child protection plan as a result of such difficulties. The legal system was also used to protect children where there was a lack of parental engagement or co-operation (Cleaver and Freeman 1995; Corby, Millar and Young 1996; Dingwall *et al.* 1983; Farmer and Owen 1995; Hunt *et al.* 1999; Iwaniec *et al.* 2004; Miller and Fisher 1992; Platt 2007; Thorpe 1994) and in a few cases care proceedings were started, a care order was made or supervision orders were extended.

Written agreements were rarely used to try to overcome difficulties in working with parents. In one such example, the local authority was granted an emergency protection order to gain access to three-year-old Freddie after concerns had been raised about the conditions he and his mother were living in. This led to a written agreement being drawn up stating that Freddie would be examined by the GP, would attend nursery regularly, the flat would be clean and that his mother would accept a programme of visits. As a consequence the local authority did not at that time seek a care order. However, in this case, the mother reluctantly complied only for a period and as concerns about Freddie continued, the local authority removed him from her care and initiated care proceedings.

Lack of involvement of fathers

In general, there was little focus on involving fathers (or father figures) in the cases in the study (see also DePanfilis 1999; Farmer and Owen 1995, 1998; O'Hagan and Dillenburger 1995; Stone 1998). In one such case the father lived in the family home but claimed not to be involved in the upbringing of the children. Children's services treated this mother as if she was a single parent, although the daughter about whom there was concern was noted to be a 'Daddy's girl'. Fathers were often shadowy figures on the files and the researchers considered that greater attempts could have been made to involve the father or father figure in a quarter (27%) of cases (see also DePanfilis 1999; Ryan 2000; Scourfield 2006; Tanner and Turney 2003). Nonetheless, there were often obstacles in the way of doing so, such as the mother's partnerships changing frequently, mothers who were not frank about the men in their lives (whether living with them or not) (Haringey Local Safeguarding Children Board 2009) and some men ensured that they were not available during social work visits. All of these issues could make men difficult to engage, even when they were having a real impact on their children.

Levels of engagement of the children

Where information was available (half of the files), there were fairly high levels of engagement by children and young people. Over three-fifths of the children were very or quite well engaged with their social workers, while only a quarter were not. (For the remaining tenth their level of engagement was variable.) Thus, a third of the children (35%) were hard to engage and these were mostly adolescents. Some children and young people (33%), though, did engage with another worker.

How far were expectations about parental standards made clear?

One way in which social workers could attempt to monitor and exert some control over cases was in making their expectations of parental standards clear (Trotter 2002), although research suggests that social workers may be uncomfortable with adopting a directive style with parents (Secker 1993). Such expectations were made clear with over two-fifths of the families, usually in the form of written agreements. Written agreements had been used in a quarter of the original returns. Where conditions were specified these included addressing drug and alcohol use, accessing support services, co-operating with children's services, attending meetings, protecting children from adults who posed a risk, maintaining appropriate conditions in the home, ensuring school attendance, attending medical appointments and providing appropriate levels of supervision. Conditions were sometimes concrete and tightly specified and at other times were rather more general. Specific expectations often related to parental alcohol use.

Expectations could be specified at various stages. Children's services could make clear to parents what improvements needed to be made while the child was at home, after concerns had been raised. Subsequently, when children were looked after, the social worker could specify the conditions the parents needed to meet for the child to be returned to them. Conditions might also be specified and written agreements drawn up at the point that the return went ahead. For example, due to a placement breakdown caused by Anna absconding, she returned to live at home with her mother and stepfather at the age of 14 with a care order in place. The conditions for the return were as follows: weekly social work visits initially, which were to reduce to fortnightly and then to monthly; for a safe and stable environment to be provided for Anna; and for her mother and step-father to co-operate with other agencies.

The consequences of not complying with specific expectations were often not made clear to parents. This occurred with Dominic's mother, Mrs Booth, when in response to deteriorating conditions in the home during Dominic's second return home at the age of five, the social worker clearly laid down the expectations of children's services. The situation did not improve and Dominic was made subject to a child protection plan. This did not succeed in motivating change and concerns continued. However, there was no evidence of a contingency plan if co-operation and change were not forthcoming, and so Dominic remained at home.

While some parents complied when conditions were set, many did not. Such situations received varying responses. In many cases children's services took action and either removed the child, started care proceedings or made alternative permanence plans. At other times no action was taken. It is worrying that a few children remained at home despite their parents not having fulfilled such expectations and occasionally children were actually returned home despite the conditions for return not having been met by the parents. Clearly, it is very important that when conditions or expectations are made, the consequences of not fulfilling them are made explicit and consistently acted on. Clear contingency plans are needed in these situations.

In general, children's services more often made their expectations explicit and acted on them when dealing with young children who were at considerable risk, since the local authority would then be confident about making alternative placement plans for them (see also Farmer and Parker 1991).

Giving parents too many chances and bringing about change in parents

In half of the cases (47%) parents had been warned that more coercive action would be taken if particular requirements were not fulfilled, for example co-operating with an assessment. The difficult practice issue was in following this through. The researchers considered that in almost two-fifths of the cases (38%) the parents had been given too many chances to make changes. For example, Peter was returned home from care on four occasions (from the age of 12 months) to a situation that was unchanged from when he had been removed. His mother consistently misused alcohol, had only once unsuccessfully gone into treatment, and had thereafter been given numerous chances to change. A care order was made when Peter was aged nine and it was agreed that there would be no further attempts at reunification. However, after several placement breakdowns, he returned to her at the age of 11. His mother continued to drink, Peter's behaviour became increasingly difficult, he had no suitable school provision and became involved in offending.

We examined how often real changes took place in parents' functioning during the whole period from first referral to the end of the five-year follow-up. There were very few cases (10) where it was possible to identify real change in relation to the parents' difficulties or their parenting during children's services involvement. In four cases there was clear evidence that the parents' mental health problems had improved, resulting in successful returns, with three parents receiving good support for their problems. There were four cases where the parents had successfully managed to address their drug (3) or alcohol misuse (1) problems. This is extremely low given that in two-thirds of families there was evidence of substance misuse problems prior to care. One young person, who had committed a serious offence against another child, spent a year in a secure unit, during which time he and his parents received treatment. This input resulted in a successful return where the young person did not reoffend. Finally, one girl was successfully returned home after the completion of family work and play therapy. This return was well planned and occurred after a gradual increase in contact.

These figures suggest that parents' difficulties often show little change in spite of the services provided for them and also suggest that more intensive help may be needed to bring about real change. This indicates the importance of practitioners remaining realistic about what has and has not changed and of looking for ways in which families can improve their functioning, such as by means of changes in family composition or the presence of extensive and targeted support. The optimism about change shown by some children's guardians, expert assessors and other practitioners does not appear to be based on strong foundations.

The effect of children's ethnicity on case management

A fifth of the children (19%) were from black and minority ethnic backgrounds, with 16 per cent of the 104 families having at least one minority ethnic child. While generally, ethnicity did not appear to affect the handling of cases, in two-fifths of the families it appeared to have some impact (see also Brophy, Jhutti-Johal and MacDonald 2005; Brophy, Jhutti-Johal and Owen 2003). Of course, it may be that ethnicity affected case management in more cases but that this was not evident from the case files. Korbin and Spilsbury (1999) stress the importance of 'cultural competence' when social workers intervene in families with black and minority ethnic backgrounds, explaining that cultural competence puts children's protection first but that this is understood within a cultural context, including identifying culturally appropriate interventions and sorting out which aspects of a family's difficulties are 'cultural', which are 'neglectful' and which are a combination of these. However, even this explanation points up how difficult it is to achieve culturally competent practice, and in addition, there is a dearth of knowledge about the child-rearing practices of particular minority ethnic groups (Dutt and Phillips 1996, 2000; Stevenson 2007). Misunderstandings about variability between cultures have been identified in a number of child death enquiries (e.g. Laming 2003; London Borough of Lambeth 1987).

In three cases it appeared that children's services did not take concerns as seriously as they might have done because of cultural factors, a situation which has been described as cultural relativism (Dingwall *et al.* 1983; Korbin 1991) or 'reconstructed racism' (Channer and Parton 1990). In two cases beatings were apparently not taken more seriously because of a view that in some cultures physical chastisement is accepted, while in a third case the physical and emotional abuse of an 18-month girl after she returned home to her parents and brothers appeared to be explained away as a cultural issue. In two other cases parents argued that it was acceptable in their own countries to leave a child alone in the house. For four other families there were problems in finding a relative who was willing to care for the child or a culturally or ethnically matched placement, while an Asian sibling group of three children were returned to their violent and emotionally abusive father because children's services were concerned that their cultural needs were not being met in foster care.

Inappropriate case closure

The researchers judged that the cases of 40 per cent of the families were closed inappropriately, that is when there was clear evidence of the presence of difficulties or where the underlying problems in the case still remained (Nottinghamshire Safeguarding Children Board 2009). For example, one case was closed soon after a 13-year-old girl had been sexually abused by three adults and without the provision of any counselling. Another case was closed against a mother's wishes at a time when she felt unable to cope with her son. In many of these families the cases had to be quickly reopened after further concerns were raised. For example, Grant first came to the attention of children's services when he was aged ten, but after an educational social worker became involved the case was closed despite concerns about his mother's hostile behaviour, the chaotic appearance of the household, and the relationship between his parents who were heroin users. The case was re-referred 10 months later due to the family's chronic problems.

Some cases were closed after children moved from one parent to the other separated parent without any assessment of this other parent's suitability. As previously noted, a small number of cases were closed due to lack of parental engagement. For example, as we have seen, after Becky's father failed to take up any of the services offered, the case was closed when Becky was 12 years old. During the next seven months, there were eight child protection referrals from neighbours, professionals and anonymous sources expressing concern about her father's alcohol use, lack of supervision, neglect and the children's contact with a known child sex offender.

Unallocated cases

As we have seen, for a third of the children there were periods during the three-year follow-up when no worker was allocated and the cases of 5 per cent of the children remained unallocated throughout this period (see Chapter 4). Thus, the lack of an allocated worker was fairly common and in at least one case no social worker was allocated for a period even though the child was subject to a child protection plan.

It was clear that in such cases drift occurred and some children were abused or neglected by their parents, with no action taken to protect them; others were not returned home when planned; written agreements were drawn up but not signed by parents; pieces of work were not completed or plans for a permanent placement were not actioned; and in one case a child with a plan for adoption remained with his birth parents.

The effect of changes of social worker on case management

As we saw in Chapter 4, only a fifth of the children (22%) had the same social worker throughout the final three-year period. Interestingly, for two-thirds of the cases, these changes of social worker did not appear to affect the handling of the case. However, for 6 per cent of cases the changes of social worker had a positive impact on case management, in a tenth of cases (10%) a negative effect, and both positive and negative effects in a further group (16%) of cases.

The allocation of a new social worker could bring a new perspective to the case. Sometimes the new social worker considered the situation to be more concerning than previous workers. For example, Emma had been on a child protection plan for two years while living with her mother. There had been little change in the situation during this time and evidence that Emma's mother Mrs Frayne continued to use drugs. Nonetheless, Emma's social worker recommended that the plan be discontinued as she felt that Mrs Frayne's care of her was good enough. When a new social worker was allocated, she immediately proposed that Emma, now aged three, should be removed from home if Mrs Frayne could not demonstrate that she was drug free.

There were other cases where new social workers changed the plans for children so that they were returned home. For example, the plan for Charlie was long-term foster care. However, due to his difficult behaviour, he had experienced a number of placement breakdowns and there were difficulties in finding him a long-term placement. A new social worker was allocated who ascertained that Charlie still had a strong desire to go home and felt that, although risks remained, Charlie's brother was doing well at home and that the risks could be minimized by a support package and close monitoring. A phased return took place when Charlie was aged 13 but he became uncontrollable and it disrupted after ten months.

However, a new social worker did not always bring a new perspective to a case. For example, when a new social worker was allocated to Darren's case, as we will see, she continued to treat the case as one of family support instead of child protection because this was how the case had been dealt with in the past, even though there was clear evidence of major child protection concerns.

In summary, changes of social worker could impact on the management of a case by prompting more proactive work or changing the plans for the child, but it often had no such effect. However, the lack of an allocated social worker often had a negative effect on cases because of drift. Of course, when there were many changes of social worker there was a lack of continuity for the parents and children and a lack of follow-through which could also affect case management.

Drift

A number of cases showed periods when the case drifted and there was little social work activity. As we have just seen, sometimes this was because the case was frequently opened and closed even when there were continuing difficulties. At other times drift occurred because of changes of social worker or when cases were unallocated for periods.

Failure to contain children

In many of the cases in the study, lack of proactive work and appropriate interventions left children exposed to adverse home circumstances for too long, so that if at a later stage they went into care their behaviour made it difficult to contain them there. This could lead to many changes of placement and sometimes absconding, and by this stage even if more specialist (and often expensive) placements and services were deployed to assist the young people, they often had limited impact.

In a third of the families, children and young people displayed very difficult behaviour and were beyond control. These children tended to be older, with most aged between 10 and 14 years old at the time of the return we focused on, and the largest number were 12 years or older at that point. For many of the children a downhill trajectory of increasingly difficult behaviour was evident. For example, as we have seen, Charlie returned home to his mother at the age of 13 after an unsettled three years in care. His behaviour was challenging and his school attendance poor. The family had struck up a close relationship with neighbours who were convicted child sex offenders. There was conflict at home between Charlie, his mother and his older brother. Charlie destroyed furniture, smoked cannabis and sniffed aerosols, and the emergency duty team described him as 'uncontrollable'. Ten months later Charlie was arrested for shoplifting and, when the police refused to return him home, he was placed in residential care. He absconded home from the unit and became a persistent offender, spending a number of periods in young offender institutions.

Parents often struggled to cope with their teenage children's difficult behaviour while they were at home, but the response of children's services did not always reflect the severity of their concerns and was sometimes minimal. For example, Justin returned home to his mother at the age of 13 but his mother was at her wits' end because she could not cope with his behaviour. He threatened and blackmailed her, refused to attend school and on one occasion smashed up the house. A referral for a foster placement was made, but no placement was found and no further action was taken. In addition, a number of children were not being contained within the education system either. Children were often excluded, temporarily or permanently, including a few younger children who were excluded from primary school.

Sixteen of the children were not containable within the care system. Typically these children were frequent absconders, displayed very difficult behaviour, were often violent and some had problems with drugs, alcohol or offending. For example, Bobby went missing from foster care at the age of 12 and when he was located was placed in a residential unit. He regularly went missing from the unit in the day and sometimes overnight. Bobby was involved in offending, including criminal damage, threatening behaviour, burglary and theft and he was thought to be using drugs. Shayla was accommodated for the second time for 14 months at the age of 11. She moved frequently as placements could not contain her drinking, drug-taking, challenging behaviour and assaults on staff.

Children's services would often deal with children who were not being contained within the care system by moving them to different types of placement. For example, children who could not remain in foster care were moved to residential care and children who were problematic in residential care were sometimes moved to specialist units, including residential schools. An alternative response when children were not containable in the care system was to return them home *faute de mieux*.

For nine young people, their difficulties were so great that they were placed in secure accommodation for one or more periods. These stays in secure accommodation usually kept the young people safe or curbed their problem behaviour for a limited period, but most of the young people resumed their risky lifestyle on being released.

Sadly, for most of these children who were beyond control and not containable, their outcomes at the five-year follow-up point were poor. For example, Norman spent a number of periods in young offender institutions for offences of theft and robbery. He continued to use drugs when he was not in prison and lived in a variety of types of temporary accommodation. He only intermittently complied with the terms of his supervision orders and was often rearrested for breaching these orders. At the five-year follow-up point he had been released from prison to his home address but his subsequent whereabouts were unknown.

However, a few young people who had been difficult to contain fared better. For example, Geoff achieved a good outcome. He had committed a serious sexual offence and was sentenced to two years in a secure unit. A psychiatrist and psychologist provided a treatment programme for him to address his sexual offending behaviour and his own sexually abusive background. Family therapy and parenting work were also undertaken with his parents. Due to his excellent progress Geoff was released from the secure unit on licence and returned to live with his parents. The psychologist and psychiatrist continued to work with Geoff and his family, and a youth offending team worker also monitored his progress and supervised his licence. Geoff remained at home until he moved to supported lodgings and then into his own flat. He did some college courses and got a job, later settling in a flat and getting married. Geoff's good outcome appeared to be linked to the high levels of treatment and intervention provided for him and his family while he was in the secure unit and after his release.

There was evidence that quite a number of children who became difficult to contain could have been helped at an earlier stage. For example, there were concerns about Andrew prior to his birth as both of his parents were drug users and frequent offenders. Despite this, he remained living with his parents and several times was made the subject of child protection plans due to neglect. By the age of eight he was referred for smoking cannabis and getting drunk. Eighteen months later he was placed in a residential therapeutic school, where he did well and was later returned to his parents. He went on to have a drug problem himself and became a prolific offender. There were opportunities, both at Andrew's birth and later, to prevent him from being further exposed to the adverse influences of his parents. Had these opportunities been taken his problematic behaviour might have been prevented.

How proactive was case management?

Finally, we consider how proactive case management had been over the entire lifetime of the case. We identified four broad patterns of management. In some cases, management had been proactive throughout, in others it had been characterized by being mainly passive. In the third group, case management had started out as proactive but had later become passive to events, while in a fourth group, the reverse was the case.

We begin by discussing the cases which began by being passive but later became proactive.

Case management that was initially passive but later became proactive

Over a quarter (26%) of the families (27 of the 104 families, affecting 38 children) were passively managed initially but were later managed proactively. Some of these cases were managed as family support cases for too long in spite of a build-up of concerns that would have made earlier child protection intervention more appropriate (see e.g. Laming 2003). For example, the Bates family was first referred when the children were aged five, four and two years old. Over the years there were numerous referrals for physical abuse and neglect and possible sexual abuse to the children. The school also expressed concern about the children's behaviour and conditions in the home. The children were not accommodated until three years later, but although a written agreement was then used, the conditions had not been met by the time the children again returned home. It was another two years before care proceedings were brought and care orders made, by which time the children were so disturbed that they needed specialist foster placements.

Needless to say, some cases showed a more complex pattern, where after passive management followed by more proactive intervention, management again became more passive later. Six of the 27 cases in this group showed this pattern. For example, from early on in their lives concerns were regularly expressed that a sibling group of three children was being neglected and their school had real concerns about them. These concerns were not viewed by children's services as serious enough to precipitate a child protection investigation and the referrals were viewed in isolation and not cumulatively in the context of previous concerns (passive). Children's services made many attempts to try to engage the mother but she remained hostile and unresponsive. Finally, the children entered care when the oldest was aged nine. The plan was for long-term foster care, since when care orders were made it was recommended that the children should not be returned to their mother (proactive). The plan remained long-term fostering until three years later when the mother began to say that she wanted the children back to live with her. At this point a more passive approach was adopted and the children were then returned home in stages without any assessment of their mother. They remained with her but their anti-social and criminal behaviour escalated (passive).

Case management that was initially proactive but later became passive

We look now at the second group of cases in the somewhat different situation where case management began by being proactive but later lost this momentum. A quarter (25%) of the families were managed this way (26 of 104 families, affecting 31 children). The pattern in these cases was for children's services departments to take action either early on in the child's life or soon after concerns about the child's welfare became evident. Appropriate action was then taken to safeguard the child and plan for the future, but as time wore on the management was no longer proactive but merely reactive to events. Sometimes, momentum was lost because although children's services departments had attempted to safeguard the children's future through the use of care proceedings, as previously mentioned, the children's guardian or an expert assessment had not been in agreement with their recommendations, so this avenue had been blocked.

For example, as we have seen, a care order was obtained on Daisy when she was three months old, after concerns about gross neglect to her and her older siblings, and she remained at home. However, after heightened concerns she was removed and it was planned that she would return home following a residential assessment only if it was successful. The assessment was unsuccessful and it was planned that Daisy would be adopted (proactive). However, the children's guardian disagreed with this decision and an independent assessment recommended that Daisy be returned home. When she was reunified on a care order she was rejected and severely physically abused by her mother and suffered further neglect. Daisy then went on to experience seven failed returns home as the situation at home had not changed (passive).

Sometimes, after proactive intervention, followed by a passive phase, case management became more proactive again. In the example which follows, the second period of proactive work was followed by another passive phase. As we have seen, Mrs Black's first three children were removed to adoptive placements because of her alcohol problems, neglect of the children and involvement with violent men. When her fourth child Sasha was born, she and her mother were placed in a residential assessment centre and moved to live independently 18 months later (proactive). Sasha was under a child protection plan until she was three. Sasha next came to the attention of children's services when she was aged nine because her mother was struggling to cope, and she had a number of periods in care. By the age of ten, she was described as sullen, unhappy, neglected and unkempt as a result of her mother's drinking problem. The local authority believed that they did not have the evidence that they would need for care proceedings and were aware of Sasha's desire to stay with her mother (passive).

By the age of 12, Sasha was on her seventh return home. Care proceedings were then initiated (proactive). However, an addictions specialist who provided an expert opinion to the court believed that Mrs Black had abstained from drinking since Sasha was last accommodated and so, instead of a care order, a supervision order was made with a plan for shared care. In the event, this ensured that Sasha continued to be influenced by her mother, who encouraged her drinking, and there was frequent violence between them. By the age of 14, Sasha had been excluded from school, was offending and was misusing drugs and alcohol. During the final three-year period Sasha had four social workers, her case was twice closed, she was a frequent offender, misused drugs and alcohol, and could not identify any supportive relative (passive).

As we have seen, in a number of cases when the local authority had sought a care order but instead a supervision order was made, the subsequent case management faltered. It may be that in this situation the social workers considered that there were few options left for them (see also Farmer and Parker 1991) and, as we have seen, there may be reluctance to attempt to initiate care proceedings a second time. However, as we saw in Chapter 5, even care orders did not ensure that management remained proactive.

Another general situation in which proactive work gave way to passive management was when children who had been appropriately placed in substitute care or residential schools were then returned home to parents whose circumstances had not improved and remained there in spite of evident difficulties. In four of the cases which followed this pattern, the return occurred after placement in a residential school. In addition, as might be expected, there were a number of children whose case management, while good in the initial stages, was later passive as they became older and no placement could contain or hold them.

Case management that was passive throughout

We now consider the 24 per cent (25) of families where case management was predominantly passive (affecting 31 children). These were some of the most poorly managed cases in the study, where children were left at risk without adequate intervention, sometimes over long periods, and where we might expect particularly poor outcomes. They included cases where there were many changes of social worker and case closures and where the concerns of other professionals were ignored. The cases were treated as family support when they were open, and abuse, neglect and parental rejection of the children were minimized. Parental problems such as alcohol and drugs misuse or mental health difficulties received little attention, so children experienced the many adversities caused by living with parents with these difficulties (see e.g. Cleaver *et al.* 2007, 2011; Forrester and Harwin 2004; Harwin and Forrester 2002; Kroll and Taylor 2003; Lynksey, Fergusson and Horwood 1994; Maluccio and Ainsworth 2003; Tunnard 2002a; Velleman 1993). Sometimes attempts to instigate care proceedings were thwarted by legal advice that there was insufficient evidence to do so, and on the rare occasions when care proceedings were instigated the outcome (and its implementation), especially the use of supervision orders, did not assist case management. In one case, when children's services wanted to remove children from their mother who had once again allowed them to see a relative who was a convicted child sex offender, the children's guardian and the court did not agree, and gave the mother yet another opportunity to show that she could keep the children safe.

Overall, there was a lack of direction and planning in these cases, little or no permanence planning and insufficient clarity with parents about what needed to change and by when and the consequences if no change took place. Sometimes the workers did not have a view of the full history of the case. In addition, it appeared that no one had oversight of the whole case, which might have led to a recognition of the extent of harm the children had suffered and the ineffectiveness of the approach taken. In two cases either the mother or both parents had learning difficulties and in another the family were travellers, which might have explained the enormous efforts to work with the family without instigating care proceedings. These are what Miller and Fisher (1992) call 'mitigating factors' and Henry (2008) calls 'defences' which can operate to dilute or soften interpretations of adverse parental behaviour. It is likely that in some of these cases the parents (usually the mother) were seen as co-operative and this reassured workers (see e.g. Cleaver and Freeman 1995; Corby *et al.* 1996; Dingwall *et al.* 1983; Farmer and Owen 1995; Hunt *et al.* 1999; Platt 2007; Thorpe 1994). Nonetheless, in a number of these cases, senior managers or the chairs of child protection reviews in the authorities wrote on file that they were very unhappy with the way the case was being handled.

An example of passive case management is shown by Frank's case. His mother had learning difficulties and had been sexually abused by her father. Her first two children were looked after by relatives or placed for adoption. When, a year later Frank was born it was not clear why children's services did not consider placing him for adoption too. There were many concerns about neglect and poor supervision and while still very young Frank was sexually abused by a neighbour and a relative. His mother actually wanted Frank and his two younger siblings to go into care, but this was not agreed. At the age of seven Frank had a fall and sustained a serious injury and from the age of eight he showed sexualized behaviour. There were also many referrals about his mother's drinking and leaving the children unsupervised. In spite of this catalogue of difficulties, Frank and his siblings were not placed on child protection plans and care proceedings were not taken. When Frank was aged ten the health visitor wrote a letter to the children's services department criticizing the lack of a proactive response to Frank's difficulties and requesting a case conference. This was refused. Frank was accommodated at the age of 11 and then had ten placements with a brief return to his mother who was overdosing and misusing drugs. When at the age of 14 he returned to his mother yet again with no improvement in her problems, the service manager expressed grave reservations on file about this return. When Frank was aged 15 care proceedings and permanence planning were discussed in a review meeting but no action was taken on either count.

In another example, Darren's mother Mrs Price rejected him and Darren was neglected, physically and sexually abused and witnessed domestic violence. There was a stream of referrals about physical abuse to Darren, his sexualized behaviour, and reports that Darren and his siblings were being left with unsuitable carers. The children were made subject to child protection plans and Mrs Price was given support, including monthly respite care for Darren and his siblings, which was described on file as a 'damage limitation exercise to expose them to good parenting experiences'. After Mrs Price moved in with Mr Hand much of the caring was undertaken by Mr Hand's mother, who drank and hit Darren and tied him up to control him. A new social worker, who found that Darren was regularly shut in his room, arranged that Darren, now aged eight, should be accommodated, but did not resist when Mrs Price demanded his return, in spite of evidence of gross neglect and Darren's resulting major emotional and behavioural problems. A multi-professional meeting to consider the multiple maltreatment to Darren did not support a move to care proceedings, although a later meeting did agree to this on the basis of new evidence that Mrs Price might be involved in drug dealing. This meeting noted that 'the level of neglect encountered by Darren was leading to a deterioration in his well-being' and it was seen especially at school that he had 'unacceptable levels of insecurity and had unreasonable responsibility for the younger children'. At this point the service manager wrote on file that he was mystified by the lack of intervention in a case of such exceptional maltreatment and cruelty.

However, local authority legal advice concluded that there was insufficient evidence to proceed, so Mrs Price was given several tasks to improve her child care and respite care was increased to fortnightly. However, this active social worker then left, the case was unallocated for two months and the case was then closed, in spite of the school's objections. The fifth social worker who was allocated to the case, when Darren was aged ten, wrote on file: 'the matter is regarded as family support rather than child protection', suggesting that the former case management style dictated the approach she then took.

This case is characterized by the local authority's lack of response to serious maltreatment to Darren. The insistence on taking a family support approach throughout seemed to lead to a lack of planning and little attention to Darren's needs or to his future. There was a great deal of inertia in this case, which was not altered even by the service manager's searing criticism, and since Darren had gone on living with his mother for so long, it appeared to become more difficult to consider decisive action to secure his future. Indeed, it could be argued that since the previous case management had condoned a poor situation, an assumed 'point of no return' occurred when poor case management led to the argument that only further poor case management was possible and it would have made a change of management more difficult to justify. (This is backed up by case file notes in which the social worker commented that since Darren had lived with rejection from his mother for nine years, 'Are we going to break this bond now via the courts?' The worker envisaged that Darren would cling to his mother and siblings 'with his existing anxious bond and the huge feeling of responsibility for his siblings'. The social worker also wrote that the children's guardian might think it was too late to move Darren from his family or only allow a supervision order.) Clearly, in addition, the poor legal advice when care proceedings were considered constituted an important missed opportunity to intervene.

In another case in this group, the child's father was a violent man who had threatened social work staff with violence and this might have had some bearing on the hands-off management in the case (see e.g. London Borough of Lambeth 1987; Miller and Fisher 1992; Stanley and Goddard 2002). Since such information would not always have been evident from the files, there may have been other cases in which threatening behaviour affected case management. In other cases in this group, returns took place which were unsuitable or where the parent had not been assessed and these were not challenged by children's services – even in one case when this occurred during care proceedings.

With many of the cases in this category, it is also clear that once appropriate action was not taken when children were young, opportunities to intervene later were severely constrained, partly by children's worsening behaviour and partly by their own difficulties in trusting adults or moving on from parents who had withheld from them the affection they still craved (Farmer *et al.* 2004). In such situations, young people often have entrenched, unresolved attachment difficulties with their parents, and even when placed in care they seek to return to parents who have been highly rejecting, neglectful or abusive to them (Moyers, Farmer and Lipscombe 2006).

Case management that was proactive throughout

We turn now to consider the quarter (25%) of families (26) where the case management was predominantly proactive (affecting 38 children). In a number of these cases an initial child protection conference was held prior to the child's birth, or care proceedings or actions to accommodate children were initiated soon after birth. In all of them, once concerns about the children's welfare had been recognized, children's services departments moved to protect children and plan for their future. The parents were still given the chance to show that they could parent their children safely, but action was taken if they could not. In this group, children from 11 families were returned successfully to their parents. These returns were generally well planned and provided with considerable levels of support. Another three children were returned to the other parent (usually removed from the mother and returned to the father). Children from 12 families had permanent placements away from their parents, with eight adopted, three in long-term foster care and one in kinship care.

For example, there were concerns about Adam prior to his birth and an initial child protection conference was held before he was born. Adam was made subject to a child protection plan and care proceedings were started after he was born, while Adam went from hospital to a residential mother and baby unit. His mother, who had learning difficulties, was very engaged with professionals and committed to caring for him. Following a positive assessment, Adam and his mother moved to a flat with an excellent support package in place. As a result of his mother's good progress a one-year supervision order was made. However, after the supervision order expired Adam's mother was hospitalized because of mental health problems. Adam was accommodated and returned to his mother for five days following the breakdown of his foster placement. He then returned to foster care at the age of two and a half and care proceedings were initiated when his mother threatened to remove him from voluntary care. The psychiatric assessment of his mother during the care proceedings gave a very poor prognosis and so the plan was for adoption.

It was heartening to find that in some cases parents' care of their children did improve and, more unusually, in one case both parents managed to become free of drugs. In this case, the initial plan was for a short period of accommodation, but due to lack of engagement from the parents, care proceedings were started. A care order was made and Dylan's plan was for long-term fostering because of his parents' continued drug use. Both parents attended drug treatment and became drug free, and Dylan's mother later applied to discharge the care order. Dylan returned home to his mother at the age of nine. His behaviour was difficult but his mother managed to cope, despite receiving only limited support.

As would be expected, in many of these cases care proceedings or child protection procedures were used effectively either to safeguard children, bring about increased co-operation from the parents or, if this was not forthcoming, to plan for permanence. However, some cases were worked with proactively without using the courts or child protection procedures.

We found that the rates of proactive practice varied by local authority from a high in one where 36 per cent of its practice was categorized in this way, to the lowest level in two authorities where only 11 per cent was. Similarly, passive practice featured in 52 per cent of the cases in one authority as compared to only 8 per cent in two others with the lowest rates. This suggests that practice did vary by local authority and not simply by which social worker or team was responsible for the case. However, since the numbers in each authority were quite low, these findings can only be regarded as indicative.

In addition, it was noticeable that in the proactive cases children were usually (65%, 17) fairly young when action was taken to protect them and secure their future and that a good number of the parents were misusing drugs (6) or alcohol (4) (10 of 26 or 38%).

Criticism of case management on the case files
Criticism of the overall case management

In a small number of cases criticisms or reservations about the management of the case were recorded on the files. In eight cases affecting 12 children, outright criticisms of the whole way the cases were being handled were recorded. In the case of Darren, noted as an example of passive case management above, the service manager had written on file:

> I am mystified by the lack of child protection intervention in this case and the lack of action over a number of years... Darren seems to me to have been systematically abused and mother has either been involved as the perpetrator of this or at least has consistently failed to safeguard and protect... Darren has been physically abused and harmed, sexually abused, shows inappropriate sexualized behaviour himself and [has been] emotionally and mentally harmed.

Three months later the same service manager told the team manager that the case notes were 'frankly rubbish' and failed to make a case for care proceedings. Four months later the service manager commented on further 'drift' on the case, reiterating that the worker needed to show that family services had been provided before care proceedings to protect Darren could be taken. Surprisingly, little action was taken in response to these criticisms and almost four years later, when Darren was a teenager who was putting himself at risk through his behaviour, the social worker reported that her supervisor thinks 'we may need to consider Darren's longer term future'. Eventually, when Darren was aged 14, care proceedings were instigated after his mother assaulted him, and a psychologist advised that Darren should not return to his mother.

In another case where two sets of care proceedings had not protected a child who was returned home each time on supervision orders, two years later the team manager commented on file that the case needed 'a statutory framework, close monitoring and an interventionist style of working'.

In a case, already mentioned, where the children were exposed to domestic violence, neglect and drug misuse, there were many referrals from the housing department, neighbours, the NSPCC and the school about neglect to the children, yet no action was taken and on one occasion the child protection team declined even to investigate a child protection referral. After care proceedings were finally taken when the older child was aged nine and the younger eight, the child protection co-ordinator highlighted the length of time it had taken to remove the children from home. Bradley was placed in foster care and a subsequent disruption meeting commented:

> It seems that the case was dealt with episode by episode. Each time there was a crisis there was some intervention and then the family went back together and the case was closed... When the children were finally removed it was when a placement became

available, rather than at a point of exceptional crisis… Although there are answers to the question of why the children were left with their mother for so long, we are left to conclude that it would have been much better for them if they had been removed much sooner.

These comments highlight the key issues in the management of this case: dealing with the case episode by episode, leaving the children too long before removal and the removal being placement-led rather than decisive action to protect the children. In spite of these criticisms, the children were later returned to their mother.

In a fourth case a child protection conference chair expressed grave concern about the management of the case and the lack of adherence to the child protection plan set out in the initial conference. The chair was concerned at the delay in starting care proceedings, which was due to chronic staff shortages. In a similar way when he was consulted about the advisability of holding a child protection conference, the child protection co-ordinator for another case involving three children agreed that a conference was needed and wrote:

I do also feel concerned that we have closed the file on previous occasions when I feel there should have been more discussion about what we might do/not do. A year ago, the police described the children as being petrified of their father…we did not do school checks at this time.

The chair of a child protection conference on Harry similarly expressed concerns that his name had:

been included on the child protection register for nearly two years and there still exist very serious concerns about [him]. There are a number of matters that warrant further consideration. Little is known about mum's drug intake, her current psychiatric state, home conditions, or the effect on the children of mum's periods in hospital.

Despite the chair's comments, there was no subsequent discussion on file about how to put this right or of taking a harder line with the mother about how things needed to change. The children's guardian noted in her report for the subsequent care proceedings on Harry that the social worker was reacting to events rather than doing proactive work to achieve lasting change.

The two other cases where there were such major concerns about case management involved children's guardians. In one the children's guardian wrote that she 'was astonished to read the number of times that Courtney's bruises had been noticed by health professionals and nothing had been done about it'. Courtney had been five months old when such bruising was first observed. In the other case, after Shayla (aged 13) had been discharged from secure accommodation, the children's guardian considered that the mother's refusal to attend an arranged assessment for them both in a specialist psychotherapy unit should not have been accepted without an alternative being put in place. She accused children's services of a passive approach where a proactive one was needed.

Disagreement with the decision to return children

In five cases there were publicly expressed disagreements with the children's services department's decision to return children home. In one, the service manager expressed major reservations about a 13-year-old girl's return to her mother. In another case, a boy who had been sexually abusing his sister and mother was being treated by the NSPCC, who were understandably critical when a decision was taken to return him home without involving them and at a time when more work was still needed. Their criticism was well founded since subsequently this boy sexually abused his sister and was violent to his mother. Yet later, after four failed returns, the authority was still considering a further reunion.

In another case where Greg had attended a residential school from the age of 9 to 12, the school reported their concern at the decision to return him to his mother (who herself was worried about managing him), given that he always returned to the school tired, hungry and in trouble with the police after the holidays. These warnings were ignored. He was then physically abused by his mother, rapidly placed in a children's home and by follow-up was homeless.

The children's guardian in another case criticized the plan for a 14-month phased return for a 10-year-old boy, considering this too long a period of uncertainty and that more work was needed with the mother before the return. In the first set of care proceedings in another case, the children's guardian disagreed with the local authority's request for the children to be returned on supervision orders. The guardian was also critical of the delay in instigating the second set of proceedings and in her report the psychologist commented that there had been a missed opportunity to safeguard the children during the first proceedings when they had returned on supervision orders.

Other disagreements and criticisms

In another case when a young man went into a secure unit, the children's guardian criticized the local authority for planning a further assessment of his parents, who she considered had been given ample opportunity to change already. She saw no reason for any further assessment of them.

Criticism of lack of response to referrals

We have noted that in many cases referrals about children were not adequately followed up. In four cases professionals criticized the children's services department's lack of response to such referrals. In one case, as we have seen, Frank had suffered a litany of maltreatment, including sexual abuse by three different perpetrators, neglect and emotional abuse as well as a serious fall. The health visitor complained about the lack of a proactive response to the risks to the children and requested a child protection conference but this was refused. Similarly, Darren's head teacher commented that it was 'truly dreadful how rejecting his mother was' of him. In a similar vein, when care proceedings were eventually initiated for Philip and his brother and sister, the children's guardian was very critical of the lack of action in following up the many referrals about his situation. These included an incident of sexual abuse by a relative when he was aged three which was not investigated, bruising on many occasions and a series of unsuitable men caring for him. Other referrals included non-attendance at school, the children being left alone and living in a very dirty house. Indeed, at a previous point when the case was closed, the team manager had noted that if such issues arose again, the follow-up needed to be more efficient and speedier.

The criticisms of case management made in all these cases seemed fully justified, so it is concerning that they so rarely led to any response. This suggests that systems need to be developed so that any criticism of case management is reviewed by senior managers as part of an audit of the entire case and a written response made to the professional concerned. Moreover, when managers themselves comment on a case, there needs to be a robust system to review the case and ensure that their directions have been followed up.

There is always the potential for disagreement between child protection conference chairs and team managers (see for example Farmer and Owen 1995) and there need to be clear avenues to broker such disagreements. It would therefore be useful if such cases were routinely referred to a more senior manager who would decide on the course to be taken. The way that some of these cases were managed and the acknowledgement by managers that children had been abused when the local authority knew about the risks might now leave the authorities open to claims for compensation for negligence or breach of human rights by the young people concerned. At the time that the decisions were taken, the law was unclear that local authorities could be liable for the decisions they made relating to child protection and child care (Case 2007), but the existence of a duty of care to children is now clear. Nonetheless, the mere fact that the decision turns out to have been a bad one does not make it negligent. The courts have accepted that professionals with responsibilities for child protection 'cannot be held liable every time genuine and reasonably held concerns about the safety of children are proved, retrospectively to be misguided' (*AD and OD* v. *United Kingdom* (2010)).

More generally, there appears to be a need to institute procedures which will deliberately cut across the kinds of processes underlying long-term case management that have been described. Having a second worker who visits with the children's social worker on a regular basis, say four or six monthly, to provide a second pair of eyes and to consider the situation and advise on case management might be useful. This could be a senior practitioner who carries a small caseload but whose principal responsibility is to provide case advice, consultancy and this kind of second opinion. In addition, regular case audits by senior managers would appear to be essential.

Now that we have considered how the cases were managed, we turn in the next chapter to look at the social workers' experiences of working with neglected children and their parents.

7

Social Workers' Perspectives

This chapter presents the views of the 37 social workers, team managers, leaving care workers and family support workers who we interviewed about 50 of the children and young people in our study. We also sought social workers' general views about issues in working with neglect.

Engaging and working with parents and children
Parents
Leaving care workers generally worked only with young people and so had little to say about their working relationship with the parents. Many of the social workers described mainly positive relationships with the parents, where parents were receptive to ideas, open to support and would contact the worker directly about problems. Their approach was to be open and honest with parents, provide emotional support, work in partnership with them, keep them informed and give praise.

Some social workers took a more directive approach. For example, with one child's mother who was an alcoholic, the worker said she had been very clear with the mother about her drinking 'by explaining to her in short, sharp, jerky movements that "You drink – no child." Simple as that'. When asked if her approach was mainly supportive or directive, another social worker said that the child protection system embodied a directive approach.

> A bit of both but I think since it's been in the [child protection system]... our concerns have been child protection obviously, there's been a lot more of the directive. It's had to be.

However, this worker went on to say that the use of the child protection system did not always sustain motivation from the parents:

Q. How well do you think the…more directive approach of the child protection system works with this family?

A. I think, I think initially it had an impact upon mum…whereby she actually realized the seriousness of the concerns because we were in the child protection arena. Although, you know, since, through the reviewing process I think…her motivation still fluctuates and she's not able to maintain the focus that actually these are the level of concerns and needs prompting and reminding that, you know, how serious everybody's concerns are.

Social workers thought it was important to strike a balance between being supportive and directive:

I think it's a balance. I hope more so the support. I hope that but I am conscious that in the past it has become directive, yes. But I think the directive is trying to be round a supportive way.

In contrast, other workers had had great difficulties in working with and engaging parents. This could take the form of parents refusing to engage at all or with particular services, or failing to respond to letters and telephone calls. Two social workers described the difficulties of working with parents who were willing to engage in getting their own needs met rather than the children's. They were demanding of time and resources and the workers had consciously to direct the focus back to the child. Another worker highlighted the difficulties of working with parents who could be deceptive and misleading with professionals. She suggested that workers needed to be prepared to put in a large amount of work and do unsociable hours in order to get the bigger picture when working with these families. At the extreme end some parents were actively hostile towards workers. In one case the social worker commented:

I think obviously dad hates social services with a passion. He takes no responsibility for his actions to the children. It's all our fault that we took them – when we didn't – they asked [to come into care].

This social worker also described the impact of this difficult relationship with the father:

My approach, at the moment is very different to before. I find working with the dad a very big struggle on a personal level because of his attitude, his argumentativeness, and I suppose originally I, sort of, rose to that and was quite argumentative back.

So I think at the moment I try to engage more in a conversation, but I'm very firm on what I won't discuss in certain areas.

Children and young people

The workers described both positive and difficult relationships with the children and it was clear that it often became more difficult to work with them as they got older. However, some children and young people were very willing to engage and social workers had good relationships with them. They described how, in trying to build a relationship with a young person, they would do enjoyable activities or have meetings where the child felt safest. Two leaving care workers emphasized that paying a personal allowance to young people gave leverage to get the young person to engage or meet them. One said that he had stopped a young person's personal allowance being paid into his bank account so that the young man had to come into the office and the worker could check if he was alright.

Being on an order with the youth offending team or probation generally increased engagement since the alternative is a return to court. One leaving care worker described renewed engagement from a young woman after she had been sent to prison. A social worker who had been involved with a young person for a very long time felt that this enduring relationship was important in sustaining the young person's engagement:

> With my help we've managed to get him out of some of those holes. I kind of think that if we'd have had a lot of different social workers involved it would have been very difficult for them to have helped him get out of the hole because it would have been like lack of relationship and lack of trust around that.

Several workers commented on the fluctuating engagement of some teenagers, with some only engaging when they wanted something or were in a crisis. One team manager described how a worker had endeavoured to work with the young woman in a planned way but ended up only managing crises:

Q. What kind of work have you done with her?

A. It has been, it's crisis management.

Q. And what does that involve?

A. Well, I mean, well we attempt not to do crisis management, we attempt to work in a planned way obviously, and the worker that's been allocated has tried to contact her and arrange to work with her and her plan, but that's not how it worked out really. So we are just responding to her crises, which at the moment are around her offending and, you know, supporting her in that, and…sorting out accommodation and finance and all those sort of things. But, although we don't want to work in a crisis management way, that is the way it's turned out.

Some young people engaged with the social worker or leaving care worker but refused to engage with other services such as the youth offending team, psychologists or mentors, while for others it was the other way round. Some of the obstacles to engaging young people were their avoidance of contact by not being in and missing appointments, all of which were fairly common: 'Yeah, he legs it most of the time (laughs) – that's a pretty good obstacle.'

Workers also had to deal with aggression and difficult behaviour and one had been slapped, punched, kicked and spat at by a young boy with problems of aggression and suspected attachment difficulties. A leaving care worker described the approach of the young person she worked with to try to get what he wanted:

I think probably the biggest obstacle was his whole belief system that if you shout hard enough and jump up and down hard enough people will give in so they can have a peaceful life.

They also had to deal with some young people's lack of trust in them, particularly if their parents were anti children's services.

There was evidence that difficulties in engaging children and young people could have an impact on the worker:

Q. Has the case posed any challenges or dilemmas for you?

A. Yes, how to motivate somebody, and how to engage with somebody that's reluctant to engage or doesn't feel at this point in his life he particularly needs the service… I'm not particularly satisfied with the work that I've done because he's so difficult to engage – that's been very frustrating.

Returns home

Of the 50 children and young people whose workers we interviewed, only 13 were living at home when the interviews took place. Of these, eight were open to leaving care workers who could not comment extensively about the suitability and success of these living situations. Those who could do so said that the benefits for children of being at home were in sustaining relationships with their parents and siblings and in the family being together. One social worker said that although a return that had recently taken place was going well, it was still in the honeymoon period and so it would not necessarily continue to do so later. Most also highlighted worries about the children being at home. These included long-standing concerns about neglect, parents' difficulties in prioritizing the needs of their children, volatile parent–child relationships, a child's fear of his father and suspected physical chastisement and children who were carers for their parents. Despite the concerns that they had, one social worker commented that they were not enough to remove the child:

> I think partly because a lot of what we've got is just things from the other children and from feelings in a way, with some evidence but not enough to go CP or to remove.

Another suggested that it was best for a child who had been at home for a substantial period of time to remain there, despite ongoing difficulties, because she was likely to respond poorly to living in foster care.

Three social workers talked about planning returns home. One described how he had carefully weighed up the pros and cons of the child returning and felt that it had a good chance of success. Another discussed a return home that was wanted by both the child and her mother and how a support plan was put in place because of the mother's drinking. The worker was hopeful that this return would succeed but felt realistically that the child would eventually return to care. A third child had returned home within the court process, which was motivated by the child and mother's wish to be together but a hefty support package was put in place to make it possible.

Interestingly, a few workers commented on how returns had been managed in the past, before their involvement. One worker was 'dumbfounded' that the children she was working with had been returned home previously as she could not believe that their father had been assessed as a fit parent. Another worker also felt that a previous decision to return the children home had not been the right one and that the local authority should have fought harder in court and argued that reunification was not the best plan for the children. They had gone on to suffer further abuse when they returned home. A third worker suggested that the local authority had actually 'reinforced a bad attachment' through trying 'years of family work' premised on the child's desire to live with her mother.

Services and interventions

A few practitioners highlighted the difficulties they had experienced with delivering the services that were needed. For example, several workers expressed concern that the children they were working with were still waiting for life story work and commented on the difficulties in getting CAMHS involvement because of their waiting lists and narrow criteria. Other workers had been unable to secure any support from adult services for their older young people.

A few practitioners made more general comments about the need for earlier help for families (Munro 2011). One suggested that therapeutic residential units should be used for children with difficulties when they were younger so that 'they've still got time to be guided and moulded'. Another felt strongly that the young people she worked with should have had more counselling when they were younger.

Several workers commented on the need for more preventative services for families, with one saying that 'neglect is one of those kind of areas where early intervention and education can have a big impact really'. There was also evidence of very good services and support being provided to some children. For example, four workers described excellent foster placements where the foster carers were friendly, communicated well with the social worker, were experienced with children with behaviour problems and had stuck by the children they were caring for. One worker highlighted the excellent input from the youth offending team, who had had weekly sessions with the young person. Two practitioners spoke highly of a mentoring scheme that was available in their authority and another had undertaken a lot of work with a child around a placement move. Other appropriate and timely services and supports that were provided were art therapy, CAMHS work on attachment, a diversion scheme run by the local youth offending team and an activity scheme during the school holidays to occupy a young person and ensure he did not become involved in offending or anti-social behaviour.

The success of children's services involvement

Most of the workers whom we interviewed thought that children's services' work with the family had been successful overall. These cases included children who were now in foster or other placements, children at home and young people living in supported or independent accommodation. Some workers explained that the department's work had been successful because since the children had been removed from home and placed in care they were happier and safer, especially when their placements were stable:

> I think since he went back into care there's a great improvement. I think he's doing really, really well. He's been in the same placement since returning to care.

> What I can say is that if Anthony had remained at home I'm convinced that we would have had a damaged child both physically and emotionally.

In another example, a child who had been looked after for an extended period and had recently returned home with a safety plan in place was considered to have been successfully protected:

> Well I don't think we're at the end of our input, so at this point I think we've definitely protected her, we're planning for her future and we're putting in place what we feel is appropriate for her future. So I'm optimistic we've done her a good service, but we're not finished yet.

Other children and young people had stopped offending, were settled in housing or were no longer dependent on children's services.

Some workers commented that services or the work they had done had contributed to these successful outcomes, including good foster and residential placements, multi-agency work, therapy or life story work. Simply being involved for a sustained period with a young person so that a good relationship could develop and the work could be done was also seen as important. In one case this consistency was provided by the worker's team:

> Somebody would always pick him up, he was never left stranded, you know what I mean, there would always be somebody that could continue if I was on holiday or whatever. And I think that consistency for Jordan I think has been the biggest thing in his life really.

A few workers attributed the improvements that they observed in the young people to them maturing over time rather than solely as a result of specific interventions:

> I think just, sort of, growing up and really getting used to living in an adult world has obviously had an impact on her, which has made her more independent and resourceful.

The picture was more mixed for several other children. For example, one young person appeared to be doing well as he was not involved in offending, but the social worker felt that his emotional needs were not being met at home. Conversely, another young person did not appear to be doing well in terms of indicators such as having stable accommodation or being in education, employment or training. However, the social worker had a good relationship with the young person and he himself felt that he was doing very well.

A number of practitioners felt that the department's work with the family had been unsuccessful overall. Many of the reasons the workers gave for this evaluation were to do with poor case management or system failures. For example, a few children had experienced numerous placement moves which the workers felt were unnecessary and one child had not been found an appropriate residential placement due to lack of funding. Some of the workers attributed the lack of successful work to poor planning or decision-making processes. For example, two commented that a child should never have been returned home and another was critical of the delay in starting care proceedings:

> Maybe we should have gone straight into proceedings then and put him up for adoption and maybe found him a family of his own. So I think we failed him really in that respect. The delay hasn't been beneficial to him at all.

Some children had had multiple changes of worker:

> They've both had changes of workers, like there's no tomorrow, and that hasn't helped, you know, and just when somebody's getting in there they move on or whatever, you know, and so I don't think the service has been great.

A few workers considered that they had tried really hard but were frustrated by the lack of engagement from the young person and had been unable to have much impact:

> I don't know, I'm going to say unsuccessful but that's partly because he won't ever engage and so it's almost as if we've never done anything with him, because you can't literally force him to do it.

The leaving care workers highlighted some particular issues relevant to working with care leavers. A few considered that they needed to be involved two or three years earlier to be able to do a good job and be satisfied with their work, and emphasized that they only have a set period of time in which to engage and work with young people, then disengage and make sure young people are not dependent on the support by the time the involvement ends. Concern was also expressed about leaving care support typically ending when young people reached the age of 21:

> Far too early, I mean…we know these children are damaged… and we're told by the age of 21 they'll all be sorted. And it's a ridiculous, kind of, concept really.

Workers' knowledge of their cases

It was notable that many of the practitioners we interviewed lacked knowledge about the history of the case. These workers had been involved with the children and young people for an average of 23 months (range 1–72 months) when we interviewed them, although in 15 cases the worker had been involved for less than a year. In particular, several leaving care workers admitted to knowing very little about the history of the case, sometimes only learning about past events from the young person:

> Q. How much do you know about things that happened in his past?

> A. Not a lot really, I just know from, 'cause I've been trying to catch up on his caseload and there's not a lot on the system about him. It's only the bits he's told us really, which isn't a lot really. He tends to like steer away from his early years, sort of thing.

Some children's social workers also lacked knowledge of the child's history. They were sometimes unaware of key events that had happened in the past, with one social worker having to print off the child's placement history to check if she had returned home recently. Another social worker said that her priority when getting a new case was to build a relationship with the young person and parents and that she would get a feel for the case by reading the key documents on file such as assessments and court reports. Despite this, it was apparent to the interviewer that this worker was unaware of the majority of the history of the case. While this highlights the importance of reading the case files in newly allocated cases, this is not an easy task for busy practitioners. There is therefore a real imperative to maintain detailed but concise chronologies.

Neglect

We asked the social workers about their experiences of working with cases of neglect more generally. Many identified how neglect could affect children. Workers had seen children who were aggressive, had behaviour problems and were offending, and others who became withdrawn and closed off. Neglected children were often considered to be insecure, to have low self-esteem and might also have developmental delay or learning difficulties. One worker suggested that emotional neglect had a lasting impact and resulted in more 'scars' that physical neglect. Practitioners thought that it was important to understand the long-term impact of neglect and that the effects were cumulative. One commented that it was easy to underestimate neglect but that its effects were insidious:

> I have heard other people who do certainly minimize neglect. And, you know, I've heard it quite often in court I have to say, you know, 'A bit of neglect it's not sexual abuse we're talking about here, we're not talking about physical abuse, you know, we're talking about a bit of neglect', for example. And I suppose, I think [neglect] has a particularly insidious way of invading the psyche of young people and in giving them issues around self-esteem and identity problems.

While many workers were able to comment on the impact of neglect on children, several commented on the difficulties of actually defining it. They highlighted that neglect was harder to define than other types of maltreatment, that there was no clear indicator that signalled neglect and that it was not clear-cut. One said that neglect was less tangible than physical or sexual abuse but that emotional abuse was even less tangible than neglect.

Practitioners commented on thresholds in neglect cases. They highlighted the difficulty of knowing where the threshold for intervention in cases of neglect should be set (Allsop and Stevenson 1995; Gardner 2008; Minty and Pattinson 1994):

> To put together a threshold document based on neglect type issues is incredibly difficult.

> Neglect is something which is very hard to determine the point at which you become significant harm…when does it become a risk to their children?

Another social worker suggested that it was not always easy to be aware when the threshold had been reached with neglect because neglect by definition tends to be cumulative over a period of time. She said: 'It's easy I think for things to deteriorate gradually without you noticing.'

Another problem facing social workers is the variation between teams and professionals about what the threshold for neglect is. A social worker suggested that one of the challenges of working with cases of neglect is that:

> It seems to be subject to different subjective responses and opinions from different professionals. This makes it difficult to judge a clear and consistent threshold and to measure change.

Another social worker felt that the assessment team in her authority had a high threshold which was 'much higher' than the threshold in her looked after children's team. A team manager highlighted the difficulty in getting the legal team and the court to agree that the threshold for action had been reached. She explained that they could not always go to court and get a care order when they felt it was necessary because legal advice would be that the threshold had not been reached. This was clearly very frustrating and it appeared that this was putting off social work professionals from taking cases to court. Similarly, social workers commented on the dilemma that it took a long time to gather the level of evidence of neglect required by courts and during that time neglect continued to impact on children, who had by then been at home so long that it might be considered acceptable for them to remain:

> You can't often get that level of evidence, it takes a long time to get and then quite often we're finding that you're going to court and because the children have been in there so long in that situation – it's considered that it's okay for them to stay there.

The practitioners made many suggestions about how to work with cases of neglect. On a practical level they suggested demonstrating to parents how to carry out domestic and parenting tasks and checking their knowledge of how to do these tasks, suggesting different ways of doing things, setting targets, giving guidance or re-educating them. Depending on the family and the worker, practitioners were sometimes direct with parents or they might work around the issues. They felt it was important to get the parents to recognize the impact of the neglect on the child. Several workers highlighted the importance of talking to children and observing how they were presenting. Gathering information from other agencies was considered to be important too, as was careful recording and monitoring.

While several practitioners commented that working with neglect was no different from addressing other forms of maltreatment, a few practitioners highlighted particular difficulties. One social worker emphasized the need to be extremely thorough in assessing and working with these cases, as neglect could be hidden. Another said that there was more chance in neglect cases of turning the situation around and of the children staying at home. However, in contrast, a few social workers expressed concerns about sustaining change in cases of neglect, about children languishing on child protection plans and about parents slipping back into neglectful ways.

We asked practitioners what kind of services they would like to see in place for neglecting families. The response was overwhelmingly about practical support in the home such as family support or home start, with many workers suggesting that such support should be regular, even daily. However, they also said that this type of support was not available as widely as was needed and was a stretched resource:

> It's about resources, about having the physical, the people, the family support workers, the, you know, the people that go out to the houses and support, and try and, you know, keep the children in the families. But they haven't got the time to go there every day or twice, it's all about resources and there isn't the money there. There just isn't.

Having considered the perspectives of social workers on working with neglected children and their parents, we examine in the next chapter the views of the parents and children themselves.

8

Interviews with Parents and Children

We were only able to conduct a very small number of interviews with parents and neglected children and young people (see Chapter 2). Here we give the views of the six parents and six children with whom we spoke. We focus on the parents' and children's views of their relationship with each other, on their returns home, sources of support and children's services' involvement. We also sought to discover how they defined and understood neglect.

Interviews with parents

Three interviews were held with mothers, one with a mother and her partner, one with a father and one with a father and the child's grandmother. At the time of the interviews the children in five families were living at home and one child was in a shared care arrangement. Three of these children had remained at home since their original return. Three had returned home for a second time after unsuccessful previous returns (and had been there for five months, nine months and three years respectively).

The parents' relationships with their children

Most of the parents were positive about their current relationships with their children. For example, one parent said they had a 'good bond' and three parents talked about the love in their relationship. Another parent said that they were 'dead close' and one described how she and her daughter got on well and enjoyed doing things together. One father was more reserved in his answers and said of his relationship with his son: 'It's fine, it's alright.' However, these relationships were not without their difficulties. One mother described how she sometimes needed to be firm with her daughter:

> We know each other that well and don't get me wrong we are really, really best of friends. But again don't get me wrong she knows when I mean business, she knows if I'm being serious...I would say to her, 'That's it, you know, it's non-negotiable. It's what I say or tough.'

In a similar vein, another mother said that her daughter could be demanding and testing and that this was not easy to cope with but that she had to:

> say things and be firm when she's trying to get her own way, you know...I mean I love her to bits, you know, I do but, you know, she is hard work.

For two parents the strain on them was evident. One was struggling to understand her daughter's recent difficult behaviour. The other described the worry, stress and health problems he had experienced as a consequence of caring for a child with significant medical problems and developmental delay.

Sources of support

Two of the parents had good support networks consisting of doctors, family, friends, workmates, the church and a community psychiatric nurse. The other parents lacked support to varying degrees. One mother only named friends as her source of support despite having significant difficulties. Three others clearly stated that they did not get much or any support and none from their families, with one father saying that he did not ask for any. As the other father put it: '[There's] nobody, only me.' However, two of these parents said that they sometimes got help from other sources such as a neighbour or the child's previous foster carer. Interestingly, in one case it was clear that the school had been very supportive to the parents when the child had gone into care.

Returns home

Several of the parents were able to describe the benefits of the child being at home. For one it meant that she and her daughter were now able to be together and this mother commented that 'It's better than her being in care.' For another mother it enabled her child to be normal: 'Bit of normality, you know, close to her friends and everything, close to school.'

One parent talked at length about how she had had to prove that she was able to cope with having the child at home. This mother had severe mental health problems and commented that she had to be in a 'strong enough position' to have the child back. The planning for the return took place within care proceedings and the mother worked well with children's services and appeared pleased that the court and children's services agreed with the return plan:

> Social services were happy, they were happy and quite, you know, happy to sort of say to the courts, yeah, you know, Angela is ready and, you know, we have no objections for that and that was how the final court hearing actually went.

However, after they returned home two parents talked about how their children had been affected by their time in care and by the separation from them. One child was described as being angry and insecure and another as feeling low after returning home. One couple talked in detail about their feelings about the child's entry to care and subsequent return home. They said several times that they felt guilty that the child had had to go into care and that when she returned home they were 'scared of losing her'. However, these parents also said that it was a good thing that their child had been looked after because, at the time, they themselves were 'messed up' and had 'crappy problems'. It was evident from the interview that they were motivated to address these problems while the child was in care and had been successful in doing so.

In contrast, the shared care arrangement did not appear to be successful. This mother said that she could not cope with her daughter living with her full-time because of her behaviour:

> I don't mind having Rhiannon at home at all, but just the way it's got…it's just been a nightmare, just totally out of control and it's like no point having a child in the house when she's trashing everything, won't listen to a word you say, out of the door when you say 'No'… About two weeks ago it was a total and utter nightmare, AWOL, you know, having the police and everything…she was just a nightmare smashing stuff up. She's kicked a big thing in her door, which has not long been replaced really since the last door, just smashing everything up… It's like once she's with certain mates, that's it, she does what she wants, and it doesn't matter what I say 'cause she won't listen to me and what can you do?… She'll be kicking off, screaming for hours… Yeah well I can't be dealing with that at the moment, you know, I struggle at times as it is, and I don't need that.

Experiences of children's services involvement

We talked to the parents about their involvement with children's services. In three of the interviews the parents were very positive about it. They described children's services as being absolutely fabulous, down to earth, helpful, a lifeline and 'the best social services I've ever met'. June and Roy described how they felt very supported throughout the process of reunification:

> They constantly told June that she's getting her back...so that was excellent... There's light at the end of the tunnel and that's what drove us.

Most of the parents said that they saw children's services as supportive and that the social worker had not tried to control them. However, in one case where there was a very structured return home the mother did not view this positively at the time:

> But I think actually, you know, at the time I was quite angry about things, you know, to be honest with you...and I was like, you know, I don't see why I should have had to have gone through all of this, and that's how I was feeling. But in hindsight I can see that actually the structure [worked] quite well, it sort of eased me slowly back into things and, you know, by the time I actually did get Georgia back I was ready to have her back.

In two cases care orders were in place, or had been in the past, and both of the parents in these cases said that they were happy with the care orders:

> What they have done is put a care order in place so, which I was in agreement with because I think obviously if anything does go wrong then they can put something in place straight away.

One parent, who described herself as an alcoholic, reflected that children's services involvement was important for the safety of her family:

> I wanted somebody to protect my children, and that's what [the social worker] did to the best of his ability. He was fabulous. Without social services my children wouldn't have really stood a chance, they would have just stayed here with me being drunk and carried on.

She also said that she felt able to telephone the social worker if she had had a drink but that when she was sober she was a 'brilliant mum'. This mother also commented on the importance of the relationship between parents and professionals and professionals' responses to parents:

I think you've got to be honest with each other, you've got to respect each other. Okay I'm an alcoholic but I'm still a human being and I'm not a bad person on the whole, so if anybody from social services treated me like an idiot because I'm an alcoholic, then I could understand somebody being a bit rude to them because I would order [them] out my house.

In addition to the way that children's services related to the parents, it was important how the parents responded to children's services:

Just to stick with it and listen to what they've got to say, and don't be angry at them because it's not their fault, you know, and if they just listened... We wanted to get Finlay back – you've got to listen to get the result. They want what we want, so it's just a connection isn't it?

I don't see them as being, you know, a threat or sort of against me, you know, I think that they're there to help and, you know, basically, you know, that's what they're there to do.

Some parents were less positive about children's services involvement. One mother commented that children's services reward bad behaviour, as the social worker had taken her daughter to a fast food restaurant after she had displayed difficult behaviour. Another father was critical of the level of visiting he had received, saying that he had only seen a social worker a couple of times since his son had returned home.

In one case the child's father and paternal relatives had reported concerns to children's services about the mother's care of the child but said, 'They didn't want to know. They weren't interested really with it.' Action was only taken when the police became involved. This family was also critical of how children's services handled the child's contact with his adopted siblings. Contact was promised but was cancelled at short notice or did not materialize.

One mother with mental health problems really valued the support given to her by children's services more recently but said that there was a point where she felt help should have been given earlier:

Well I think initially when I first became ill...not last year but the year before, I think for a good year I was sort of asking for help and I feel that, you know, I wasn't listened to then...and I actually just became progressively worse and ended up going into hospital, and I think that that could have been prevented. And Aleesha going into care could have been prevented as well.

Services

Most of the parents described a variety of services that they and their children had received. These included counselling, parenting courses and assistance from mental health workers. We asked them to comment on how useful they had found these. Several parents had received counselling at various points in their lives and two had found it helpful:

> Q. And when you had counselling before did you find it useful?

> A. Yeah, she was nice, yes seems good.

However, two parents commented that that it had not been particularly useful:

> I've had counselling since I was 15 and it's still not worked.

> I had to buy a relaxation tape for a pound, and the sound of dolphins and that wasn't going to do nothing for me at that time so. But no it's just, I just, ever since I just papered over the cracks really.

Two parents received support from a community psychiatric nurse and both found this service very helpful:

> Yeah, me CPN nurse yeah – Barry – he's wicked yeah. It's very good… I see him near enough every other day.

Treatment for alcohol misuse problems had been provided for two parents. One mother had attended a treatment programme but relapsed:

> I went to rehabilitation and detox…two years ago, I used to go every day and I improved…this was treatment for my alcoholism. Then I relapsed and for one month I had to go to the project but not participate, then I was able to participate again and… things improved. When I was there I went to AA regularly and did what's called 'shares', where you talk to other people about your difficulties. But in the end it was too much for my head to cope with, I found the shares and the life story work too much pressure, so I relapsed again… I attended for five months every day. I'm disappointed with myself. Guilt with me is the killer, I still feel it. I've learned a lot about myself, they strip you down in places like that – but I like hiding away.

This mother went on to relapse again and had continued drinking ever since.

The other mother with alcohol problems had also been to Alcoholics Anonymous and was mostly sober, with episodes of binge drinking. Her daughter had the support of neighbours who provided a safe house for her during these drinking episodes and looked after her mother when they occurred:

Q. Have you ever been offered support for your alcohol problems?

A. I used to go to AA and stuff like that, so I used to do everything off my own bat… We do need social services right, but when I'm sober I'm a pretty confident person, I'm good at my job, I do it well, I'm a good mum… And I run a very good home, it's only when I'm drinking…so when I'm sober I get together all the bad things and sort them out. So I do everything positive to counteract it happening again to the best of my ability, do you know what I mean?

A few of the parents had received help with parenting. One mother attended a parenting class which was not effective with her child's behaviour. She also received advice about behaviour management but did not see this as helpful. Another mother was very enthusiastic about a 12-week Webster-Stratton parenting course she had attended, saying that it had helped her to understand things and that the people who ran it were great. It helped improve her confidence and she was sad when it ended. One couple spent a period in a residential unit with their daughter prior to her return home. They received help with their parenting, which they found useful, and they really liked the staff there. The couple felt that it was a 'refresher' and said that they still continue with the routines that they learned there:

M That place was so helpful, like it re-booted, you know, we both had children before Morgan…and [without it] we wouldn't have had a clue would we?

F It was like refreshed again, it's really, yeah it's very good.

M And that still stays in us now, today, we get everything ready [for dinner], we tidy the house [and continue with those routines].

A father who had attended an anger management course had found it helpful. He said that he had been able to take parts of it away and put them into practice and had learned a lot. One mother who was having financial difficulties emphasized that the financial support she and her daughter received was very important and said that this was the thing that she would want more of in an ideal world.

In contrast, one father said that he did not receive any services. Another said that the only service he had received was short periods of babysitting which had not given him enough time to go to the supermarket. In one of the three closed cases, there were clear unmet needs for support. This father was struggling to cope with a child with a significant disability and little support was in place. Interestingly, one mother suggested that, once a case had been closed, children's services should do a follow-up phone call every couple of years to ask if everything was going well and if they needed any support. She also suggested that this could be in the form of a drop-in centre where you could go if you needed help and advice. Another mother suggested that there could be more help for parents at weekends.

Neglect

We also talked to the parents about the neglect the children had experienced. Two said that the child had only been neglected while living with the other parent. In one of these cases the information collected from the file supported this claim but in the other case it appeared that the child had also been neglected by the parent who we interviewed. Four of the parents indicated that the child had experienced neglect while living with them. For example, one mother said:

> When I'm drinking I just drink, and that's neglect whichever way you look at it. If I can't cook the children a meal at the age of 11 and 12 I'm not looking after them, am I?

However, it appeared that some aspects of her parenting were not neglectful as she went on to say:

> But through all my drinking I've never ever missed one of the children's appointments, never ever.

Two mothers with mental health problems described how their children had experienced neglect while at home. One mother said that her depression and drinking had made her self-absorbed and the other said that her child had to witness her mental illness and take on a caring role. Another mother said of the rows she used to have with her partner: 'It's abuse and it's neglect ain't it basically?', while one mentioned missed appointments:

> Q. Sometimes social workers might think if a parent doesn't take a child to health appointments that could be thought of as neglect, what do you think about that?

A. Sometimes I can't leave the house, so it could apply to me, sometimes I find it difficult to do things.

One mother was able to describe how she felt when children's services said that she had neglected her children:

Horrible (laughs) you know, you don't want to neglect your children do you, do you know what I mean, you feel awful.

We also talked to the parents more generally about what they felt might constitute neglect and some of them were able to give insightful descriptions:

Well I mean to not listen to your children I think, poor hygiene, don't feed them the right foods, don't give them any time to themselves, you know, of yourself, you know, you don't play with them at all, you don't take them out, you don't, you know, treat, make their lives, you know, feel special.

Another mother said that neglect was not looking after a child properly or not giving them cuddles or playing with them. Not feeding or clothing a child and keeping them in their bedroom was the description given by another parent. Finally, one parent gave a long list of things that could be neglect, which included: not feeding the child, not keeping them safe, the parent putting their own needs first, leaving the child alone, leaving the child with someone you do not trust and letting the child go out on their own.

Interviews with children and young people

At the time of the interviews, the six young people were aged between 11 and 19 years old. Three were boys and three girls. Three of the young people had remained at home since their original return. One young woman was living with her boyfriend and his mother following a series of residential and foster care placements after her return broke down, followed by a period in supported accommodation. Two young people were in foster care after their returns home had been unsuccessful, one having been there for a year and the other for seven months.

The children's current progress and achievements

Most of the children we interviewed appeared to be progressing reasonably well. For example, one young woman was at college, had a good group of friends and talked about the social activities she did with them.

Another boy who had developmental delay and medical problems talked enthusiastically about his love of football. Two other boys also talked about hobbies and activities that they did in their spare time. Most of the young people were positive about school and two had received certificates or awards from school or college for their progress.

However, there was evidence of difficulties in one case where a girl had been in trouble with the police. More worryingly, we interviewed a young woman whose life appeared to be very chaotic. She had no stable housing and had a boyfriend who made aggressive phone calls to her throughout the interview. She said that she was anorexic and worried a lot about things.

Sources of support

All of the young people we interviewed said that they had someone they could talk to if something was worrying them. Three said that they were able to talk to their parents and two mentioned friends as being able to help them:

> My mates are there for me, if I say anything to 'em, ain't it, they'll, kind of, help me out.

Another young man said that he would talk to his social worker or teachers if he had any problems. Conversely, one young person said that she had told teachers at school that she was being bullied but that nothing had happened. Helpful chats with grandparents about the past were mentioned by one young person and another young woman had a mentor as a source of support. However, one young person said that her sources of support were limited because her boyfriend 'doesn't let me have friends'.

However, not all the young people would readily use the sources of support that they had. One young woman said that she could talk to people if she wanted to, but that she would be very reluctant to do so:

> A. No, I wouldn't put the stress on somebody else's shoulders, I don't really see the point when all they're going to do is sit and worry about it. What's the point in two people worrying about stuff? So I don't really bother… If it was a life or death and I had to, it probably would be either my sister or my friend, that's it.
>
> Q. Yeah, but you wouldn't, you'd be very reluctant to do that?
>
> A. Yeah, I wouldn't, it would have to be like, either jump off a bridge or talk to someone (laughs) so that would have to be the situation I'd have to be in.

Experiences of living at home, including returns

Three of the young people were living with a parent. One young woman explained that she had demanded that she return home to her mother, otherwise 'I'll just go back with my mum anyway'. She considered that the return had worked out really well, apart from when her mother drank. These periods of drinking would last a few days and occurred approximately monthly. The young woman would look after her mother and the house during these times, which she did not mind doing as she said:

> Me and my mum are very close, so I don't mind looking after her when she drinks.

However, she also said that she was unhappy about her mother's drinking and that her family life differed quite a bit from that of her friends, in that it was more stressful and she had to do more housework and step in when her mother was drinking.

> I do a lot of housework but a lot of my friends don't do housework at all which I find very wrong. Like when my mum drinks I have to step in.

This young woman had confided in her close friends about her mother's drinking, so she was not lying to them when she said she had to care for her mother and was unable to go out with them. Another young man who was living with his father said that his family life was 'normal' and 'much better' than care or living with his mother.

Some of the young people also talked about their previous experiences of living at home. Three talked about the arguments they had had with their parents when they were living with them. Nonetheless, one of them said that she thought her family life at the time had been the same as her friends' and a young man said that everything had been good at home. He described his family life at home as better than that of his friends, who had earlier bedtimes and set mealtimes. It appeared that the latter two young people may have been idealizing their past experiences at home somewhat.

One young woman was realistic about her previous time when at home. She said that her father was a drinker and that people who drink are wasting their lives. This young woman explained that she had had to do a lot of caring for her younger siblings at the time, including preparing meals for them and getting them ready for school.

Experiences in care

The two young people who were in foster care said that they felt safe and looked after there. However, one girl said that she missed her siblings and wanted to go home. She explained that she understood the reasons why she could not go home but disagreed with them. The other young man said that he had been angry and surprised that he had had to go back into foster care. He had gone to a foster placement where the carers were 'old and horrible' so he threatened to hurt himself and was moved to his current placement. He now wanted to return home and was angry about an incident where he felt he had been unfairly punished by the foster carers and said he hated it in care. Both of these young people had retained contact with their parents and appeared close to them.

Three young people reflected on their previous experiences in care. One young woman said that she had really enjoyed it and had liked the manager of one of the children's homes. However, the other two were less positive. Both said that they had not been listened to while there. One young woman described how she was 'passed around' and that people did not really talk to her about why she was moving and when, nor did she have a choice about where she went. She described her varying experiences with different foster placements:

> Some people did make you feel welcome… There's only a few that I stayed in my room quite a bit and thought well I don't particularly want to get to know them 'cause they don't like me.

A young man responded to a question about whether people listened to him about what he wanted to happen:

> Definitely not. You had to, like, act up to get listened to, if you know what I mean, say like in school. So you have to cause a bit of trouble so they'll come and, like, listen to what you want.

Reflecting back on the past

We asked the young people to reflect on their past experiences, what they would change if they could and who was responsible for what had happened to them. One young woman said that she would change her behaviour so that she could be back living with her mother, while a young man said that he would have changed the foster placement where he had been unhappy.

The young people had mixed feelings about who was responsible for what had happened to them. One young woman said that she blamed her stepmother who made her angry and her father for abandoning her. She also partly blamed her mother, who still misused alcohol:

> I blame my mum a little bit, but I don't blame her, but I know I've got mixed emotions about why my mum, about my mum and that. I love her to bits like, but I do blame her a bit because I understand it's an illness that she's got. But it's still a bit of her fault 'cause she kept going, so kind of her fault too.

Another young person said that he blamed his stepfather for what had happened while he was living with his mother, but also saw his mother as being at fault:

> Yeah, but I don't blame my mum ain't it, because, you know, I love my mum, but it's partly her fault as well like. I often miss her now.

Experiences of children's services involvement

The young people were asked about their experiences of children's services involvement both past and present. Children's services were no longer involved with two of them, one of whom was rather negative about his previous experiences. He felt that social workers had 'bribed' him to behave at school while he was in foster care by saying he could see his mother only if he was good. He also felt let down that children's services had said that they would arrange for him to have contact with his adopted siblings but this had not materialized.

Two of the young people who currently had leaving care workers or social workers were positive about them. They saw them as helpful, got on well with them and could ask them for help. One said his social worker got money for him but he wished she visited him more often. In contrast, one young woman was more negative, saying that she did not see her current social worker very much and that she did not help her. She also said that the leaving care team did not help her and that she had wanted a different leaving care worker. She said that children's services had not helped her when she was having difficulties and that generally they did not give people enough money. She had financial difficulties and felt that she had been passed between the council and children's services for housing provision, which made her angry:

> Well I'm not even with the council, I'm not, even if I go there to ask for that, they'd just send me back to social services, 'Go back to social services.' Well I had a go at them one time. I said,

'Well, social services are doing fuck all for me so I want you to do something for me', and they're like, 'No we can't do nothing for you, go back to social services.' I'm like, 'Oh you're taking the piss.'

Services

Several of the young people talked about the services that were provided and how useful they were. Most thought that support from Connexions had been useful, although one young woman said that they had given her only one option about work in the future and she had wanted more. One young person had a mentor and a drugs worker and rated both of these professionals highly, while another took part in activities organized by an independent fostering agency which he enjoyed.

One young person had taken up the option of counselling but went to only one session:

Q. Did you just see them once?

A. Yeah, it's not good to…make a counsellor cry, so (laughs) I felt, kind of bad, so I didn't go again.

Q. And I'm interested to know…what were you hoping to get from going there?

A. I was hoping to get a little bit of stress relieved, off my shoulders about my mum, my dad, and stuff like that, everything. So I thought well I'll go and see her and see what happens, you can only try once, and plus my college recommended it, so I went. It didn't work out so I said, 'I'm not going again.'

One young woman had received a lot of support from her college, including help with her coursework. She had also attended a confidence-building course at the college and made friends through the course.

Interestingly, a young person whose mother was an alcoholic tried to find help for her. She looked on the internet for someone to help her mother but only found services that she had already tried. She also asked for advice about how to stop drinking from someone who had done so. They said it was just down to willpower, which the young person had not found helpful.

Three wishes

At the end of the interviews, we asked the young people what they would wish for if we gave them three wishes. Two of the young people gave wishes that concerned being successful as adults. One wanted to find a partner who would treat her well, to have a nice house and get a good job.

A number of the young people gave wishes that concerned their parents and families (see also Farmer *et al.* 2011; Ward 1995). One young person whose mother had an alcohol problem wished that her mother would never drink again, for her close family not to have money worries and for her nephew to grow up safe and happy. Another young woman wanted to stay in contact with her mother when she was grown up. A young man who was in care said that he wanted to return home to his mother and never wanted to go into care again as he hated it. Finally, one young woman's only wish was to move out of the town she lived in.

Neglect

We asked the young people more generally what kinds of things might constitute neglect. Some of them were also able to reflect on whether their experiences in the past had involved neglect. Interestingly, the two young people who we thought had probably had the most chronic experiences of neglect in the past were unable to say what neglectful behaviour might be. They both said that they did not know and avoided further questioning.

Some of the other young people were able to say what they thought neglect was. One young person said it was 'parents leaving you to get on with what you want', which was similar to the explanation he gave as to why it was good when he lived at home. This boy said that he had not been neglected while living at home, showing that young people do not always identify the parenting that they receive as neglectful (see Rees *et al.* 2011). Another young person was a little unsure of his explanation but said that neglect was 'mental abuse' and that it was also 'not feeding you as much'. A young woman gave several examples of what might be neglectful behaviour and said that 'there's loads of forms of neglect'. Interestingly, she commented that neglect was a harsh word to use about her experiences when her mother was drinking and that her mother made up for it when she was sober, so it did not matter:

> When my mum was drinking, well neglect's a bit of a harsh word isn't it really? I'd say we had to care for ourselves...but she makes up for it when she's sober, so it doesn't really matter.

Now that we have explored the views of the children and parents, we examine in the next chapter the children's progress and outcomes.

9

The Children's Progress and Outcomes

This chapter describes the key events that occurred for the children during the full five-year follow-up period with a particular focus on the final three-year period. Their progress and outcomes are considered on a range of dimensions, including placement stability and their well-being at follow-up.

The outcomes of the returns

The stability and quality of the returns

By the two-year follow-up, half of the 138 original returns had ended, mostly because of a breakdown in relationships between the parents and children. Another 44 per cent of the reunions were still continuing and the outcome of the returns was not known for the remainder.

Three years later, by the five-year follow-up, the proportion of returns which had disrupted had risen to 65 per cent. Just 29 per cent were continuing at this point (or had been when the case was closed) (see Table 9.1).

Table 9.1 Stability of the original returns at the two follow-up points

Outcome	At two-year follow-up		At five-year follow-up	
	Number	Percentage	Number	Percentage
Continuing	61	44	40	29
Ended	69	50	90	65
Not known	*8*	*6*	*8*	*6*

Researcher ratings of return quality were made as follows:

- **Good quality** – returns that were positive or adequate for the child. This category included cases where there were some difficulties or adverse incidents but, on the whole, circumstances for the child were adequate or good.

- **Borderline** – returns that included circumstances or incidents that were likely to be harmful for the child *or* where the parents were having difficulties managing the child, but where we did not consider that the return should have ended, either because the difficulties were not sufficiently serious or because, on balance, care would not have been a better option for the child.

- **Poor quality** – returns that were unacceptably harmful for the child and/or significantly limited his/her life chances, such that either they had ended or in our opinion should have been ended *or* where the parent was totally unable to cope with or contain the child's behaviour.

At the two-year follow-up, a quarter of the returns were rated as of good quality, 15 per cent as borderline and 58 per cent of poor quality. (A few cases were excluded as they were closed before there was adequate information to assess their quality.)

By the five-year follow-up point, fewer (18%) of the returns were considered to be of good quality and more (72%) were of poor quality. (See Table 9.2).

Table 9.2 Quality of the original returns at the two follow-up points

Outcome	At two-year follow-up		At five-year follow-up	
	Number	Percentage	Number	Percentage
Good quality	33	25	23	18
Borderline	19	15	11	8
Poor quality	75	58	93	72
Not known	*3*	*2*	*3*	*2*

Table 9.3 shows the relationship between the stability and quality of the returns at both time points. As can be seen, over half of the continuing returns were of good quality for the children, but for two-fifths of the children who remained at home their returns were borderline or harmful.

(The two returns of good or borderline quality which had ended were young people who had moved from home to independent living by choice rather than because of difficulties at home.)

Table 9.3 Original return stability by quality at the two follow-up points

Original return quality	At two-year follow-up		
	Continuing (n=61)	Ended (n=69)	Overall (n=130)
Good quality	33 (54%)	–	33 (25%)
Borderline	19 (31%)	–	19 (15%)
Poor quality	7 (11%)	68 (99%)	75 (58%)
Not known	*2 (3%)*	*1 (1%)*	*3 (2%)*
Original return quality	At five-year follow-up		
	Continuing (n=40)	Ended (n=90)	Overall (n=130)
Good quality	22 (55%)	1 (1%)	23 (18%)
Borderline	10 (25%)	1 (1%)	11 (8%)
Poor quality	6 (15%)	87 (97%)	93 (72%)
Not known	*2 (5%)*	*1 (1%)*	*3 (2%)*

Safeguarding during the final three-year period

During the two-year follow-up period, three-fifths of the children (59%)[1] were maltreated. Two-fifths (39%) were neglected, a quarter (25%) physically abused, and a fifth (20%) emotionally and 5 per cent sexually abused. (These figures do not add to 100% as children experienced multiple forms of abuse.)

For most (99) of the cases that were open at any point between the two- and five-year follow-ups (n=102), there was sufficient information on file to consider re-abuse rates. We found that half (48%) of the children had been abused or neglected during the final three-year follow-up, with neglect most common and sexual abuse much rarer. This rose to

---

1   This compares with 46 per cent of children who were maltreated in the reunification study (Farmer *et al.* 2011), which also included children who had not been neglected.

64 per cent when we consider only the children who had spent time with their parents (see Table 9.4). Nonetheless, three children were abused or neglected while living away from home.

Table 9.4 Abuse and neglect during the final three-year period

Abuse or neglect	Percentage of all children (n=99)	Percentage of children at home at any point (n=75)
Any abuse or neglect	48	64
Neglect	39	53
Physical abuse	20	27
Emotional abuse	10	14
Sexual abuse	2	1

Of the 48 children (48%) who were abused or neglected during the final three-year period, 33 had also been maltreated during the two-year follow-up period, suggesting the continuity of risks for children. Nonetheless, 15 children who were maltreated during this period had not been subject to abuse or neglect previously, so new risks could emerge.

Neglect

During this final three-year period, educational or cognitive neglect (67%), often including poor school attendance, was most common (see Table 9.5) but physical and supervisory neglect were also frequent. Emotional and medical neglect occurred less often (for details about these types of neglect see Chapter 3).

Table 9.5 Types of neglect experienced during final three-year period

Type of neglect	Children who experienced neglect during the final three-year period (n=39)	
	Number	Percentage
Educational or cognitive neglect	26	67
Physical neglect (including nutritional neglect)	25	64
Supervisory neglect	24	62
Emotional neglect	16	41
Medical neglect (including neglect of mental health needs)	12	31

Most children (80%) experienced multiple types of neglect. Twenty-eight per cent of them experienced two types, a quarter (26%) three types and 18 per cent experienced four. The remaining 8 per cent experienced all five types of neglect (see Figure 9.1).

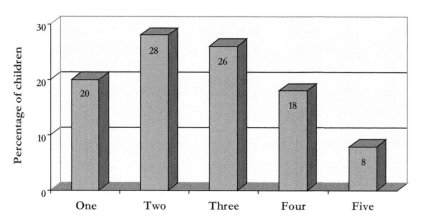

Figure 9.1 Number of types of neglect experienced during final three-year period (n=39)

Of the 39 children who were neglected during the final three-year period, for two-fifths (38%) it was minor, for half (49%) it was moderately severe and for 14 per cent very severe (see Chapter 3 for details of these ratings). For just over half of these children (53%) the neglect was a chronic problem, although for 47 per cent it was more episodic.

Child protection and the courts

Child protection concerns were raised for about two-fifths (40%) of the children during the final three-year period, which was half of the children who were at home at any point during this period. In addition, child protection concerns were raised about one young person while she was in care, as she was frequently absconding and associating with known sex workers. The majority of these concerns (84%) were about abuse or neglect (with neglect most common, followed by physical abuse), while the remainder concerned parental difficulties, such as alcohol misuse. For almost a third (30%) of the children where child protection concerns were raised, these concerns were not single referrals but were multiple concerns raised by different people or at different points in time.

In a few cases these safeguarding concerns led to child protection plans being made. Four children (4%) had been subject to a child protection plan at the start of the final three-year period. A further seven were placed on plans later (three under the category of emotional abuse, four under neglect). Thus, a tenth of children (11%) were on a plan at some point during this period. In addition to these children, there were live child protection concerns about another seven children at the five-year follow-up point, relating to neglect, physical and emotional abuse and in one case sexual abuse.

At the start of this period, two-fifths (43%) of the children had already been made the subject of a care order. Most (70%) remained on care orders throughout the final three-year period or until the order expired on their 18th birthday. Six of the children were adopted and in one case the care order was discharged and replaced with a residence order to relatives. Another six children had their care orders discharged while they were living at home with a parent. Thirteen per cent of the children were the subject of care proceedings during this period – care orders were made on nine, supervision orders on three and one set of proceeding had not been concluded. Thus, in total, just over half of the children (52%) were the subject of a care order during the final three-year period. Of these children on care orders, nearly two-thirds (65%) were at home at some point during this period.

Adversities and parental difficulties during the final three-year period

During the final three years, almost a third of the children (32%) had been exposed to poor parenting, characterized by inconsistent discipline, aggressive or unresponsive parenting, a lack of stimulation or low levels of warmth and affection. This was 45 per cent of children who had spent any time at home.

Some of the children also lived in households where parents (or occasionally kinship carers) were struggling with difficulties such as domestic violence, drug or alcohol misuse, mental health or health problems, learning difficulties, inappropriate sexual activity (such as prostitution, open use of pornography or having multiple partners), marked instability (characterized by multiple house moves or by a very chaotic and unpredictable environment for the child), anti-social behaviour and offending (see Table 9.6).

Table 9.6 Parental or carer difficulties during
the final three-year period

Difficulty	Percentage of all children (n=102)	Percentage of children at home at any point (n=75)
Alcohol misuse	22	31
Mental health problems	20	27
Domestic violence	18	22
Drugs misuse	14	19
Health problems	12	13
Marked instability	11	15
Offending	8	11
Anti-social behaviour	7	10
Learning difficulties	4	6
Inappropriate sexual activity	3	3

Encouragingly, over half of the children (52%) had not experienced any of these parental adversities during this period, although a third (31%) had experienced two or more (range 0–8, mean 1.15, sd 1.58). Of the 75 children who had spent any time at home, only a third (36%) had not experienced any of these adversities, although 40 per cent had been exposed to two or more (range 0–8, mean 1.49, sd 1.65).

Exposure to social and environmental difficulties, such as poor home conditions, overcrowding, financial problems and social isolation were not uncommon (see Table 9.7).

Table 9.7 Social and environmental adversities
during the final three-year period

Adversity	Percentage of all children (n=102)	Percentage of children at home at any point (n=75)
Overcrowding	20	25
Particular financial problems	20	27
Poor home conditions	16	21
Social isolation	14	30

Of the 75 children who had spent time at home, half had not experienced any of these social and environmental difficulties but a third (32%) had experienced one and 18 per cent had been exposed to two or more.

Combining the data on abuse and neglect, parental adversities and social and environmental adversities, we found that 37 per cent of the children were not abused or neglected, nor were they exposed to any parental, social or environmental adversity during the final three-year period. However, this was true for only a fifth (19%) of the children who had spent any time at home during this period.

The children's relationships with their carers

The researchers judged that the child's relationship with their current carers was good in most cases (63%) and satisfactory in 19 per cent. Eight per cent of the children had some difficulties and a tenth had serious difficulties in their relationship with their current carers, such as regular conflict, lack of support and affection.

For the children who were not at home at the five-year follow-up, a quarter of children (26%) had good relationships and contact with their birth parents and for a further 15 per cent it was satisfactory. However, for the remaining 59 per cent of children there were some or serious difficulties in these areas. For these children, contact could cause them distress and arrangements were often difficult to manage (see also Farmer et al. 2004).

The children's progress

In terms of children's progress, we considered a wide range of children's difficulties during the final three-year period. Behaviour problems and underachievement were most common at some point during follow-up (64%

and 56% respectively), while sexually abusive behaviour and prostitution were least common (1%). Nonetheless, many children had fewer difficulties by the five-year follow-up, with, for example, only 28 per cent of children displaying behaviour problems at this point, although underachievement at school was a continuing issue for nearly half (49%) of the children (see Table 9.8).

Table 9.8 Children's difficulties during the final three-year period

Behaviour	Not an issue	An issue at any point during the final three-year period	Still an issue at the end of the final three-year period (five years from the original return)
Developmental delay	92%	8%	8%
Emotional problems	62%	38%	16%
Suicide attempts/ self-harm	86%	14%	3%
Eating problems	90%	10%	5%
Lack of self-confidence	72%	28%	16%
Child passive/ withdrawn	94%	6%	2%
Behaviour problems	36%	64%	28%
Aggression towards others	56%	44%	13%
Violent behaviour	67%	33%	9%
Child beyond control	77%	23%	10%
Hyperkinetic problems	85%	15%	12%
Drugs misuse	75%	25%	10%
Alcohol misuse	80%	20%	3%
Offending	60%	40%	6%
Non-attendance at school	58%	42%	14%*

School exclusion	80%	20%	5%*
Underachievement	44%	56%	49%*
Poor language skills	93%	7%	5%
Attachment problems	89%	11%	1%
Conflict/hostility with parents/carers	64%	36%	10%
Associating with deviant peer group (inc. gangs)	75%	25%	3%
Victim of bullying	79%	21%	3%
Bullying others	93%	7%	1%
Concerns about physical presentation	80%	20%	3%
Sexualized behaviour	93%	7%	2%
Sexually abusive behaviour	99%	1%	0%
Concerning relationships	94%	6%	0%
Risky sexual activity	87%	13%	4%
Involvement in prostitution	99%	1%	1%

* These figures were calculated using a reduced sample size as 18 young people were no longer of school age at the five-year follow-up point.

Thirty-four young people had reached the age where they were eligible to take their GCSEs. Of the 27 young people where information was available, 19 per cent obtained one GCSE at grade A* to G or a GNVQ. A further 7 per cent took their GCSEs but did not appear to have obtained any passes. The remaining 74 per cent did not take any GCSE exams. Nine young people went on to post-16 education to study for vocational qualifications and one to work-based training/an apprenticeship. After leaving school or post-16 education or training, only one young person was working and 13 were unable to find or hold down a job. A further five could not work due to disability, caring responsibilities or being in prison.

Five young women were pregnant during the final period, resulting in three live births, one miscarriage and one pregnancy that was still continuing (for which a pre-birth conference was arranged because of concerns that the young woman had neglected a previous child). Only one of the three young mothers was caring for her baby without raising concerns.

In order to ascertain the extent of the difficulties the children had experienced, we counted the number that each child had shown at any point during the final three-year period. The average number of difficulties experienced was 5.18 (range 0–19, sd 4.47). Only 15 per cent of children experienced no difficulties during the final three-year period, while a fifth experienced ten or more difficulties (see Figure 9.2).

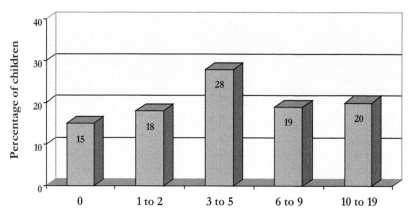

Figure 9.2 Number of children's difficulties during the final three-year period (n=94)

As would be expected, the older the children the more difficulties they had experienced (t (92)=0.36, p<.001).

Children's outstanding needs

As shown in Table 4.4 in Chapter 4 we had recorded three key areas where the researchers considered that children needed some or more support. Two-fifths of the children (42%) were considered to have no outstanding needs during the final three year period. For the remaining children their unmet needs were varied. Support with alcohol or drugs problems was most often needed (by 85% and 53% of young people with these difficulties). This was followed by help with living independently (32%), assistance with finding or keeping a job (27%) and individual support, such as mentoring (21%). Smaller proportions needed help to understand their history, with anger management, mental health assistance or work on their offending behaviour.

Outcomes in terms of stability and pathways

We turn now to consider the outcomes for the children by the end of the five-year follow-up.

The children's placements and pathways

As we have seen, 29 per cent of the returns were still continuing at this point. We now look at the subsequent placements for the 86 children who moved to live elsewhere after their original returns ended (and about whom we had this information).

The average number of different living arrangements (placements in care, custody or with kin, periods at home and independent living) experienced by children in the five years after the end of the return was 5.86 (sd 5.5), with the lowest being one and the highest 30. Over a quarter of the children (29%) had been in only one or two subsequent living arrangements or placements, while a third (32%) had had between three and five (see Figure 9.3). A further 27 per cent had had between six and ten such arrangements, with 12 per cent of children experiencing 11 or more. The older children had the highest number of living arrangements (r (84)=0.36, p=.001).

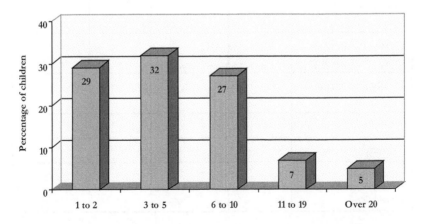

Figure 9.3 Number of subsequent living arrangements after end of original return (n=86)

Of the 86 children, 34 (40%) stayed away from home for the remainder of the five-year follow-up, while 52 (60%) spent some time at home. On average, the children had a further 1.9 periods at home (including returns from care and other moves home from elsewhere) (range 1–5, sd 1.18), with over half (55%) of the children and young people having only one further period at home, 22 per cent having two further episodes and the remaining 23 per cent having three or more periods at home.

The latest information on file indicated that, at the five-year follow-up point, half of the children (49%) were living at home and one was living in a shared care arrangement. Eleven children (8%) were living in family and friends placements and the same number had been adopted. Sixteen per cent of children were in a foster placement and a tenth were living in hostels, lodgings or were living independently. A further three young people were in custody or prison (see Table 9.9).

Table 9.9 The children's living arrangements
at the two follow-up points

Living arrangements	At five-year follow-up point		At two-year follow-up point	
	Number	Percentage	Number	Percentage
Living at home	68	49	91	66
Foster placement	22	16	25	18
Residential care/ school	0	–	8	6
Hostel, lodgings or independent living	13	10	1	1
Family and friends placement	11	8	8	6
Adoptive placement	11	8	2	1
Custody/prison	3	2	2	1
Shared care	1	1	0	–
Unknown	*9*	*6*	*1*	*1*

In order to make sense of the varied histories of the children, we grouped them according to their placement 'pathways' during the five-year follow-up period. The first group was made up of the 40 children whose original returns were still continuing. We divided the 86 children whose returns had ended into five other groups, based on their subsequent movements (see Table 9.10).

Table 9.10 Placement pathways (n=126)

Placement pathway	Number	Percentage
Original return continuing	40	29
Subsequent return	15	11

Stability away from home
   In care
   Family and friends placement
   Adoption
	36
	18
	7
	11
		26
		13
		5
		8

Unstable mix of care and return (ending in return)	13	9
Unstable mix of care and return (ending in care placement/independent living/custody)	16	12
Unstable care experience	6	4
Outcome of original return unknown	*8*	*6*
Original return ended but subsequent placements unknown	*4*	*3*

CHILDREN WHO REMAINED AT HOME IN A SUBSEQUENT RETURN

After the end of the original return, 10 children were looked after before returning home again, while five moved directly to the other separated parent and stayed there. This case example illustrates a typical subsequent return:

Box 9.1 Case example – Subsequent return

Lauren originally returned home at the age of eight months after a seven-month period in care, which included a residential assessment with her parents. The return went well initially and care proceedings ended in a supervision order. After the order expired a year later, the case was closed. There were two referrals three and four years later and a number of requests for financial assistance; however the case was not reopened.

Almost four years after Lauren went home she was made the subject of a police protection order as her mother had been assaulted by her father. They were both under the influence of alcohol and both had injuries. Lauren was placed in foster care and it was planned that she would return home as soon as possible. A risk assessment was carried out and her parents were by then receiving support from the mental health team, the alcohol advisory service and were to attend an anger management course. After just over a month in care Lauren returned home. A family support worker visited regularly and the case was subsequently closed.

STABILITY AWAY FROM HOME

The children who were in stable placements away from home included 11 who were placed for adoption, seven in family and friends placements and the remaining 18 who were in stable long-term care placements. A number of these children (18%) moved directly from the original return to their stable placement away from home, but it took longer for the other children to move to a stable placement, with an average of 15.5 months elapsing before they were placed stably (range 0–51, sd 16.62). Eight (22%) had experienced subsequent returns home from care.

Box 9.2 Case example – Stability away from home

Concerns about drug use, domestic violence and Corey's mother's mental health problems led to Corey being accommodated at the age of 18 months. Corey's parents were encouraged to address their drug problems but concerns about domestic violence and drug use still continued. Despite these concerns it was decided that Corey would return to the care of his mother after having been in care for approximately a month (original return). His father was sentenced to a term of imprisonment and his mother's drug tests were initially negative.

However, the situation deteriorated with Corey being neglected and his mother's drugs use increasing. Corey was reaccommodated after being at home for 19 months so that his parents could seek drug treatment and an assessment of their parenting skills could be undertaken. Care proceedings were started and a care order was obtained. During this time it was concluded that neither of Corey's parents were able to care for him adequately and that adoption would be the plan. A matching panel was held and Corey was matched with an adoptive couple. Corey was adopted at the age of five years and the case was subsequently closed.

UNSTABLE MIX OF CARE AND RETURN (ENDING IN RETURN)

The 13 children in this group had experienced one or more subsequent unsuccessful returns home or had unstable care experiences after the original return, but were living at home at the five-year follow-up point. These children had had between 4 and 30 (sd 6.87) different living arrangements subsequent to the return. At the five-year follow-up point it was planned that eight of these children would remain with a parent, but there was no clear plan for the remaining five.

Box 9.3 Case example – Unstable mix of care and return (ending in return)

There were concerns that Jerome was being neglected from early on in his life and he was accommodated at the age of three and a half. Jerome's time in care went well initially and a care order was obtained. There were numerous plans to return Jerome to his mother, but these were delayed because of delays in assessments, concerns about the influence of Jerome's older brother, who was at home, and reluctance on the part of his mother. The plan for Jerome was changed to long-term foster care, but, following his unhappiness in care, he returned to live with his father and paternal grandparents after four years in care (original return).

This ended seven months later when his father left the household, but the paternal grandparents continued to care for Jerome. However, when they could not cope he was placed back with his mother. During this return, there were concerns about Jerome's school attendance and his mother's mental health.

Eighteen months later his mother was admitted to a psychiatric ward and Jerome went to live with his grandmother for a week and then moved in with his older brother's girlfriend. This lasted for four months until Jerome elected to move to live with another brother and his girlfriend. When Jerome was 15 years old, his brother and girlfriend were no longer able to cope with Jerome's challenging behaviour and he returned to live with his mother.

UNSTABLE MIX OF CARE AND RETURN (ENDING IN CARE
PLACEMENT/INDEPENDENT LIVING/CUSTODY)

The 16 children in this group had experienced one or more subsequent unsuccessful returns home and were living away from home at the five-year follow-up (but not stably). These children had had between 4 and 26 (sd 6.18) different living arrangements subsequent to their original return. The future plans for this group of children at the five-year follow-up point were very varied. The plan was unclear for six. Seven young people would be moving to or remaining in independent living. The plan for one child was to return home and two others were to move to a long-term foster placement.

Box 9.4 Case example – Unstable mix of care and return (ending in care placement/independent living/custody)

Tamar was removed under a police protection order at the age of 11 and placed with foster carers after bruising was observed to his face. After a short period in care, Tamar refused to return to his foster placement and remained in his father's care (original return). His father found it increasingly difficult to keep Tamar safe as he was continually absconding and after almost two months at home, Tamar was placed with foster carers. He then had two placements in residential units but frequently absconded and was excluded from school. It was felt that Tamar needed a specialist school, so he moved to a residential school out of the area after ten months in residential units. The school placement went well and after a year there Tamar began having weekend respite with foster carers. The local authority began to consider returning Tamar to the local area, given his progress at the school.

Unfortunately, following the departure of the social worker, this transition was rushed and badly managed and Tamar ended up absconding home to his mother from his respite foster carers. Tamar initially appeared to settle at home with his mother but started offending and displaying violent behaviour. After over a year of being at home, Tamar's mother could no longer cope with his behaviour and he was placed in a hostel. After this he ended up living on the street until his mother said he could stay with her temporarily. The housing department were unable to help him as he had made himself intentionally homeless by not co-operating with family members. Mediation was suggested but both and Tamar and his mother refused this. Tamar was then ejected from his mother's flat and moved to temporary accommodation, where he remained at the end of the five-year follow-up.

UNSTABLE CARE EXPERIENCE

Following the end of their original returns, the six children in this group had not subsequently returned home but had had unstable experiences in care characterized by frequent moves and/or placement breakdowns (between 3 and 19 different placements, sd 5.85). At the end of the five-year follow-up, one young person was living with foster carers, two were living with relatives, one was in a hostel and two were living independently. It was planned that the young person in foster care would remain there. One of the young people living with relatives was to move to independent living in the future.

Box 9.5 Case example – Unstable care experience

As we saw in Chapter 4, Ben's extended family were unable to cope with his behaviour and requested that he be accommodated at the age of 13, as his father was in prison and he had not had any contact with his mother for two years. His mother then contacted children's services and said that she wished to care for Ben full-time. After contact was started with his mother, Ben absconded home from foster care (original return) and the case was closed as Ben had only been accommodated.

There were a number of referrals and assessments while Ben was at home but he remained there for 15 months until he was accommodated following a scuffle with his mother. Ben was placed in a residential unit and then spent four months in a secure unit as a result of a detention and training order due to numerous offences he had committed, including assault, criminal damage, breach of the peace, racially aggravated assault, arson and theft.

Upon his release he was fostered for a week but that quickly broke down due to his difficult behaviour and he went into residential care. A specialist residential placement with educational and therapeutic provision was sought and Ben moved to the identified placement after almost a year at the residential unit. Unfortunately, Ben was asked to leave this placement after seven months because of his behaviour and absconding. Ben then moved to temporary supported lodgings. After a year there Ben had to leave because of his abusive and aggressive behaviour and offending. With few options available, Ben went to live with his grandparents, where he was living at the five-year follow-up point.

In conclusion, when comparing these six groups, some clear differences are apparent (see Table 9.11). The children placed stably away from home were younger and had experienced lower levels of previous adversity. Although these children ended up in permanent alternative placements, some had still experienced a number of moves beforehand and a number had returned home again after the end of the original return. The unstable mix of care and return (ending in care or another placement) was perhaps the most unstable group. A significantly higher proportion of these children had been looked after before the original return and they had had the highest number of previous returns home. After the return ended, this group had the highest number of subsequent living arrangements and of subsequent returns home. They also experienced the highest levels of further abuse or neglect.

The children who were still in their original returns had the most stable experiences. However, the extent of further abuse or neglect these children experienced while at home was quite concerning. The majority of the children in the unstable care experience group were accommodated and they were the least likely to have been looked after previously. These children did not return home again after the end of the original return but had high levels of subsequent movement and could not be sustained in stable placements away from home. Overall, as can be seen, many children experienced high levels of placement movement and this was particularly true for the three unstable groups.

Table 9.11 Summary data for six placement pathways

	Continuing return (n=40)	Subsequent return (n=15)	Stability away from home (n=36)	Unstable mix of care and return (ending in return) (n=13)	Unstable mix of care and return (ending in other placement) (n=16)	Unstable care experience (n=6)
Age at start of return (mean)	7.2	7.27	5.69*	11.9*	11.25*	11.33*
Returned with legal order in place	53%	53%	53%	39%	44%	33%
Looked after prior to care period before original return	38%	53%	61%	46%	75%*	33%
No. of times returned home prior to return (mean)	1.2	1.75	1.4	2.2	2.3	1
No. of adversities prior to care period before original return (mean)	5.2	5.93	4.56*	6.15	5.9	6

No. of living arrangements after return (mean)	N/A	2.27	3.28	9.62	11	8.33
No. of subsequent returns home from care after original return (mean)	N/A	0.8	0.31	1.5	1.9	N/A
Abuse or neglect during original return	43%	47%	81%	62%	75%	83%
Further abuse or neglect (during final three year period)	56%	38%	39%	64%	75%	33%

* Significantly different from the children in the other groups, p<.05.

N/A = not applicable.

Stability outcome

In order to simplify these groups further, we assigned them to three overall outcome categories (see Table 9.12):

- **At home** – includes continuing original return and subsequent return groups.

- **Stability away from home** – includes children placed stably in care, family and friends placements, or adoption.

- Unstable – includes the two groups of children who had an unstable mix of care and return and the unstable care experience group.

Table 9.12 Stability outcome categories (n=126)*

	Number	Percentage
At home	55	43
Stability away from home	36	29
Unstable	35	28

* The sample size is less than the full sample of 138 as there were 12 cases where either the outcome of the original return was unknown or the child's placement(s) after the return were unknown.

The children in these three stability outcome categories differed in terms of their age and the levels of difficulty they were experiencing during the final three-year period. The child's age at the start of the original return was significantly related to the stability outcome categories (F (2, 123)=20.67, p<.001) with the children in the stability away from home group having been youngest (mean 5.7 years), followed by the children at home (mean 7.2 years), while the unstable group had been the oldest at return (mean 11.5 years).

The levels of the children's difficulties during the final three-year period were also related to their stability outcomes. The children in the unstable category tended to have had a much greater level of difficulties than those in the at home and stability away from home groups. Suicide attempts/ self-harm, violent behaviour, the child being beyond control, drugs and alcohol misuse, non-attendance at school, school exclusion, attachment problems, conflict/hostility with parents or carers and risky sexual activity were all significantly more likely to occur in the unstable group than the at home or stability away from home groups. There was a statistically significant difference too in the levels of aggression towards others, with the children who were stably placed away from home displaying the lowest levels (19%), followed by the at home group (38%) and then the unstable group (69%). Offending was significantly higher in the unstable group (63%) than in the at home group (30%), which was in turn higher than in the stability away from home group (7%). However, it is important to note that the age of the children at the original return in the three stability outcome categories was significantly different, as we have seen. It is therefore probable that the higher likelihood of typically 'adolescent' behaviours in the unstable group is due to their older ages.

Children in the unstable category had also shown a significantly higher number of behavioural difficulties as compared with those in the other groups (F (2, 91)=19.45, p<.001). Again, this is likely to be because of their older age.

Children in the unstable group had more often been accommodated when looked after than those in the other groups, although this difference was not significant. There was, however, a relationship between the local authorities and stability outcomes (see Table 9.13). Authority C had a much lower proportion of cases (15%) in the at home category and a much higher proportion (54%) in the unstable group when compared with the other six authorities. This was not explained by differences in the children's ages, as the ages of the children did not differ significantly between local authorities.

Table 9.13 Local authority and stability outcome categories

	At home (%)	Stability away from home (%)	Unstable (%)
Authority A	61	23	16
Authority B	43	36	21
Authority C	15	31	54
Authority D	70	10	20
Authority E	31	38	31
Authority F	41	36	23
Authority G	60	20	20

Chapter 10 will further explore the factors which were associated with particular outcomes.

Independent living

As noted earlier, 10 per cent of the young people were living in hostels, lodgings or were in independent living arrangements at the five-year follow-up. By the end of this period 19 young people had had some experience of living independently. Most of them (15) were in the unstable outcome group, with a few falling into the stable away from home category. For most of these young people (68%) their accommodation was in the form of a council, housing association or private tenancy. The remainder were living in bed and breakfast accommodation (3), a house share (1), a hostel (1) or a foyer (1). Details of independent living were not consistently recorded on files, so the following figures should be interpreted with some caution. There was sufficient information to determine that four young people had experienced poor home conditions while living independently and six had had financial problems. Two young people appeared isolated while living independently and five had had difficulties managing generally. A tenth (11%) of the young people had made multiple attempts at living independently and four had been homeless at some point. Bearing these difficulties in mind, we judged that 7 of the 15 young people, where sufficient information was available, had managed to sustain a period of independent living that lasted three months or longer where they appeared to be coping well and were living in accommodation of a satisfactory standard.

Outcomes in terms of the children's well-being
Child's well-being

A researcher rating of the child's overall well-being at the five-year follow-up point (or the point the case was closed if earlier) was made. There was sufficient information to rate 130 of the 138 cases. The following categories were used:

- **Good** – the children in this group were making good progress. They had few problems in relation to health, emotional and behavioural problems, social interaction and education, training or work. Where problems were identified they were only minor and likely to be in only one or two areas. Any problems the child did have were not impacting on their overall progress and well-being.

- **Satisfactory** – the children in this group were faring reasonably well but they were likely to have a number of minor difficulties or a more significant difficulty which was causing them some problems. The children were likely to be receiving appropriate help for particular difficulties. However, the impact of these difficulties was not significant and there were likely to be other areas where the child was doing well. The child might have had more pronounced difficulties at an earlier stage but these had improved.

- **Poor** – the children in this group were likely to have a number of more major difficulties. However, some positives could be identified such as an area where the child had few difficulties or the fact that they were engaging with support. The impact of pervasive problems could perhaps be tempered by the support children were receiving or the quality of the placement they were in.

- **Very poor** – these children had pervasive problems such as drug or alcohol misuse, offending or severe emotional and behavioural problems which affected most aspects of their life and functioning. These children were likely to have multiple significant problems and there was often evidence of a downward spiral or deterioration.

Almost a third of the children (29%) had good outcomes in terms of their well-being, for a further third (33%) their well-being was satisfactory, a quarter (25%) had poor well-being and for the remaining 13 per cent it was very poor (see Table 9.14).

Table 9.14 Child's overall well-being at five-year follow-up point

Well-being	Number	Percentage
Good	37	29
Satisfactory	43	33
Poor	33	25
Very poor	17	13

As might be expected, there were differences in the children's overall well-being according to their stability outcomes (see Table 9.15). Almost a third (29%) of the children in the at home group had good overall well-being, for more than a third (38%) it was satisfactory, but a third had poor (31%) or very poor (2%) well-being. Almost three-fifths (58%) of those placed stably away from home had good well-being and for a third it was satisfactory. In contrast, only 3 per cent of the unstable group had good overall well-being, while 70 per cent had poor or very poor well-being. (This is similar to Wade and colleagues' (2011) finding that the most vulnerable children in terms of outcome were those who had experienced unstable reunification.) These differences were statistically significant (χ^2 (6)=48.08, p<.001). The one young woman in the unstable outcome category who had good well-being had managed to turn things around for herself despite the significant levels of adversity (including neglect, emotional and sexual abuse) and instability that she had experienced. She had a fairly stable job and was studying at colleges for qualifications relating to this work.

Table 9.15 Child's overall well-being according
to stability outcome category

	At home (%)	Stability away from home (%)	Unstable (%)
Good	29	58	3
Satisfactory	38	31	27
Poor	31	8	35
Very poor	2	3	35
Total	100	100	100

For the purposes of analysis, the poor and very poor categories were combined and will hereafter simply be called 'poor'. We found that the child's age at the start of the return was significantly related to well-being (F (2, 127)=14.47, p<.001), with the children with good well-being having been youngest (mean 5.5 years) at that point, followed by the children with satisfactory well-being (mean 7.4 years), and the children with poor well-being having been the oldest (mean 10.2 years).

Whether children had been voluntarily accommodated when looked after was also significantly associated with well-being (χ^2 (2)=7.03, p=.03). Children with poor well-being were much more likely to have been accommodated when they entered care, perhaps explained by the fact that older children are more likely to be accommodated. Children with poor well-being were also more likely to have a parent who had had alcohol misuse problems before they returned than children who had satisfactory or good well-being (χ^2 (2)=6.94, p=.023).

There were some differences between the local authorities in the proportion of children in each of the well-being categories (see Table 9.16). Authorities E and G had slightly more children with good well-being. Authority C had the highest proportion of children with poor well-being and authority G had the lowest. Some of this difference is likely to be explained by the local authority variation in stability (see Table 9.13), as well-being and stability were significantly associated with each other.

Table 9.16 Local authority and well-being outcome categories

	Good (%)	Satisfactory (%)	Poor/ very poor (%)
Authority A	26	42	32
Authority B	31	23	46
Authority C	29	14	57
Authority D	25	25	50
Authority E	36	36	28
Authority F	23	50	27
Authority G	40	40	20

Again, Chapter 10 will explore further the factors which were associated with particular outcomes.

The quality of children's living arrangements

We also rated the quality of the children's living arrangements at the end of the five-year follow-up (or the point the case was closed if earlier). This was based on how well the placement or arrangement met the children's needs and how likely they were to do well there. A quarter of the children (24%) were in good quality living arrangements at the five-year follow-up point, for 37 per cent it was satisfactory and for 39 per cent it was poor or very poor (see Table 9.17).

Table 9.17 Quality of child's living arrangements at five-year follow-up point

Quality	Number	Percentage
Good	33	24
Satisfactory	50	37
Poor	36	27
Very poor	16	12

The quality of the children's living arrangements was significantly associated with their overall well-being at the five-year follow-up point (χ^2 (9)=206.83, p<.001). Children who were doing well were more likely to have good quality living arrangements and children who were doing poorly were more likely to have poor quality ones. However, the two ratings did not always correspond. There were 11 children whose well-being was not as good as the quality of their living arrangements. These were all children who were in foster placements and who were experiencing fairly substantial emotional and behavioural difficulties. One of these children had recently moved from home to foster care and her well-being was still compromised due to her recent experiences at home. The remaining children had been in foster care for longer periods of time and had long-standing difficulties. These children were likely to need long-term therapeutic input to address their difficulties.

Box 9.6 Case example – Child with poor well-being in a good-quality placement

Rasheed was moved to foster care at the age of nine, after he alleged that his father was hitting him. Rasheed's behaviour in foster care could be erratic and attention-seeking at times, but he was doing well academically. At the five-year follow-up point Rasheed had been in the same foster placement for a year and nine months and the carers had coped fairly well with his behaviour, which was still of concern. Rasheed had said he wanted to kill himself and just before the follow-up he had been put on report at school for bullying, being stubborn, running off and talking to imaginary people. There were concerns that he was suffering from an identity crisis.

Conversely, there were 15 children whose well-being was better than the quality of their living arrangements. Twelve of these children were living at home, two were living independently and one was living with relatives. The well-being of the children in these placements was good or satisfactory in spite of their parents' difficulties, poor parenting or the risks to the child. These children may have been more resilient than others and were perhaps receiving crucial support, for example from children's services, relatives or school. A number of these cases illustrate the difficult dilemmas involved in returning children home to parents who have difficulties such as alcohol misuse difficulties or mental health problems.

Box 9.7 Case example – Child with good well-being in a less satisfactory living arrangement

Lucy returned home to her mother Mrs Smith at the age of 12. Mrs Smith was an alcoholic and had periods when she engaged in binge drinking. When this occurred, Lucy had to take on more responsibility in the household such as completing domestic tasks and taking care of her mother. At the five-year follow-up point Lucy remained at home living with her mother. She had obtained some GCSEs and was studying a foundation course at college. She had a good relationship with her mother and had friends at college. Her health was good but she would sometimes get upset with her mother when she was binge drinking.

Ethnicity

Interestingly, children's ethnicity was significantly associated with both of our outcome variables (see Table 9.18). Black or minority ethnic (BME) children were more likely to be stably at home than white children (67% v. 38% respectively) and less likely to be unstable (8% v. 32% respectively). Similar proportions of children in both groups were placed stably away from home (BME 25%, white 30%). Additionally, BME children were less likely to have good well-being (12% v. 32% respectively) and more likely to have satisfactory well-being (52% v. 29% respectively). Similar proportions of children in both groups had poor or very poor well-being (BME 36%, white 39%).

Table 9.18 Ethnicity and outcome variables

Outcome variables		BME* (%)	White (%)
Stability	At home	67	38
	Away from home	25	30
	Unstable	8	32
	Total	100	100
Well-being	Good	12	32
	Satisfactory	52	29
	Poor/very poor	36	39
	Total	100	100

*BME = black or minority ethnic.

Some of this variation may be explained by the fact that our two outcome variables are significantly related to each. However, when the figures are examined in detail it is clear that the difference in the stability outcome category is only part of the picture (see Table 9.19). Overall, over two-thirds of all children stably at home had satisfactory or poor well-being. However, the proportion of BME children who were stably placed at home and had satisfactory or poor well-being was much higher (94%), with only 6 per cent of BME children stably at home and having good well-being there (compared to 29% in the sample as a whole). We found that a surprisingly large proportion of BME children who were placed stably away from home had poor well-being (33% v. 11% in the whole sample), which might be explained by slowness to make permanent placements away from home for these children.

Table 9.19 Relationship between stability
and well-being for BME children

	At home (%)	Stability away from home (%)	Unstable (%)
Good	6	33	0
Satisfactory	63	33	50
Poor/very poor	31	33	50

We looked at other factors which might explain the differences in our outcome variables between the BME and white children. There was no significant difference in the age at first referral or the age at the original return between the BME and white children. BME children were no more likely to have siblings in the sample than the white children and there were no consistent differences in placement pathways in relation to the local authorities in which the BME children were concentrated. A detailed examination of the case summaries suggested that some of the returns of the BME children were concerning given the risks to the child and the lack of planning and assessment around the return. It could be that a desire to return children to their birth families had overridden or obscured potential concerns about these returns and that this was more prevalent for BME children. However, given that the number of BME children in our study is only small (n=26), these findings should be interpreted with some caution and only suggest that BME children may have different outcomes. This is an area for further research, particularly in relation to reunification.

In summary, five years after the original return to their parent(s), two-fifths of the children (43%) were living stably at home, either in the original return or a subsequent one. A further 29 per cent of children had achieved permanence in adoption, foster care or a family and friends placement. The remaining 28 per cent of children had had unstable experiences following the end of their original returns and a number had already made attempts at independent living. The children with unstable outcomes had significantly more difficulties than the others, had been significantly older when they went home and ended up with poorer overall well-being.

In the next chapter, the factors which help to explain children's outcomes will be examined.

10

Explaining Outcomes

This chapter describes the factors which are associated with our outcome variables and discusses the multivariate analysis that we used to understand how the different factors interacted and contributed to explaining outcomes.

Outcome variables

In the previous chapter we described our two outcome variables and how they were devised. The stability variable describes the children's placement pathways over the five-year follow-up period. Children who were still in their original returns at the five-year follow-up point were grouped with children who had achieved stability in a subsequent return to form the 'stable at home' group (43%). The children in the 'stable away from home' group (29%) were in stable foster, kinship or adoptive placements. The third 'unstable' group of children (28%) had had unstable experiences in care or unstable moves between care and home.

Our second outcome variable related to the children's overall well-being at the five-year follow-up. Children who had good well-being were making good progress and had very few difficulties (29%). The second category included children who were faring reasonably well but who had some minor difficulties. These children were coded as having satisfactory well-being (33%). Children who had poor or very poor well-being (38%) had more major difficulties which impacted on their progress and functioning.

Stability

Our approach to examining the ways in which different factors interacted and contributed to outcomes was exploratory, given the lack of previous research and theory in this area to guide the selection of variables. In order to establish which variables might be related to stability at the bivariate level we divided our independent variables into groups. We found that a large number of variables were significantly related to our stability outcome variable (see Appendix 1, Table A1.1). This is likely to be because some of the variables were measuring very similar things or the same thing at different time points. Additionally, the relationship of some factors (e.g. behaviour problems) with the outcome variable is likely to be explained by their relationship with another variable (e.g. age) which is itself significantly related to the outcome variable. Therefore, these findings should be interpreted with some caution. Relationships were considered to be significant if $p<.02$. This more rigorous significance level was used due to multiple comparisons with one outcome variable.[1]

A number of child factors which were in evidence before the return were significantly related to the stability outcomes (see Appendix 1, Table A1.1). The children in the stable away from home group were the youngest when they first entered care and the youngest when they returned home. The next oldest group were those who ended up stably at home, while the unstable group were the oldest at these points.

Before returning home, the children in the unstable group had, more often than the others, had behavioural and emotional problems, shown sexualized behaviour, been in conflict with their parents or been excluded from school. Children in the stable away from home group had experienced the fewest number of adversities before returning home, followed by those placed stably at home, while those with unstable outcomes had experienced the most. Indeed, in keeping with this, young people in the unstable group had experienced the most emotional abuse, were more likely to be rejected or singled out for rejection, and had more often experienced very severe neglect. The two stable groups had experienced a similar number of types of neglect before being looked after, with the unstable group experiencing significantly more, possibly partly because these children were older.

In terms of case management before return, specific conditions were more often set for the parents of children in the two stable groups, while the parents of children in the unstable group had least often received any specialist help at this point and these children were more likely to return home in an unplanned way. It was more likely that all the problems had been addressed prior to the return in the two stable groups than in the unstable group. The same proportion of children (53%) in the stable at home and stable away from home groups were subject to a legal order at the start of the return, while fewer children in the unstable group

---

1   A large number of variables were related to our outcome variables, thus inflating the Type 1 error rate. Therefore, a Bonferroni adjustment was made to reduce the family-wise error rate due to multiple comparisons with one outcome variable.

(40%) were returned home on orders and more had been accommodated, although these differences were not significant.

In addition, children in the stable away from home group were most likely to have returned home with siblings, while few children in the unstable group did so, probably related to their age differences. During reunification, the parents of the children in the stable away from home group received the most support from specialist and informal sources, while the parents of children in the unstable group received the least.

As would be expected, a number of factors relating to the progress of the returns were associated with stability. Poor parenting skills and poor home conditions were identified most frequently in the unstable group. There was evidence of parents' inability to cope in many of the cases in the unstable group, while this was less common in the other groups. Children in the unstable group showed the most emotional and behavioural problems and conflict with parents, and were more often beyond their parents' control.

When looking at case management from the first referral until five years after the original return, the cases of children who ended up with unstable outcomes had more often been inappropriately closed, decisions had not been followed through and more often there had been missed opportunities to prevent further harm. A clear focus on the key issues was most likely to have been maintained in the stable away from home group (perhaps because of the permanence plans for these children), followed by the stable at home group, while this occurred less frequently in the unstable group. Overall, proactive case management was most often a feature of the stable away from home and the stable at home groups, and had least often occurred in the unstable group. Passive case management was most often apparent in the unstable group.

Predicting stability

Because the sample size was modest and had limited numbers within each outcome category, the three-part stability variable was recoded into a dichotomous variable. The stable group, which consisted of the 'stable at home' and the 'stable in care' group, was compared with the unstable group.

We undertook a series of forward stepwise regressions to establish a subset of variables to enter into a final regression model. Included in these stepwise regressions were variables found to be significant in the bivariate analysis (which had small amounts of missing data and were not highly correlated with other predictors) and a few important variables from the small amount of previous relevant research. Together, the variables took account of the child's experiences before entering care, factors during the care episode, the making and progress of the return and the overall management of the case. (Variables relating to the final three-year period were excluded, as only 102 of the 138 cases were open at any point during this period and thus the sample size would have reduced considerably.) For a list of the variables used in the regression analyses see Appendix 1.

There were a number of other factors which might have been potentially important predictors, but it was not possible to include these in the regression analyses because of missing data. In relation to the return these included: the presence of poor parenting skills, parental drug and alcohol misuse, informal support and the child returning home with siblings.

The regressions showed that three variables were most predictive of the likelihood of a stable placement. These variables were:

- the child's age at the original return
- changed household membership at the start of the return
- the local authority variable.[2]

One other variable was significant: that is whether the child had emotional problems before returning home. However, it was not entered into the final model because there was too much missing data. This is an area to be considered in future research. The results of the final model including the three variables are presented in Table 10.1.

Table 10.1 Hierarchical logistic regression predicting stability: final model block entry

Independent variable	B	SE	Wald	df	Sig	Exp(b)	95% CI for Exp(b)
Child's age at return	−0.389	0.083	22.076	1	<.001	0.678	0.577–0.797
Changed household membership (at start of return)	1.242	0.536	5.364	1	.021	3.462	1.21–9.904
Local authority	2.308	0.694	11.049	1	.001	10.05	2.578–39.182

2   This was a binary variable which compared one authority (C) which had very different practices with the remaining six authorities. A series of correspondence analyses were undertaken which established that authority C was rather different in terms of both of our outcome variables and in relation to overall case management. See Table 9.13 in Chapter 9 for the differences in the stability outcome variable according to local authority.

The likelihood of being in a stable placement decreased as the child's age increased. For every year of increase in the child's age at the start of the return, the odds of not being in a stable placement five years later increased by a factor of 1.47. However, if the child was returned to a changed household then the odds of being in a stable placement increased by a factor of 3.46, suggesting that the arrival or departure of a parent's partner or a move to the other (usually less troubled) parent often signals improved parenting. In addition, if a child was not looked after in authority C they were ten times more likely to be in a stable placement. However, the confidence interval for the local authority variable was very wide, probably as a result of grouping local authorities for the purposes of comparison and the fact that some authorities had small numbers, so this finding should be viewed with some caution. All the authorities had some children who were not in stable placements (see Table 9.13). The final regression model correctly predicted 84 per cent of the cases overall, 63 per cent of the unstable cases and 92 per cent of the stable cases. This suggests that the children's outcomes were affected by a combination of the characteristics of the child and the return households and also by case management, which varied by local authority.

The intention in this exploratory study was to develop a model that would identify the predictors of stability. The strict requirements of the regression analyses limited the extent of our multivariate analysis. Therefore, we used CHAID (Chi-Squared Automatic Interaction Detector) analysis to explore further the differences between our three stability outcome groups. CHAID uses the most significant predictor from a range of independent variables to segment the sample. The groups are then further split, again using the best predictors, until there are no more significant predictors or the groups have reached their minimum size. The results are then presented in an easy to interpret tree diagram. CHAID is useful for dealing with categorical outcome variables and also copes well with different levels of measurement within the predictor variables. Additionally, missing data is not as problematic within CHAID analysis as in regression analyses. CHAID is an exploratory technique and the findings are suggestive of relationships that are present in the data, so further research with a larger sample size is needed to confirm these relationships. The CHAID analysis both confirmed the findings from the regression analyses and revealed other factors which may be important.

The overall misclassification risk of the tree was 31.7 per cent (SE=0.041), indicating that by using these variables we correctly classified 68.3 per cent of all children to their stability outcome group. However, the tree was more successful at predicting the stable away from home and unstable groups (80% and 80.6% respectively correctly classified) than the stable at home group (52.7% correctly classified).

The results of the regression and CHAID analyses showed that the child's age at return was highly significant in predicting stability. More specifically, the CHAID analysis indicated that children who returned home over the age of six were more at risk (and those over 12 at return were most at risk) of having a subsequent unstable placement pathway (while this only occurred for one child returned home under the age of three). It also appears that case management is key to outcomes. Children who were reunified under the age of three had the highest chance of a permanent placement in care if the return was not successful (58%), while those who returned home between the ages of three and six were only half as likely to be placed stably away from home (31%). The chances of this outcome fell still further for children aged 6 to 12 (21%) and over 12 at return (14%). There was also evidence that, if concerns were raised about children aged between three and six at return, then they were often acted upon, resulting in children moving to permanent placements elsewhere.

However, when children returned home, even at the age of six or over, their cases appeared to be less well managed and the rates of unstable outcomes rose. For example, children who returned home over the age of 12 who had first been referred to children's services below the age of three, had the highest chance of falling into the unstable group. These children had been known to children's services for many years, yet it appeared that little effective action had been taken to prevent them from having unstable care experiences. For children reunified over the age of 12, but first referred over the age of three, none ended up in permanent placements away from home, suggesting a lack of permanence planning for these children.

For children aged between 6 and 12 at return, it was evident that the build-up of neglect was a major predictor of instability. This could be because children who experienced larger numbers of types of neglect had more problems and, thus, instability was more likely. Equally, it could be that the children who had many experiences of neglect lived with families with more significant problems, which resulted in unstable experiences for the children. This finding might also suggest that if there was more intervention to tackle neglect then fewer children would have later unstable experiences.

In addition, the finding that among children who returned home between the ages of 6 and 12, even those who had been exposed to a high number of kinds of neglect could achieve stability at home if they were returned to changed households (58% did so), suggests that practice needs to focus on ensuring that real change is achieved in these families before children are reunified (see also Farmer *et al.* 2011; Wade *et al.* 2011).

Well-being

As with the previous analysis for the stability outcome variable, we divided the independent variables into groups in order to explore their relationships with the well-being outcome variable. Many of the factors that related to well-being were the same as those relating to stability, which is not surprising given that the two outcome variables are related to each other. We found that a large number of variables were significantly related to our outcome variable (see Appendix 1, Table A1.2). This is likely to be because some of the variables were measuring very similar things or the same thing at different time points. Again, relationships were considered to be significant if $p<.02$.

The children who ended up with good well-being were the youngest when they first entered care and when they returned home, and those with the poorest well-being at follow-up had been the oldest at these stages. Children with poor well-being had the most behaviour problems and were more likely than others to be in conflict with their parents and siblings. Children with good well-being had the least problems in these areas.

As might be expected, the number of adversities they had previously experienced was highest for children who ended up with poor well-being and lowest for those with good well-being. Children with poor well-being had experienced the most physical and sexual abuse, while those with good well-being had much less often been emotionally abused. The children with poor well-being had also much more often experienced very severe neglect and high numbers of types of neglect.

When specific conditions had been set for the parents before return, children more often had good well-being later, suggesting that they were carefully managed (which in turn was also probably related to their younger age). The returns of those children with poor well-being were more likely to have been unplanned and the timing accelerated. There was also more likely to have been pressure from the child for the return among those with poor well-being. In contrast, children with good well-being had more often than others had exceptional support for the return from their caregivers (especially foster carers) (see Farmer *et al.* 2011) and all their problems had more often been addressed before reunification.

Again, the parents of children with good well-being had received the most support from specialist and informal sources, while the parents of children with satisfactory and poor well-being received lower levels of such support. During reunification, the parents of children with later poor well-being had parented poorly most often, been unable to cope, had children with behaviour problems who were beyond their control, and had been in conflict with their children more often. In addition, these children went on to have the most placements in care and returns home over the whole period.

When considering case management from the first referral until five years after the original return, the cases of children who ended up with poor well-being were more likely than others to have been inappropriately closed. Moreover, intervention had only been galvanized by trigger incidents, while neglect to children had more often been marginalized. Failures to safeguard children had been evident most often for children who had poor well-being at outcome, as had passive case management. Overall, proactive case management had occurred most often for children with good well-being and least often for children with poor well-being.

Finally, two measures of placement movement over the five-year follow-up period were related to well-being. The children with poor well-being had a greater number of different living arrangements over the five-year follow-up and a greater number of returns home from care compared to the children with satisfactory well-being. The children with good well-being had the smallest number of different living arrangements over the five-year follow-up and the fewest returns home from care.

Predicting well-being

Regression analysis was undertaken using the same process as for stability and using a very similar set of potential predictor variables. Notably, the number of different placements (or living arrangements) the child had had during the five-year follow-up and whether the child had ever been the subject of care proceedings were added. These variables were not included for stability as they represented part of the process of achieving or not achieving stability. Again, variables were only included if they did not have large proportions of missing data and were not highly correlated with other variables. For a list of the variables used in the regression analyses see Appendix 1.

A series of regressions revealed that two variables were most predictive of the likelihood of good or satisfactory well-being. These variables were:

- child behaviour problems before the original return
- failure to safeguard the child (at any point during the case).

One other variable was significant in the regressions: the number of different living arrangements (or placements) the child had over the five-year follow-up period. However, it was not entered into the final model because it had too much missing data. The results of the final model are presented in Table 10.2.

Table 10.2 Hierarchical logistic regression predicting good/
satisfactory well-being: final model block entry

Independent variable	B	SE	Wald	df	Sig	Exp(b)	95% CI for Exp(b)
Child did not have behaviour problems prior to the return	1.746	0.548	10.169	1	.001	5.733	1.96–16.766
Child adequately safeguarded (absence of a failure to safeguard)	1.27	0.51	6.189	1	.013	3.559	1.309–9.677

If the child did not have behaviour problems before returning home, the odds of having good or satisfactory well-being at follow-up increased by a factor of 5.73. If the child was adequately safeguarded overall then they were three and a half times more likely to have good or satisfactory well-being than if they were not.

The final regression model correctly predicted 75 per cent of the cases overall, 83 per cent of the children with good or satisfactory well-being and 64 per cent of the children with poor well-being. It suggests that children's outcomes in terms of their well-being were affected by children's characteristics and by case management issues.

Again, we used CHAID analysis to explore further the differences between our three well-being outcome groups. The overall misclassification risk of the tree was 36.9 per cent (SE=0.042), indicating that by using these variables we correctly classified 63.1 per cent of all children to their well-being outcome group. However, the tree was more successful at predicting the poor well-being group (82% correctly classified) than the good and satisfactory well-being groups (54.1% and 48.8% respectively correctly classified).

This analysis showed that children who had behaviour problems before returning home were more likely than others to have poor well-being at the five-year follow-up point. This highlights the persistence of these behaviour problems, since children with difficult behaviour at follow-up were also much more likely than others to have poor well-being. For children who had behaviour problems before return, case management did have an influence on their outcomes in terms of well-being. If the case management approach had not marginalized the neglect the children had experienced, then they were more likely to end up with satisfactory or good well-being. Similarly, if the neglect was not marginalized but case management had nonetheless failed to safeguard children, then they had an increased chance of having poor well-being. This suggests that, for children who have problems, it is possible to manage the case in ways which help to improve their well-being at a later stage.

For children who did not have behaviour problems before reunification, the long-term consequences of having already experienced a larger number of types of neglect are evident. Children were much more likely to have poor well-being if they had experienced more than eight kinds of neglect incidents before return home (these children were no more unlikely to be neglected during the return than others, so it was their prolonged exposure to neglect before entering care which contributed to their poor well-being.) Interestingly, BME children who had no behaviour problems before reunion and had experienced eight or fewer types of neglect beforehand were less likely to have good well-being than other children in this situation. On examining these cases in more detail it was evident that several of the children were still at home or had remained at home for long periods in returns where they were being neglected or physically chastised. As suggested in Chapter 9 it may be that a desire to return BME children to their birth families had overridden or obscured potential concerns about these returns.

Now that we have examined the factors that were statistically related to our two types of outcome, we consider in the final chapter the implications of our study findings for policy and practice.

11

Implications for Policy and Practice

Practitioners have very little research to inform them about which kinds of case management or combinations of services keep neglected children safe and contribute to improved outcomes. Since cases of neglect often need long-term interventions, the aim of this study was to help to fill gaps in our knowledge about how risks are assessed and managed over time and to identify predictors of child outcomes when cases are followed up over a five-year period. This research focused on 138 neglected children from seven local authorities who had been returned to their parents in a set year, with most of the children drawn from the sample in our previous research on reunification. The reunification study had followed up these children for two years from the original return. This study followed them up for another three years, providing the rare opportunity of following up a group of children for five years in all. Since the study focuses on neglected children who had been returned home from care, these children are likely to be at the more severe end of the spectrum. (The sample did not include neglected children who had never entered care or those who did so and stayed there.)

This chapter draws together the key findings from the study and notes some of the implications for policy and practice. First, the findings about the profile of children and families, the services provided and case management will be revisited, then the children's progress and outcomes over the five years will be considered, paying attention to the factors that were related to outcomes. In the second section we look at the issues which emerged from the study. The use of the words 'statistically significant' will be used sparingly in this chapter, but it should generally be assumed unless stated otherwise.

Key findings
The children's early experiences

All the children in the study had been neglected. Most (81%) had experienced a lack of appropriate supervision and many had also been physically neglected (83%) or not taken to medical appointments. Over three-quarters of the children had been emotionally neglected and almost half experienced neglect of their education or their need for stimulation. Most children experienced multiple types of neglect. For a tenth of the children the neglect that they experienced was minor, for over half it was moderately severe and for over a third very severe. Parents who misused alcohol significantly more often than others very severely neglected their children and supervised them inadequately.

In addition, most (84%) children had also been emotionally, physically or, more rarely, sexually abused. So although this is primarily a study of neglected children, some of the findings are likely to apply more widely to children who come to the attention of children's services departments.

The children's parents themselves had severe and long-standing difficulties. Almost half had experienced abuse and neglect when they were growing up, nearly a third had been in care and over a quarter had already had children looked after or adopted.

Most of the children experienced parental domestic violence (74% of families) and substance misuse (66% of families). In over two fifths of the families, children had been living with a parent with mental health problems. By the time the children in the study entered care, most were living in single parent (64%) or stepparent families (20%).

It is important to highlight the fact that concerns were voiced about these children from early in their lives, providing the potential for early intervention to help them, with over half of the children having been referred to children's services before the age of two, including a third referred before birth. Three-quarters had been brought to children's services attention by the time that they started school. Yet, as we will see, quite often children's services involvement continued over many years without sufficient action being taken to protect the children. This in turn had a direct relationship with poor outcomes for children at the five-year follow-up point.

The total number of adversities (other than neglect) experienced before entering care was noted, including adverse parental behaviours such as domestic violence, drug or alcohol misuse and poor parenting skills, the death of a parent, abuse and exposure to a convicted sex offender. Most children (70%) had experienced between four and nine such adversities.

Only four children (3%) had experienced one or no adversities other than neglect.

Many of the children in the study showed difficulties, some of which were attributable to the neglect or other types of parenting deficits that they had experienced. These included children who had very delayed development or poor speech, did not put on weight, had missed a great deal of school, had decayed teeth or untreated medical conditions, children who were over-responsible for their parents or siblings, those who had emotional and behavioural problems, were anxious, withdrawn or suicidal, or, on the other hand, were aggressive, violent, offended or misused drugs or alcohol.

Services during the final three-year follow-up period

The services provided during the first two years of the returns for the whole group of children from which our subsample of neglected children was drawn have already been described in the reunification study (Farmer *et al.* 2011). For this research we recorded the services and interventions provided for parents and children over the next three years.

Services for parents

We recorded services during this three-year period for the 52 sets of parents (68 children) whose cases had been open for at least three months and where the child had been at home for at least one month during this period. The services which had most often been provided were assistance with mental health problems (50%) and with financial difficulties (45%). Help for parents who misused drugs was patchy, with only 38 per cent of such parents getting any service and even fewer of those with alcohol problems (16%) receiving help (see also Farmer *et al.* 2011). Most of this support was short term, with only a fifth of parents receiving help which went on for more than six months.

A quarter of the parents received no support at all during this period. Three-fifths of them needed more help, particularly with their children's behaviour, their parenting skills, alcohol and drugs problems and domestic violence. The parents of the older children received significantly *less* support than those with younger children, even though many of these parents were struggling with their adolescent children's serious emotional and behavioural problems.

Parents in the interviews said that they appreciated social workers who showed them respect and were clear with them about the consequences of not meeting conditions, such as not drinking (see also Farmer *et al.* 2011), but some parents were critical of low levels of visiting, of children being rewarded for bad behaviour or of promised actions not materializing. Some had found the services provided useful but others had not. Two of the six parents interviewed had either received no help or received too little to be useful, while one father was struggling to cope with a child with serious health difficulties with very little support.

Services for children

We had information on the services provided to 93 of the 102 children whose cases were open for at least three months during the final three-year period, since we could consider services to them whether or not they went home. Help with drugs misuse had been forthcoming for almost half (47%) of the young people who had needed it and about a quarter also received assistance with independent living skills, counselling or mental health help, but only 8 per cent of those who needed it received assistance with alcohol misuse problems. It was noticeable that work on parent–child relationships (3%) was very rarely provided. Again, most of the support was short term.

Almost a third of the children did not receive any formal support during this three-year period. Three-fifths of the children needed more assistance. Help with alcohol (83%) and drugs misuse difficulties (53%) were most needed, followed by assistance with mental health problems, living independently, finding a job and education. A third of the children had periods when they did not have an allocated worker and only a fifth of the children had the same social worker throughout the three years.

The older children received *more* types of help than younger ones but were also more likely than younger children to be receiving *insufficient* support, presumably because older children were experiencing greater levels of difficulty. Children in the stably at home outcome group received fewer types of support than those placed stably away from home, who in turn received fewer types of support than those in the unstable category who received the most. This relationship is partly explained by the differences in the ages of children in the three groups (children in the unstable group were the oldest) and the fact that cases of children stably at home were more likely to be closed.

Adequacy of services

Overall, the match between the needs of the cases and the services provided was thought to be very good or good in only just over a quarter of the cases, while it was fair (42%) or poor (9%) in others, and in a fifth of the cases there was little or no support.

The qualitative analysis of case files and interviews revealed that even when some services were provided, they were often not at a sufficiently intensive level to meet the severity of parents' and children's needs in order to make and sustain change, while a few families lacked even basic social work support. In only a relatively small proportion of cases (10%) did real and lasting change take place in parents' capacity to look after their children, usually as a result of very intensive and sometimes prolonged services. This may be one reason why a significant predictor of stable returns home was not changes in parents' ability to cope but, instead, when there had been changes in the household to which children returned (for example, the presence of a new positive parent figure or a move to the other parent).

We found that court orders and child protection plans did not make a significant difference to the services provided at this stage, as court orders had done during the first two years of the original return (Farmer *et al.* 2011).

Case management

In addition to considering the services provided, the way in which cases had been managed was examined, looking right back to the first referral and going through until five years after the children returned to a parent. Almost three-quarters of the children were subject to a child protection plan (72%) and two-thirds (67%) to care proceedings at some stage during this period.

A range of issues affected case management. Some of these related to the characteristics of the parents and children, others to practice, while still others were at the system level either for children's services departments or in the wider system involving the courts and other professionals.

Practice issues
RESPONDING TO REFERRALS
After the children were returned to their parents, children's services departments received referrals expressing concern about the safety and welfare of almost three-quarters of them. In as many as three-fifths of the families such referrals about risks to the children, mostly about abuse or neglect, were not adequately followed up or insufficient action was taken to make them safe.

ASSESSMENT

Assessments were infrequent overall except in care proceedings where it was noticeable that specialist assessments could be helpful in making decisions as to whether or not children should be returned to their parents. Sometimes this was the only time in the case when there was clarity of planning for the child. Lack of assessment at other times could mean that the level of risk involved in returns to parents was not known, and without assessment, services were less likely to be provided.

LACK OF PARENTAL OR CHILD ENGAGEMENT

There were difficulties in engaging over two thirds of the mothers and half of the father figures. In addition, parents actively resisted or attempted to sabotage work in two-fifths of the cases. However, in a fifth of families where there were problems in working with the parents, the case was closed for this reason.

In general, there was little apparent focus on involving fathers and the researchers considered that greater attempts could have been made to involve the father or father figure in a quarter of cases. In addition, a third of the young people were not easy for social workers to engage.

DEALING WITH NEGLECT

Dealing effectively with neglected children was a considerable challenge. We found that sometimes the neglect was marginalized and other issues took centre stage, and at times the sheer number and range of child and family problems made working with the families especially difficult (Gardner 2008).

In half of the cases a clear focus on the key issues in the case had not been maintained at times by children's services. Moreover, as we have seen, in a considerable number of families key problems had not been addressed by children's services, in particular parental alcohol and drugs misuse, domestic violence, mental health problems and poor parenting. In addition, a major gap in services was in the provision of direct help with children's behavioural problems, particularly advice on behaviour management for their parents and direct work with children, including therapeutic work. Children whose behavioural problems or risky behaviours were not addressed often went on to have poor outcomes as their behaviour deteriorated and some became increasingly involved in offending or drugs use.

Although there were many reports of children suffering chronic neglect, including lack of stimulation, failure to put on weight, missed medical appointments and missed school, there was little evidence of consistent monitoring of these deficits and of children's weight and height, which could have formed the basis of a case in court. Indeed, it was relatively rare for entry to care to take place because of an accumulation of concerns about children. Decisive action in cases of neglect often awaited a trigger incident of physical or sexual abuse or a particularly serious incident of domestic violence.

LACK OF KNOWLEDGE OF CHILDREN'S CASE HISTORIES

Linked to this, a good number of the workers we interviewed lacked knowledge about the history of the case and they were sometimes unaware of key events that had happened in the past. This meant that long periods of stagnation where little had been done to protect children were not recognized and social workers could lack an overview of how concerns were mounting up or of how the case had been managed in the past, which might have provided guidance as to what might or might not work in the future.

GIVING PARENTS TOO MANY CHANCES

The researchers considered that in as many as two-fifths of the cases (38%) the parents had been given too many chances to make changes.

EXPECTATIONS ABOUT PARENTAL STANDARDS

One way to deal with a deteriorating or fluctuating situation is to lay down clear expectations about parental standards and monitor these closely. Expectations were clearly made of parents in two-fifths of the families but were lacking in the others. Expectations had been laid out in the form of written agreements in a quarter of cases in relation to the return. It was difficult, however, if parents did not comply and action was not always taken in response.

THE EFFECT OF CHILDREN'S ETHNICITY ON CASE MANAGEMENT

In two-fifths of the BME families the children's ethnicity appeared to have an impact on the management of the case, with referrals sometimes taken less seriously or not acted on or children remaining with, or returning to, parents where they were at risk.

System level issues
UNALLOCATED CASES

When cases were unallocated some children were maltreated by their parents with no action taken to protect them, others were not returned home when planned, work was not completed or plans for a permanent placement were not actioned.

THE EFFECT OF CHANGES OF SOCIAL WORKER ON CASE MANAGEMENT

Changes of social worker could impact on the management of the case by prompting more proactive work or changing the plans for the child, but it did not necessarily have this effect. Of course, when there were many changes of social worker there was a lack of continuity for the parents and children, and more likely to be a lack of follow-through of planned interventions.

INAPPROPRIATE CASE CLOSURE

The researchers judged that the cases of two-fifths of the families were closed when there was clear evidence of the presence of difficulties or that underlying problems in the case still remained.

Securing children's safety and making plans for the future

In addition to considering these general issues in managing cases, we examined how well child protection plans and care proceedings had helped to safeguard children and ensure that plans were made for their future.

Safeguarding

In half of the families there was clear evidence of a failure to safeguard children, that is children's services were involved but children went on to experience further abuse or neglect, which could have been prevented. At the time that children were not protected, the child was not on a child protection plan or subject to a care or supervision order in only 29 per cent of these families. It was clear then that child protection plans and court orders were sometimes not effective in keeping children safe.

In some cases children returned home to completely unsuitable situations, sometimes with children's services' agreement and in as many as half of the families children had experienced two or more failed returns home. In some of these cases it appeared that the children were being repeatedly returned home to circumstances that remained essentially unchanged. Indeed, many social workers spoke in the interviews about returns they were involved in, where although they had concerns about the children, these were not sufficient to warrant removal, and some had major reservations about returns that had pre-dated their involvement.

Children subject to child protection plans

In a fifth of the families the researchers considered that child protection plans should have been used to protect the children when they were not, and at other times children had experienced neglect and abuse over long periods before they were placed on a child protection plan. Where children who were clearly at risk were not on plans, there were major variations by local authority, with this applying to 42 per cent of children in one authority and to none in two others. Thus, it appears that the threshold for child protection plans in some local authorities was set too high or it was perceived to be so.

Child protection plans were used in 72 per cent of the cases at some point between the first referral and the five-year follow-up point, but in two fifths of these cases they had not been effective in safeguarding children. Sometimes there were continuing referrals about abuse and neglect to children on plans which did not reach the threshold for more coercive action. There was a greater tendency for continued neglect to attract less intervention than physical or sexual abuse, but a number of children suffered continuing physical abuse which social workers had come to view as 'acceptable' in some way. Child protection plans were much less often used for older children in relation to their risk-taking behaviour and they did not appear to be a very effective vehicle for change in these situations (see also Rees *et al.* 2011).

The use of care proceedings

In at least 15 families (14%) care proceedings were not taken in spite of children living in highly unsatisfactory situations, and the researchers judged that proceedings had been needed. In four of these cases it was stated on file that it was thought that there was insufficient evidence for care proceedings. It was clear that some legal departments were excessively cautious and that sometimes managers had not felt able to challenge their advice.

In two thirds of the cases care proceedings were used at some point. However, the researchers judged that more than a quarter of the children had been left too long before being removed from their parents. Of the children who experienced further episodes of care during the final three-year period, just under a third (30%) were also judged to have been left too long before being removed. In such cases, children suffered prolonged neglect and sometimes also other forms of abuse, but the usual response was one of family support. Once such a pattern of non-response was established it could become entrenched and incidents were often viewed one by one rather than their cumulative impact being recognized.

Once children's cases reached court, supervision orders were made on 34 of them but they failed for over three-fifths (62%), as the situation at home broke down. These supervision orders did not provide adequate protection for the children or sufficient motivation to ensure that parents maintained any improvements evident before the orders were made. In several of these cases, particularly where a parent was addicted to substances, especially alcohol, it was clear that more coercion was needed to prevent parents relapsing.

Care orders with plans to return children to a parent were made on 32 children but these returns broke down in most cases (87%). For three children, after the care orders were discharged, care proceedings were initiated on a second occasion and these three children were adopted. Of the other 25 children only seven achieved stability. Clearly, the decisions made during care proceedings are crucial, since although more decisive action to secure children's futures could be taken on children on care orders, it was noticeable that subsequent permanence planning was absent for most of them.

Care orders with plans for permanence outside the family were made on 21 children. These succeeded for most (76%) of them, although five children did not achieve a stable permanent placement.

Taken together, the plans made during care proceedings did not work out in three-fifths (62%) of the cases. These findings present a major challenge. If care proceedings do not succeed in ensuring that children are protected and helped to find a stable future either with a parent or in permanent substitute care, then the system is failing children.

Case planning and plans for permanence

For half of the children the decision was made at some point that they should be cared for away from home permanently. For a third of these children the plans for permanence were later abandoned or changed and most of them were returned home. In addition, for over a third of all the children, case planning had been inadequate, and in ten cases there was very little planning of any sort.

The effectiveness of case management

Four broad patterns of case management emerged. The first group of cases (26% of the families) were those which were passively managed initially but where management later became proactive. Some of these cases were managed as family support cases for too long in spite of a build-up of concerns that would have made earlier child protection intervention more appropriate.

The case management for a quarter of the families (25%) was initially proactive but later became passive. The pattern in these cases was for children's services departments to take action either early on in the child's life or soon after concerns about the child's welfare became evident. Appropriate action was then taken to safeguard the child and plan for the future, but as time wore on the management was no longer proactive but merely passive.

Case management that was passive throughout was the pattern in 24 per cent of the families. In these cases, children were left at risk without adequate intervention, sometimes over long periods. They included cases where there were many changes of social worker and case closures, and where the concerns of other professionals were ignored. The cases were treated as family support when they were open, and abuse and neglect and parental rejection of the children were minimized. Parental problems such as alcohol and drugs misuse or mental health difficulties received little attention, so that children experienced the many adversities caused by living with parents with these difficulties. Sometimes attempts to instigate care proceedings were thwarted by legal advice that there was insufficient evidence to do so.

Overall there was a lack of direction and planning in these cases, little or no permanence planning and insufficient clarity with parents about what needed to change and by when and the consequences if no change took place. Sometimes the workers did not have a view of the full history of the case and it appeared that managers often did not have oversight of the whole case, which might have led to a recognition of the extent of harm the children had suffered and the ineffectiveness of the approach taken. Nonetheless, in a number of these cases, senior managers or the chairs of child protection reviews in the authorities had written on file that they were very unhappy with the way the case was being handled.

Case management was proactive throughout in a quarter (25%) of the cases. In a number of these cases an initial child protection conference was held prior to the child's birth, or care proceedings or actions to accommodate children were initiated soon after birth. In all of them, once concerns about the children's welfare had been recognized children's services departments moved to protect children and plan for their future. The parents were still given the chance to show that they could parent their children safely, but action was taken if they could not. In many of these cases, care proceedings or child protection plans were used effectively to protect children, bring about increased co-operation from the parents or, if this was not forthcoming, to plan for permanence. In addition, occasionally cases were worked with proactively without using the courts or child protection procedures.

We found that the rates of proactive practice varied by local authority from one where 36 per cent of its practice was proactive to two authorities where only 11 per cent was. Similarly, passive practice featured in 52 per cent of the cases in one authority as compared to only 8 per cent in two others. In addition, it was noticeable that in the proactive cases children were usually young when action was taken to protect them and secure their future.

Parents' and children's views of neglect

While it has been found that when confronted, parents may dispute the suggestion that they have neglected their children (Farmer and Owen 1995), and views about appropriate parenting may vary between professionals and parents, nonetheless our interviews suggested that parents did have clear views about what constitutes neglect.

Four of the parents considered that their children had been neglected while living with them because of their mental health problems, domestic violence or substance misuse, and the parents gave detailed descriptions of what they thought of as neglect. Since these parents had made considerable effort to get their children back, it is likely that other parents might be less willing to take responsibility for their part in their children's neglect.

Interestingly, the two young people who had experienced the most chronic neglect were unable to answer a general question about what neglect is. This may suggest, as other research has found, that some children may regard the parenting they receive as normal rather than seeing it as neglectful (McGee *et al.* 1995; Rees *et al.* 2011). Other children saw neglect as being left to do what you wanted, left to care for yourself, being 'mentally abused' or not being fed. One young person reluctantly acknowledged that she was somewhat neglected when her mother drank. This also illustrates the dilemma for young people in acknowledging parenting deficits in parents to whom they are attached.

Re-abuse and children's return outcomes at the two- and five-year follow-up points

At the two-year follow-up, 59 per cent of the children had been abused or neglected after returning to a parent. During the next three years, half of the children (48%) whose cases were open at any point were abused or neglected. Most of these were the same children (33/48), which shows the persistence of maltreatment in many families.

By the two-year follow-up, half of the 138 original returns had ended. Three years later the proportion of returns which had disrupted had risen to 65 per cent and only 29 per cent of them were still continuing. Similarly, at the two-year follow-up, a quarter of the returns had been rated as being of good quality and 58 per cent as of poor quality. By the five-year follow-up, fewer (18%) of the returns appeared to be of good quality, whilst the proportion where the quality was poor had risen to 72 per cent.

The children's progress during the final three-year period

A wide range of difficulties was experienced by the children and young people during the final three-year period. Behavioural (64%) and emotional (38%) problems, poor school attendance (42%) and underachievement (56%) were common and a considerable proportion of children also showed violent behaviour (33%), were offending (40%), experienced conflict with their parents or carers (36%) or had problems with drugs (25%) or alcohol (20%). There were improvements in some of these difficulties by the end of the five-year follow-up, so that, for example, by that point slightly fewer children were showing emotional or behavioural problems, aggression or poor school attendance, although more were hyperactive or were underachieving at school. As would be expected, more of these problems were in evidence when children were with their parents than when they were in care (see also Wade *et al.* 2011), although rates of offending, non-attendance at school and underachievement were almost the same whether children were at home or looked after at the end of this period.

The average number of such difficulties experienced by children during the final three-year period was 5.18 (range 0–19). Only 15 per cent of children experienced no such problems, while a fifth experienced ten or more. The children in the unstable outcome category (see below) had higher levels of difficulties than those in the other two outcome groups, as would be expected because of their older age.

Children's outcomes
Stability outcomes

We assigned the children to three outcome categories at the end of the five-year follow-up. Two-fifths of the children (43%) had achieved stability at home (in the original or a subsequent return). A further 29 per cent of children had achieved permanence in adoption, foster care or a family and friends placement, while the remaining 28 per cent of children had had unstable experiences in care or in a mix of care and returns.

Well-being outcomes

A researcher rating of the children's overall well-being at the five-year follow-up point was also made. Almost a third of the children (29%) had good outcomes in terms of well-being, for a further third (33%) their well-being was satisfactory, while two-fifths (38%) had poor well-being.

Children's well-being and stability outcomes were related. Children in the stability away from home category were more likely to have good overall well-being (58% did so), while those in the at home category were fairly equally spread over the good, satisfactory and poor categories, with a worrying third having poor well-being. Children in the unstable group were most likely to have poor well-being (70%).

The factors that were related to outcomes

We investigated which factors were related at the bivariate level to our two outcomes. We found that a large number of variables were significantly related to both of our outcome variables.

STABILITY OUTCOMES

The child's age at return was significantly related to outcome, with the stable away from home group being youngest (mean 5.7 years), followed by children stably at home (mean 7.2 years), with the unstable group the oldest (mean 11.5 years). Children in the unstable group had also most often experienced very severe neglect, emotional abuse and rejection.

Other factors which were associated with stability outcomes were related to children's behavioural, emotional and other problems before return, service provision, how the returns progressed and how their cases had been managed. There was more likely to be inappropriate case closure and decisions that were not followed through in the unstable group, while a clear focus on the key issues was most likely to be maintained in the stable away from home group. There were missed opportunities to prevent further harm most often in the unstable group. Overall, proactive case management was most often a feature of the stable away from home and the stable at home groups, and had least often occurred in the unstable group. Passive case management was most often apparent in the unstable group. There were also clear local authority differences, with a much higher proportion of children in the unstable group in one authority and fewer in that authority ending up stably at home, when compared with the other six authorities.

Further analysis revealed that the child's age at return, changed household membership when they went home (see also Harwin *et al.* 2003; Wade *et al.* 2011) and which local authority they lived in, were the most significant predictors of the likelihood of a stable outcome. For every year of increase in the child's age at the start of the return, the odds of not having a stable outcome increased by a factor of 1.47. However, if the child was returned to a changed household (changes in the parent's partner or return to the other parent), then the odds of having a stable outcome increased by a factor of 3.46. In addition, children who were not looked after in the poorest performing authority were ten times more likely to end up with stable outcomes.

CHAID (Chi-Squared Automatic Interaction Detector) analysis was used for further exploration of the differences between our three stability outcome groups. This analysis suggested that children who were *under the age of six* at return were most likely to find stability in an alternative placement if the return was not successful.

For children who returned home *over the age of six* there was a heightened risk of having a subsequent unstable placement outcome, much less chance of ever achieving a permanent placement in care and indications that their cases were less well managed. Children returned over the age of 12 had a very high risk of having unfavourable outcomes.

WELL-BEING OUTCOMES

Many of the factors which were significantly associated with the well-being outcome variable at the bivariate level were the same as for the stability outcome. For example, children who were younger at the start of the return had the best well-being five years later (average 5.5 years), followed by those with satisfactory well-being (average 7.4 years), while the children with poor well-being had been the oldest at that point (average 10.2 years). In addition, children with poor well-being had more often experienced very severe neglect and the highest number of kinds of neglect. Children who had good well-being were the least likely to have experienced emotional or physical abuse and those with poor well-being most likely to have been sexually abused. In addition, children with poor well-being were much more likely to have been accommodated when they were looked after, no doubt due partly to the link with older age but also probably with the lower levels of assistance provided for accommodated children.

Interestingly, children who ended up with poor well-being were more likely than others to have previously been exposed to parental alcohol misuse. This is a problem for which few services were provided, which generally did not trigger adequate intervention, and yet was related to the most severe neglect. The children in the poor well-being group had also had the highest number of returns to a parent during the five-year follow-up period, suggesting the importance of more decisive action to prevent oscillation between home and care and the need to implement permanence plans for such children. In addition, there were major local authority differences: in one authority 57 per cent of the children ended up with poor well-being as compared with only 20 per cent in another, suggesting that variations in policy and practice were influential.

Further analysis revealed that children's behaviour problems before return and a failure to protect them were the most significant predictors of poor well-being at follow-up.

CHAID analysis also showed that behaviour problems before return were associated with poorer well-being, indicating the persistence of behavioural difficulties and their link with later poor outcomes. When children did have behavioural difficulties, they nonetheless ended up with better well-being where the neglect they experienced had not been marginalized by professionals and they had been protected. This suggests that it is possible to manage these children's cases in ways which may improve their well-being. In addition, children without behaviour problems before going home were much more likely to end up with poor well-being if they had experienced a high number of types of neglect, which again argues for earlier intervention to assist them.

Overall, these analyses show that the characteristics of the children (such as their age at return and experiences of neglect), combined with the characteristics of the family at return and the ways their cases are managed, all affect children's long-term outcomes.

Issues

The findings raise many issues for policy and practice, some of which are principally related to working with children who are neglected, while others have wider relevance.

Age

It was clear throughout the study that practice with older children and adolescents was far less proactive and sure-footed than that with younger children (see also Farmer *et al.* 2011). Authorities were more at a loss as to how to intervene effectively with young people with behaviour problems or with those who had started to offend or get involved in high risk behaviours; and some of these young people rapidly became hard to contain at home or in care. Services for adolescents were often insufficient to meet their needs and help for their parents was scarce. Specialist placements in residential care, therapeutic residential units and residential schools were sometimes helpful, but too often ended precipitately when funding was withdrawn or adolescents became less co-operative, leading to hasty and ill-judged returns.

However, it was sobering to find that the age cut-off after which children more often ended up with unstable outcomes and more rarely achieved permanence outside the family (in long-term fostering or with kin and not just in adoptive placements) was as low as *six* years at the time of the return. While it is encouraging that generally very young children provoke interventions from professionals to protect and provide permanence for them, it is worrying that once children are of school age, action to safeguard them and plan for their future is often lacking. The fact that most of the children in the study had been known to children's services departments before they started school, yet many went on to have poor outcomes, underlines the missed opportunities to intervene decisively very much earlier (Munro 2011).

Ethnicity

Children's ethnicity appeared to have a bearing on the way that their cases were managed and on their outcomes, with referrals not always acted on and children sometimes remaining with parents who were a risk to them. It was interesting to find that significantly more BME children than others ended up stably at home (67% v. 38%), but in keeping with this, fewer ended up with good well-being (12% v. 32%) and more had satisfactory well-being (52% v. 29%) than white children. On the other hand, it was encouraging that fewer BME children had unstable outcomes (8% v. 32%), while similar proportions in both groups achieved stability away from home (BME 25% v. 30%). A surprisingly large proportion of BME children who were placed stably away from home had poor well-being (33% v. 11% in the whole sample), which might be explained by the slowness in making permanent placements away from home for these children.

It is important that children's safety is always a priority and that similar parental standards are expected whatever the ethnicity of children and their families. The number of BME children in our sample was small, so these findings should be interpreted with caution. Further research in this area might be useful.

Working with unco-operative parents

Given that most of the parents in the study did not readily co-operate with social workers, practitioners need skills in engaging parents and working effectively in the face of non-co-operation, hostility and aggression (see e.g. Ferguson 2005; Gardner 2008; Stanley and Goddard 2002). While social work education emphasizes anti-oppressive practice and forging partnerships with parents, there is a need for more training for social workers in working with non-compliant parents (Laming 2009), who form a substantial part of the statutory caseload of child care social workers.

Working with neglect

The difficulty of amassing sufficient evidence to make a case in care proceedings in relation to neglected children needs to be addressed. First, there needs to be greater understanding of the kinds of evidence which will be needed to make a case in care proceedings, and local authority legal departments need to share their understanding about this with social workers and identify exactly what they can do about it. Second, this needs to be translated into a new way of working in which social workers (and other agencies) continuously monitor and build-up evidence of children's progress or lack of it, including charting children's weight gains, developmental and other progress, and gathering and recording information from other agencies. Workers need to record all referrals about children on their caseloads and the action taken in response, as well as all incidents of abuse and neglect in a readily accessible format. This of course would not mean that such children were always heading for care proceedings, but that a case can be made without delay for those who do require proceedings.

Where local courts are reluctant to make care orders in cases of neglect and are known often to make no order or only supervision orders, very senior managers need to hold talks with court personnel and regional CAFCASS managers in order to find a way forward. Avoiding taking care proceedings in such situations, as appeared to be happening in at least one of our local authorities, appears to have a detrimental impact on children's outcomes.

Reunification practice

There appears to be a presumption in many cases that children will be reunified with their parents in the absence of extreme contraindications to doing so. This is broadly in tune with legislation. However, it should not mean that children are returned to parents who are likely to maltreat them, unless monitoring and appropriate safeguards are in place. Indeed, our previous research showed that the disruption rates for reunification varied widely by local authority and that different practices were leading to different outcomes, especially in relation to older children (Farmer *et al.* 2011; see also Dickens *et al.* 2007; Schofield *et al.* 2007; Sinclair *et al.* 2008).

This study and our previous research on reunification found that the concerns which led to entry to care had often not been addressed before children returned to their parent(s). This suggests that assessment and decision-making need to focus more explicitly on what needs to change *before* return is possible, with targets clearly set and monitored by means of using conditions. There needs to be much more clarity about the standards expected of parents *during* reunification (Trotter 2002), the timescales for changes to be made, the consequences if these standards are not maintained and a clear contingency plan, which is put into action, if changes are not forthcoming (Biehal 2006; Farmer 2009; Farmer *et al.* 2011). If parents are unable, with appropriate assistance, to meet the standards expected (and preferably set down in written agreements – see Biehal 2006; Farmer 2009), then this may mean that they are unable to care for their children and other plans need to be made. Without this, children may remain for long periods with parents whose care is unsatisfactory, until (if they are lucky) there is a trigger event which propels them into care. Of course, alongside such assertive practice there needs to be intensive packages of assistance for parents and children. In addition, more decisive action needs to be taken when children oscillate between home and care, since children with the highest number of returns to parents in this study ended up with the poorest well-being. Local authorities would benefit from identifying such children and reviewing their practice with them.

The White Paper (Department for Education and Skills 2007) which led to the Children and Young Persons Act 2008 promised revised guidance addressing the need for effective care planning to ensure that work is undertaken while children are looked after and that appropriate services are provided for children and parents when the children return home. As a result, the Care Planning, Placement and Case Review Regulations (Department for Education 2010b) expect that children's services will hold a review before voluntarily accommodated children return to their parents. It is required that a 'child in need' plan is drawn up identifying the areas in which parental capacity needs to be strengthened and identifying the services needed by the children and their families. This is to ensure that their returns succeed (regulation 39) and that these plans are regularly reviewed. (The regulations continue as before to be specific about how returns of children on court orders are managed.)

The introduction of the Public Law Outline has also provided an opportunity to sharpen reunification practice, since prior to care proceedings parents are invited to a meeting to discuss their children's welfare and this will clearly spell out what needs to happen for a family to be reunited. It is to be hoped that in high risk cases, intensive help over a defined period combined with written agreements may help to identify those parents who are able to make changes within the timescales needed by their children and those who cannot (see also Ward *et al.* 2011).

There is a need for much greater recognition that reunification work is highly skilled, demanding and time-consuming. If return practice is to become more effective, then reunification also needs to be made a clear strategic priority backed up by protocols informed by research and linked to multi-disciplinary training (The Who Cares? Trust 2006). It might also be useful in future if inspections gave more specific focus to this area of practice.

There is an ongoing difficulty in getting reunification work onto the policy agenda and it is rarely the focus of practice initiatives. There may well be an argument for making it a specialization in its own right (Farmer 1992), especially in view of the high risk nature of the work and the particular skills it requires.

Services

Although a range of services was offered to parents and children, they tended to be short-term and not very intensive. Some parents and children received no services at all. As a result, in a considerable number of cases, few or none of the major problems in the family had been addressed. It is important to note that receiving specialist help was associated with children having good well-being (and lack of specialist help with unstable outcomes). In the few instances where much more extensive help was available, real change could occur. This would argue for access to a range of resources, which could be provided intensively to parents to see whether or not they can respond and make the changes that would enable their children to live safely with them. In addition, the potential for foster carers to take an extended role in supporting children and parents into and during returns could usefully be recognized and developed (Farmer *et al.* 2011).

The fact that older children were given more support, but that it was often insufficient to meet their needs (and that their parents received the least help), points to the need for more tailored services for adolescents and their parents (see also Rees *et al.* 2011; Wade *et al.* 2011). In particular, there is a need for more focused work with young people with behavioural and emotional problems who enter care, and with their parents, and also more consistency in arranging tailored support packages to help to make these returns work. Some of the techniques and 'wrap-around support' packages from Treatment Foster Care (see e.g. Chamberlain, Moreland and Reid 1992; Chamberlain and Reid 1998) might be applied to reunification, while the use of support care (Cosis Brown, Fry and Howard 2005; Greenfields and Statham 2004) or short breaks/respite care (Bradley and Aldgate 1999) might play an important part in maintaining these placements, providing positive relationships for young people and avoiding oscillation in and out of care.

Help with substance misuse problems

Our previous study on reunification showed that there were high recurrence rates for parental alcohol and drugs misuse when children returned home and that when this was the case children were significantly more often neglected and abused. This may have been because parents were not sufficiently motivated to tackle their substance misuse or because they had too little support to do so. In this study too, there were significant gaps in the services for parents with drugs misuse and particularly alcohol misuse problems, so that children were returned to such parents and suffered continuing adversities as a result of living with them (see also Farmer *et al.* 2011). It is also notable that children whose well-being was poor were especially likely to have been living with parents with alcohol misuse problems.

Often social workers believed that parents had stopped drinking or using drugs (or moderated their use) before the children were returned, when they had not. There appeared to be insufficient understanding about substance misuse (or an inaccurate assessment as to the extent of the problem) such that many social workers expected parents to be able simply to moderate or stop their drinking or drug use with little or no intervention. Moreover, our findings suggest that the alcohol misuse is sometimes normalized by workers. Social workers need much more training in the recognition of substance misuse and in assessing its nature and severity and the associated harm to children. They also need more training in making realistic assessments about prognosis that will not be overwhelmed by the 'misplaced optimism' (Forrester and Harwin 2004) that was often evident in this and other studies (Farmer *et al.* 2011; Harwin and Forrester 2002). Training is also needed in undertaking appropriate interventions, case management and care planning.

Other research (Cleaver *et al.* 2007) has also shown low levels of referral to drug and alcohol agencies, with more referrals for drugs than for alcohol difficulties. Social workers need to be able to access specialist help for parents. Ways also need to be found to ensure that children's social workers and drug and alcohol workers work much more closely together to help parents with addictions, keeping the child's best interests central (see, for example, Cleaver *et al.* 2011; Harwin and Forrester 2002; Kroll and Taylor 2003; Velleman 1993, 2002). In future, the Family Drug and Alcohol Courts, which have been piloted (Harwin *et al.* 2011), may provide an important way forward, and the government's drug strategy also highlights the need for prompt access to treatment for drug-using parents (H.M. Government 2010). This is especially important in view of the strong link between substance misuse and a range of other parenting problems (see e.g. Advisory Council on the Misuse of Drugs 2003; Cleaver *et al.* 2011; Kroll and Taylor 2003; Tunnard 2002a, 2002b; Velleman and Orford 1999), including abuse and neglect (Chaffin *et al.* 1996; Farmer *et al.* 2011; Kelleher *et al.* 1994).

There is clearly a need to review reunification practice in cases where parents misuse alcohol or drugs, to introduce clear expectations that parents will be required to undergo treatment (see Farmer 2009; Gossop, Marsden and Stewart 2001; Maluccio and Ainsworth 2003) before children are returned to them and that their substance misuse is closely monitored and reviewed before and during return. The findings of this and our previous study point not only to the need for a greater use of available services but also to consideration of routine drug or alcohol testing of parents with substance misuse problems before and during returns.

Case management
Counteracting inescapable 'errors'
Most of the reports arising from child death enquiries recommend changes to safeguarding policy at the macro level and imply that a new set of fixes will sort out the problems. However, our findings on case management over time suggest that there are important processes which will *always* affect

case management negatively and which therefore need to be deliberately interrupted.

The high proportion of cases where referrals about risks to children were not adequately dealt with and where neglect was marginalized needs to be understood, since in these situations children were often not sufficiently protected. It appeared that sometimes each incident was viewed in isolation and it is likely that some social workers were unaware of the full histories of the children for whom they were responsible. Referrals from neighbours or relatives were at times ignored, and abuse and neglect were often normalized when workers had become desensitized to maltreatment (Daniel *et al.* 2011; Stevenson 2007). This is completely understandable since practitioners will wish to find the most positive construction of events in relation to families with whom they are engaged. Many practitioners appeared to have developed a fixed view of their cases, which were not swayed by contrary information, and this psychological process has often been commented on in the literature (see e.g. Farmer 1999; Munro 1996, 1999, 2005a; Reder and Duncan 1999; Reder *et al.* 1993).

In addition, it can be difficult to maintain an accurate perspective on the extent of children's difficulties because of the habituation associated with long-term work or to take action in situations which have been implicitly condoned for some time (Farmer and Parker 1991). Ascertaining the appropriate threshold for action appears to be particularly difficult in cases of neglect (see also Brandon *et al.* 2008a). At the same time, some departments may be keen to keep the numbers of children in care down, partly because of costs and also because of a perception of the poor outcomes of looked after children (see e.g. Baxter 1989; Berridge and Cleaver 1987; Triseliotis *et al.* 1995), which recent research has strongly challenged (Wade *et al.* 2011; Ward *et al.* 2011). These processes need to be recognized as inescapable and dealt with accordingly. They were not usually a result of staffing problems within children's services.

If such processes are inescapable, then the way forward may be to find ways to counteract them as far as possible. This might be done by a second social worker (for example, an advanced or senior practitioner) doing a joint visit in all ongoing cases where there are child protection issues at a set frequency of, say, every four or six months. This would provide a second pair of eyes to review the situation and advise on case management (see also Laming 2009). While these joint visits could be undertaken by team managers, it might be preferable for someone else to undertake them, since team managers may have set the norm of non-intervention or non-action which is the problem.

Visits could usefully be accompanied by a review of the entire case so that the patterns of action or inaction could become more visible. While joint visits might initially be seen as threatening to social workers, it would need to be made clear that the aim was to assist them in their practice and provide consultancy and that this will help to share responsibility for difficult cases. Such sharing might also help in the recognition of when thresholds for intervention have been reached and assist in avoiding practice being responsive only to specific incidents of abuse, rather than responding to an accumulation of neglect. Skilled supervision also has a major role to play here (Brandon *et al.* 2008a). In addition, regular case audits by senior managers would appear to be essential in order to maintain an overview of all cases to ensure that practice remains proactive.

Up-to-date chronologies on children are vital and should record all referrals about risks and all incidents of maltreatment, and these should be consulted when new referrals are received and also at every case review. There also needs to be an expectation that workers will read and absorb the contents of case files when they take on a new case. At present, workers sometimes have an ahistorical view of cases which means that they may overlook the ways in which their cases have been (and are being) managed and focus only on the present without this important context.

Thresholds for intervention

The social workers who we interviewed said that neglect was harder to define than other types of maltreatment, since there was no clear indicator that signalled neglect. They talked of the difficulty of knowing where to draw the threshold for intervention in cases of neglect and how to be aware when that threshold had been reached, especially as a situation can deteriorate gradually without being noticed. Another problem facing social workers was the variation between social work teams (for example between intake and long-term teams) and between different professionals in relation to the threshold for neglect. In particular, it could be hard to get the legal team to agree that the threshold had been reached (Brandon *et al.* 2008a) and to gather evidence sufficient to take the case to court within the children's timescales.

As we have seen, in many cases referrals about risks to children were not seen as reaching the threshold for action to intervene. In addition, in about a fifth of the families, the researchers considered that children should have been placed on child protection plans – and in a similar proportion care proceedings should have been instigated – when they had not. Even when children were eventually subject to child protection procedures or court intervention, quite often they had been left too long before these actions were taken. In all these cases the threshold for action had been set too high: children continued to be abused and neglected and there appeared to be no mechanism for identifying these cases as in need of intervention. As previously mentioned, regular joint visits by a second worker (and robust review) might assist in recognizing when thresholds for intervention have been reached.

In addition, when children were returned home on supervision or care orders and these returns broke down, thresholds for further action appeared to be set so high that there was little evidence of action to protect them or plan for their future (see also Farmer and Parker 1991), an issue to which we will return.

Children who are the subject of a child protection plan

The finding that 42 per cent of the children who were the subject of a child protection plan were not safeguarded requires consideration. In such situations children were neglected and emotionally or physically abused while living with their parents, sometimes over long periods, while they were subject to the scrutiny of child protection procedures.

This is surprising given that these cases would have been subject to child protection review meetings at regular intervals. However, research has reported on the under-evaluation of risks at child protection conferences (Corby and Mills 1986). Moreover, child protection reviews can also be subject to weaknesses in process, so that they may not question the original construction of risk or case management. This can then have an enduring influence on the way in which later risks to children are interpreted (Farmer 1999; Haringey Local Safeguarding Children Board 2008; Munro 1996; Sinclair and Bullock 2002).

In quite a number of cases it was clear that the social worker was hoping that child protection procedures would provide an incentive for a parent to stop drinking or using drugs or that domestic violence would diminish, but all too often there was no improvement. Quite often child protection plans did not assist in engaging the parents, or they produced insufficient impetus to effect parental change, or any change was only short-lived. Some parents did not comply with the child protection plan. While services were often forthcoming, parents did not always engage or attend sessions.

When neglect was the primary category there would usually have been no child protection enquiry. As a result, this part of the process, which can have a major impact on parents and persuade them of the seriousness with which children's services view concerns (Brandon *et al.* 1999; Department of Health 1995; Farmer 1993) was lacking. Sometimes there were continuing referrals about abuse and neglect to children on child protection plans and these did not reach the threshold for more coercive action or even, on occasion, were not investigated. There were also a number of reports that child protection plans were discontinued at a stage when the parent looking after the children was not coping.

These findings suggest that there may have been weaknesses in the child protection plans or their implementation, which were not being picked up sufficiently robustly at child protection reviews (as appeared to have occurred in the Baby Peter Connelly case (Haringey Local Safeguarding Children Board 2008, 2009)). It is also possible that review conferences did not always have all the information about events since the previous review. It is therefore suggested that a full record of all referrals about children and about actual or suspected child maltreatment, plus the follow-up action taken, should be presented at every child protection review. Review members can then form an opinion about parental progress in the light of full information about continuing concerns about their parenting and about the children's progress. It also needs to be made clear at every review exactly how far children's needs are or are not being met by their parents and where there are deficits exactly how these needs will be met. This may be by the provision of additional services while children remain at home or action to move children into care. Needless to say, being subject to a child protection plan does not of itself provide protection, but it may be that the sharing of responsibility for cases with other agencies in child protection procedures leads to a lessened sense of responsibility or of urgency by the case responsible social workers and their managers (see also Farmer and Owen 1995).

It would be helpful if internal case audits regularly addressed the quality of child protection plans and the adequacy of safeguarding being provided for children subject to such plans.

Statutory and child protection reviews

The fact that many of the children in the study were not effectively safeguarded, were returned again and again to maltreating parents and lacked permanence plans, brings into question the quality not only of child protection reviews but also of the statutory reviews. As with child protection reviews, it is not clear which part of the review process was weak – whether it was the quality of the information brought to the reviews, the deliberations of group members, group processes or chairing, or a combination of these. There is an expectation that these reviews will consider children's progress and safety but it appears that this needs to be done more robustly than at present.

Child protection conference chairs and independent reviewing officers now have mechanisms for getting case management decisions reviewed if they are not satisfied with the actions of the team manager and social worker and for getting disagreements arising in reviews adjudicated on, for example if the chair thinks more proactive work is needed than the social worker or team manager. In addition, if a review notes a lack of improvement in a child's circumstances with no adequate plan to address this or there is dissent about whether care proceedings should be considered, then the case needs to be referred to a senior manager for consideration about whether the approach being taken is justified. The statutory guidance for independent reviewing officers (Department for Children, Schools and Families 2010a) is intended to address these kinds of issues, with the intention that review chairs drive improvements in care planning. In addition, it may be that independent reviewing officers and child protection conference chairs should be expected to draw out on a regular basis the children about whom there is most concern and summarize their cases, so that they can be scrutinized by senior managers.

There also needs to be a much stronger mechanism in place so that if a decision to return children in care proceedings does not work out, proactive planning does take place which ensures that new permanence plans are then made and put into action. Some local authorities have 'Children's Panels' or 'Permanence Panels' which review permanence plans for all looked-after children. Such panels would be well placed to ensure that these and other children (such as those subject to repeat failed returns) do not fall through the holes in the system or become subject to 'planning blight'.

Since cases being dealt with as family support are not subject to review, consideration needs to be given as to whether they should be formally reviewed or whether some kind of case audit would pick up those which need more active intervention.

Monitoring of practice

There is a need for more effective monitoring of practice within children's services, with higher management response if service managers or professionals from other agencies have concerns about the way a case is being managed. Any criticism of case management needs to be reviewed by senior managers as part of an audit of the entire case and a written response made to the professional concerned (see also Laming 2009).

Moreover, when managers themselves comment on case management, there needs to be a clear system to ensure that their directions have been followed up. Indeed, the way in which some of these cases were managed and the acknowledgement by managers that children had been abused, when the local authority knew about the risk, might now leave the authorities open to claims for compensation for negligence or breach of human rights by the young people concerned.

The use of care proceedings

The poor outcomes for children returned to their parents on supervision orders or care orders calls into question the decision-making in these cases in the court arena. As we have noted, sometimes children's guardians and expert assessors had been too anxious to give parents the benefit of having another chance, even though a deeper reading of the history might clearly have shown that this was not advisable (see also Dicken 2007).

Clearly, it is crucial that expert opinions and, indeed, those of children's guardians are carefully weighed and tested in court, especially as it has been found that lack of self-confidence on the part of social workers in their own expertise means that they are wary of challenging children's guardians (Iwaniec et al. 2004). Yet this can mean that long experience of lack of change by parents in a case is cast aside in favour of a recent and one-off assessment which ignores this history (Stevenson 2007).

There has been evidence before that supervision orders sometimes prove ineffective (Hunt and Macleod 1999; Hunt et al. 1999) and this was shown again in this study. In most of these cases the children's services department had wanted care orders, but sometimes as a result of the children's guardian's recommendation, or occasionally that of a specialist assessment, supervision orders were made. Indeed, in a few cases it was clear that the local authority believed (rightly) that a supervision order would not be a strong enough order. With a supervision order, the local authority has no right of entry to the child's home and no right to remove the child. There is also no direct way of enforcing a supervision order (Masson et al. 2008b). These supervision orders did not provide adequate protection for the children or sufficient motivation to ensure that parents maintained any improvements evident before the orders were made.

These findings suggest that the use of supervision orders should be scrutinized since they provided an appearance of some intervention without having much substance. Only a minority of failed supervision orders led to a renewed application for a care order (and few did so rapidly), even when this was clearly needed (see also Hunt and Macleod

1999; Iwaniec *et al.* 2004). More often moves were made to close cases once the orders expired. One issue here is that the local authority has to start fresh care proceedings and re-prove the grounds for an order where a supervision order has failed. The current situation, involving the need for court proceedings lasting many months to begin again from scratch, appears to place the barrier to securing adequate protection for children too high in such cases. Moreover, workers appear to lack confidence that a case that has resulted in a supervision order will lead to a care order on a later occasion, even when it is clear that the supervision order has not worked. It may be that the efficacy of supervision orders in their current form should be questioned.

It was of concern that where children were returned to a parent on a care order, most of these returns broke down and few of these children subsequently achieved a secure placement with their parents, or in care, or had permanence plans made for them at a later stage. Some were doomed to oscillate between home and care. As previously mentioned, there needs to be a much stronger mechanism in place for planning for these children.

These findings would suggest that the system would be improved if the judge or magistrate reviewed all cases (or at least those which end in supervision orders or returns on care orders) every six months after they have been decided, in order to assess whether the disposition has safeguarded children and ensured that they have a secure and permanent base (see also Harwin *et al.* 2003). Alternatively, although this would be less effective, it would be useful if the medium-term outcomes of decisions made on the basis of expert assessments and children's guardians' recommendations could be relayed to them to enable these professionals to get feedback on the efficacy of their recommendations. Magistrates and judges might also benefit from feedback on how decisions to return children in care proceedings have worked out in practice. It is encouraging that these suggestions have been taken up in the Family Justice Review (2011). In the absence of feedback to judges, magistrates, children's guardians and expert assessors on how well their decisions have worked out, it is hard to see how they can improve their practice. This study found a very worrying failure rate in their decisions, which did not appear to be attributable to lack of support services to children and parents.

Factors related to children's outcomes five years on

While some of the factors which were associated with outcomes were related to the children's characteristics (e.g. age and behaviour problems), many of them related to how their cases were managed. The fact that children over the age of six had a greater chance of ending up with unstable outcomes and much less chance of achieving a permanent placement in care emphasizes the crucial importance of early intervention with children and families and the need for more proactive practice with school-aged children. In a similar way, the finding that children with a high number of neglect experiences often had unstable outcomes and poor well-being, and that this was also true of those long known to children's services before return, also highlights the need for earlier and more effective intervention.

The relationship between more severe neglect (and other maltreatment) and poor outcomes in terms of instability and poor well-being would suggest the detrimental impact of maltreatment on children and the need to be vigilant in ensuring that children who are living with, or have been returned to, their parents are not experiencing continuing abuse and neglect. The findings also emphasize that social workers need to ensure that there are improvements before children are returned home, and that these are often brought about by positive changes in household membership.

Moreover, the fact that children who had been accommodated often had poor well-being by follow-up is related not only to their older age but also shows that the less rigorous way in which these cases are managed has negative consequences (see also Farmer *et al.* 2011). There is therefore a need for authorities to develop clearer policies and procedures to guide reunification practice for all children, particularly those who are accommodated. Policies need to take account of how resources to assist in preparation for and maintenance of returns can be readily accessed. This includes assistance for children and young people with behavioural and emotional difficulties and intensive help with behaviour management for their parents.

Local authority variation

When cases were managed proactively, children's outcomes were much better than when they were not. There were major local authority variations in how proactively cases were managed, leading to very much better outcomes in some authorities than others, in terms of both children's stability and their well-being. These differences in local authority practice require attention so that all can come up to the standard of the best.

Conclusion

In conclusion, work with neglected children and their families is demanding. It generally requires medium- to long-term work during which concerns about the children are likely to accumulate, but it is very difficult to have a clear view about when the threshold for more protective action has been reached. If these very real and inescapable challenges are recognized, then there is much that can be done to improve practice with neglected children. Although children's and parents' characteristics are part of the equation, we found that how cases were managed also has a powerful influence on children's outcomes. Most of the children in the study were known to children's services departments before they started school, yet too few were adequately protected and many opportunities to intervene were missed. As a result, too many children ended up with poor outcomes in terms of unstable care careers and poor well-being. This study suggests that, despite the fact that many practitioners do excellent work with neglected children and their families, there are many barriers to good practice and these need to be robustly addressed if more children are to have a safe and secure future either with their parents or in a permanent placement outside the family.

Appendix

Table A.1 Factors related to stability (n=126 or less where indicated)

Independent variables		Stability at home	Stability away from home	Unstable	Sig
Child factors					
Age at first entry to care (in years) (n=124)	(Mean)	5.6	3	7.6	$F (2, 121)=13.4$, $p<.001$
Child's age at 2001 return (in years)	(Mean)	7.24	5.69	11.51	$F (2, 123)= 20.67$, $p<.001$
Child has emotional problems (prior to return) (n=123)	No Yes	43% 57%	74% 26%	17% 83%	$\chi^2 (2)= 23.18$, $p<.001$
Child has behaviour problems (prior to return) (n=125)	No Yes	44% 56%	75% 25%	14% 86%	$\chi^2 (2)= 26.46$, $p<.001$
School exclusion (prior to return) (n=103)	No Yes	77% 23%	96% 4%	41% 59%	$\chi^2 (2)= 21.46$, $p<0.001$
Conflict with parents (prior to return) (n=122)	No Yes	75% 25%	85% 15%	26% 74%	$\chi^2 (2)= 31.96$, $p<.001$
Child sexualized behaviour (prior to return) (n=120)	No Yes	87% 13%	82% 18%	60% 40%	$\chi^2 (2)= 8.94$, $p=.011$

Independent variables		Stability at home	Stability away from home	Unstable	Sig
Adversities prior to return					
Total number of adversities prior to care period	(Mean)	4.4	3.56	5	$F_{(2,123)}=$ 6.18, p=.003
Emotional abuse of child prior to care period	No Yes	31% 69%	61% 39%	17% 83%	$\chi^2_{(2)}=$ 15.92, p<.001
Child rejected (n=115)	No Yes	81% 19%	81% 19%	51% 49%	$\chi^2_{(2)}=$ 10.78, p=.005
Child singled out for rejection (n=115)	No Yes	88% 12%	90% 10%	63% 37%	$\chi^2_{(2)}=$ 10.63, p=.005
Severity of neglect	Minor/ moderate Very severe	65% 35%	72% 28%	40% 60%	$\chi^2_{(2)}=8.77$, p=.012
No. of neglect incidents experienced	(Mean)	6.69	6.86	10.06	$F_{(2,123)}=$ 8.43, p<.001
Care and case management factors prior to return					
Specific conditions for parents prior to return (n=125)	No Yes	56% 44%	66% 34%	89% 11%	χ^2 $_{(2)}=10.31$, p=.006
Specialist help for parents during care period (n=121)	No Yes	43% 57%	39% 61%	72% 28%	$\chi^2_{(2)}=8.82$, p=.012
Original return planned	No Yes	18% 82%	17% 83%	43% 57%	$v^2_{(2)}=8.73$, p=.013
All problems addressed prior to return (n=124)	No Yes	64% 36%	58% 42%	91% 9%	χ^2 $_{(2)}=10.88$, p=.004

Return household factors					
Returned with siblings (n=109)	No Yes	48% 52%	38% 62%	83% 17%	χ^2 (2)=14.18, p=.001
Return support factors					
Specialist support for parent during return (n=121)	No Yes	51% 49%	44% 56%	82% 18%	χ^2 (2)=12.01, p=.002
Informal support during return (n=113)	No Yes	42% 58%	27% 73%	63% 37%	χ^2 (2)=8.31, p=.016
Return progress factors					
Poor parenting skills during return (n=105)	No Yes	50% 50%	29% 71%	14% 86%	χ^2 (2)=10.18, p=.006
Poor home conditions during return (n=119)	No Yes	81% 19%	65% 35%	52% 48%	χ^2 (2)=8.12, p=.017
Parent inability to cope during return (n=125)	No Yes	59% 41%	64% 36%	20% 80%	χ^2 (2)=17.22, p<.001
Child emotional problems during return (n=109)	No Yes	60% 40%	77% 23%	41% 59%	χ^2 (2)=8.5, p=.014
Child behaviour problems during return (n=113)	No Yes	47% 53%	68% 32%	19% 81%	χ^2 (2)=16.01, p<.001
Conflict with parents during return (n=110)	No Yes	70% 30%	88% 12%	37% 63%	χ^2 (2)=19.01, p<.001
Researcher ratings of return					
Child beyond parental control during return (n=117)	No Yes	73% 27%	86% 14%	19% 81%	χ^2 (2)=37.17, p<.001

Independent variables		Stability at home	Stability away from home	Unstable	Sig
Case management					
Inappropriate case closure (n=123)	No Yes	75% 25%	72% 28%	41% 59%	χ^2 (2)=11.87, p=.003
Decisions not followed through/ indecisiveness (n=114)	No Yes	86% 14%	83% 17%	60% 40%	χ^2 (2)=8.54, p=.014
Clear focus on key issues maintained (n=112)	No Yes	47% 53%	37% 63%	73% 27%	χ^2 (2)=9, p=.011
Missed opportunities to prevent further harm (n=119)	No Yes	77% 23%	63% 37%	34% 66%	χ^2 (2)=15.99, p<.001
Balance between support and control (n=124)	Support Control Even/ varied	39% 40% 21%	8% 50% 42%	46% 28% 26%	χ^2 (4)=14.74, p=.005
Type of case management approach 3 groups	Proactive Passive Mixed	38% 20% 42%	45% 8% 47%	3% 40% 57%	χ^2 (4)=21.54, p<.001

Variables entered in stages into regression analyses for the stability outcome variable

Child's age at first entry to care

Emotional abuse prior to return

Total number of adversities experienced prior to return

Child emotional problems prior to return

Child behaviour problems prior to return

Specific conditions prior to return

Original return planned

Specialist help for parents during care period

Legal order at return

Child's age at return

Previous failed returns prior to original return

Length of time in care (care period prior to the return)

Child on child protection register at start of care period

Return to parent with mental health problems

Concerns reported during return

Behaviour problems during return

Specialist support for parents during return

Returned to changed household membership

Other agency supervision during return

Was the child ever on the child protection register?

Type of overall case management approach

Failure to safeguard the child (at any point from first referral to five-year follow-up point)

Local authority variable

Child's ethnicity

Table A.2 Factors related to well-being (n=130 or less where indicated)

Independent variables		Good	Satisfactory	Poor/ very poor	Sig
Child factors					
Age at first entry to care (in years) (n=127)	(Mean)	3.57	5.02	7.1	$F_{(2, 124)}$= 9.2, p<.001
Child's age at 2001 return (in years)	(Mean)	5.54	7.35	10.24	$F_{(2,127)}$ = 14.47, p<.001
Child has behaviour problems (prior to return) (n=129)	No Yes	73% 37%	50% 50%	14% 86%	χ^2 (2)=31.62, p<.001
Conflict with parents (prior to return) (n=124)	No Yes	82% 18%	74% 26%	40% 60%	χ^2 (2)=18.84, p<.001
Conflict with siblings (prior to return) (n=104)	No Yes	93% 7%	72% 28%	63% 37%	χ^2 (2)=7.99, p=.018
Adversities prior to return					
Total number of adversities prior to care period	(Mean)	3.73	4.3	5.04	$F_{(2,127)}$= 5.85, p=.004
Physical abuse of child prior to care period	No Yes	59% 41%	37% 63%	28% 72%	χ^2 (2)=8.98, p=.011
Emotional abuse of child prior to care period	No Yes	54% 46%	23% 77%	28% 72%	χ^2 (2)=9.67, p=.008
Sexual abuse of child prior to care period	No Yes	86% 14%	81% 19%	56% 44%	χ^2 (2)=12.31, p=.002
Severity of neglect	Minor Moderate Very Sev	16% 60% 24%	14% 60% 26%	2% 40% 58%	χ^2 (4)=16.58, p=.002
No. of neglect issues experienced	(Mean)	6.78	6.4	9.18	$F_{(2,127)}$= 6.56, p=.002

Care and case management factors prior to return					
Specific conditions for parents prior to return (n=129)	No Yes	43% 57%	69% 31%	76% 24%	χ^2 (2)=10.55, p=.011
Original return planned	No Yes	11% 89%	19% 81%	38% 62%	χ^2 (2)=9.63, p=.008
Return accelerated	No Yes	70% 30%	74% 26%	38% 62%	χ^2 (2)=15.31, p<.001
Pressure from child for return (n=107)	No Yes	64% 36%	57% 43%	32% 68%	χ^2 (2)=8.61, p=.014
Exceptional support by caregivers prior to return (n=122)	No Yes	68% 32%	83% 17%	95% 5%	χ^2 (2)=10.97, p=.004
All problems addressed prior to return (n=124)	No Yes	42% 58%	74% 26%	88% 12%	χ^2 (2)=21.89, p<.001
Return support factors					
Specialist support for parent during return (n=126)	No Yes	35% 65%	63% 37%	67% 33%	χ^2 (2)=9.68, p=.008
Informal support during return (n=117)	No Yes	23% 77%	54% 46%	51% 49%	χ^2 (2)=8.8, p=.012
Return progress factors					
Poor parenting skills during return (n=110)	No Yes	50% 50%	37% 63%	17% 83%	χ^2 (2)=9.31, p=.01
Parent inability to cope during return (n=128)	No Yes	70% 30%	49% 51%	36% 64%	χ^2 (2)=10.03, p=.007
Child behaviour problems during return (n=117)	No Yes	82% 18%	49% 51%	13% 87%	χ^2 (2)=38.42, p<.001
Conflict with parents during return (n=112)	No Yes	85% 15%	82% 18%	37% 63%	χ^2 (2)=25.17, p<.001

Independent variables		Good	Satisfactory	Poor/ very poor	Sig
Researcher ratings of return					
Child beyond parental control during return (n=122)	No Yes	91% 9%	70% 30%	32% 68%	χ^2 (2)=31.83, p<0.001
Case management					
Inappropriate case closure (n=124)	No Yes	73% 27%	75% 25%	49% 51%	χ^2 (2)=8.06, p=.018
Specific incident galvanized intervention (n=125)	No Yes	77% 23%	83% 17%	57% 43%	χ^2 (2)=8.07, p=.018
Neglect marginalized (overemphasis on other issues)	No Yes	84% 16%	100% 0%	72% 28%	χ^2 (2)=13.95, p=.001
Failure to safeguard the child	No Yes	65% 35%	65% 35%	24% 76%	χ^2 (2)=20.7, p<.001
Type of case management approach 3 groups	Proactive Passive Mixed	54% 3% 43%	32% 19% 49%	8% 38% 54%	χ^2 (4)= 28.73, p<.001
Placement moves					
No. of living arrangements over five year follow-up	(Mean)	3.15	4.3	9	F (2, 127)= 12.16, p<.001
No. of returns home (from care) over five-year follow-up	(Mean)	0.19	0.7	1.32	F (2, 127)= 10.32, p<.001

Variables entered in stages into regression analyses for the well-being outcome variable

Child's age at first entry to care

Total number of adversities experienced prior to return

Child emotional problems prior to return

Child behaviour problems prior to return

Specific conditions prior to return

Original return planned

Specialist help for parents during care period

Legal order at return

Child's age at return

Previous failed returns prior to original return

Length of time in care (care period prior to the return)

Child on child protection register at start of care period

Behaviour problems during return

Emotional problems during return

Other agency supervision during return

Specialist support for parents during return

Returned to changed household membership

Conditions for parents during return

Neglect marginalized

Child ever the subject of care proceedings

Type of overall case management approach

Failure to safeguard the child (at any point from first referral to five-year follow-up point)

Number of placements over five-year follow-up

Local authority variable

Child's ethnicity

References

Abbott, D., Morris, J. and Ward, L. (2001) *The Best Place To Be? Policy, Practice and the Experiences of School Placements for Disabled Children.* York: Joseph Rowntree Foundation/York Publishing.

AD and OD v. *United Kingdom* 28680/06 (2010) ECtHR para 84.

Advisory Council on the Misuse of Drugs (ACMD) (2003) *Hidden Harm: Responding to the Needs of Children of Problem Drug Users.* Report of an inquiry by the Advisory Council on the Misuse of Drugs. London: Home Office.

Allin, H., Wathen, C.N. and MacMillan, H. (2005) 'Treatment of child neglect: A systematic review.' *Canadian Journal of Psychiatry 50*, 8, 497–504.

Allsop, M. and Stevenson, O. (1995) *Social Workers' Perceptions of Risk in Child Protection: A Discussion Paper.* University of Nottingham: School of Social Studies.

Antle, B.F., Barbee, A.P., Sullivan, D., Yankeelov, P., Johnson, L. and Cunningham M.R. (2007) 'The relationship between domestic violence and child neglect.' *Brief Treatment and Crisis Intervention 7*, 4, 364–382.

Arata, C.M., Langhinrichsen-Rohling, J., Bowers, D. and O'Brien, N. (2007) 'Differential correlates of multi-type maltreatment among urban youth.' *Child Abuse and Neglect 31*, 4, 393–415.

Bancroft, A., Wilson, S., Cunningham-Burley, S., Backett-Milburn, K. and Masters, H. (2004) *Parental Drug and Alcohol Misuse: Resilience and Transition Among Young People.* York: Joseph Rowntree Foundation.

Barn, R. (2006) *Improving Services to Meet the Needs of Minority Ethnic Children and Families.* Research and Practice Briefings, Research in Practice: Totnes. Accessed on 8 April 2009 at www.rip.org.uk/publications/ecm-research-briefings.

Barnes, J., Ball, M., Meadows, P., McLeish, J., Belsky, J. and the FNP Implementation Research Team (2008) *Nurse-Family Partnership Programme: First Year Pilot Sites Implementation in England, Pregnancy and the Post-Partum Period.* Report to the Department of Children, Schools and Families and Department of Health. Institute for the Study of Children, Families and Social Issues Birkbeck: University of London.

Barnes, J., Ball, M., Meadows, P., Howden, B. *et al.* (2011) *The Family-Nurse Partnership Programme in England: Wave 1 Implementation in Toddlerhood and a Comparison between Waves 1 and 2a of Implementation in Pregnancy and Infancy.* London: Department of Health.

Baxter, S. (1989) *Fostering Breakdown: An Internal Study.* Belfast: Department of Health and Social Security.

Berridge, D. and Cleaver, H. (1987) *Foster Home Breakdown.* Oxford: Basil Blackwell.

Biehal N. (2006) *Reuniting Looked After Children with their Families: A Review of the Research.* London: National Children's Bureau.

Bifulco, A. and Moran, P. (1998) *Wednesday's Child: Research into Women's Experience of Neglect and Abuse in Childhood, and Adult Depression.* London and New York: Routledge.

Bradley, M. and Aldgate, J. (1999) 'Short-Term Family Based Care for Children in Need.' In M. Hill (ed.) *Signposts in Fostering: Policy, Practice and Research Issues.* London: British Agencies for Adoption and Fostering.

Brandon, M., Belderson, P., Warren, C., Gardner, R. *et al.* (2008a) 'The preoccupation with thresholds in cases of child death or serious injury through abuse and neglect.' *Child Abuse Review 17*, 5, 313–330.

Brandon, M., Belderson, P., Warren, C., Howe, D. *et al.* (2008b) *Analysis of Child Deaths and Serious Injury Through Abuse and Neglect: What Can We Learn? A Biennial Analysis of Serious Case Reviews 2003–2005.* London: Department for Children, School and Families.

Brandon, M., Sidebotham P., Bailey S. and Belderson, P. (2011) *A Study of Recommendations Arising from Serious Case Reviews 2009–2010.* London: Department for Education.

Brandon, M., Thoburn, J., Lewis, A. and Way, A. (1999) *Safeguarding Children with the Children Act 1989.* London: The Stationery Office.

Brandon, M., Thoburn, J., Rose, S. and Belderson, P. (2005) *Living with Significant Harm: A Follow-up Study.* London: NSPCC.

Bridge Child Care Consultancy Service (1995) *Paul: Death Through Neglect.* London: Bridge Child Care Consultancy Service on behalf of Islington ACPC.

Brophy, J., Jhutti-Johal, J. and MacDonald, E. (2005) *Minority Ethnic Parents, their Solicitors and Child Protection Litigation.* Research Series 5/05. London: Department for Constitutional Affairs.

Brophy, J., Jhutti-Johal, J. and Owen, C. (2003) 'Assessing and documenting child ill-treatment in minority ethnic households.' *Family Law 33,* October, 756–764.

Browne, K.D. and Lynch, M.A. (1998) 'The challenge of child neglect.' *Child Abuse Review 7,* 2, 73–76.

Burke J., Chandy J., Dannerbeck A. and Wilson Watt J. (1998) 'The parental environment cluster model of child neglect: an integrative conceptual model.' *Child Welfare 77,* 4, 389–405.

Carter, V. and Myers, M.R. (2007) 'Exploring the risks of substantiated physical neglect related to poverty and parental characteristics: A national sample.' *Children and Youth Services Review 29,* 1, 110–121.

Case, P. (2007) *Compensating Child Abuse.* Cambridge: Cambridge University Press.

Cawson, P. (2002) *Child Maltreatment in the Family: The Experience of a National Sample of Young People.* London: NSPCC.

Cawson, P., Wattam, C., Brooker, S. and Kelly, G. (2000) *Child Maltreatment in the United Kingdom: A Study of the Prevalence of Child Abuse and Neglect.* London: NSPCC.

Chaffin, M., Kelleher, K., and Hollenberg, J. (1996). 'Onset of physical abuse and neglect: Psychiatric, substance abuse, and social risk factors from prospective community data.' *Child Abuse and Neglect 20,* 3, 191–203.

Chamberlain, P., Moreland, S. and Reid, K. (1992) 'Enhanced services and stipends for foster parents: Effects on retention rates and outcomes for children.' *Child Welfare 71,* 5, 387–401.

Chamberlain, P. and Reid, J.B. (1998) 'Comparison of two community alternatives to incarceration for chronic juvenile offenders.' *Journal of Consulting and Clinical Psychology 66,* 4, 624–633.

Channer, Y. and Parton, N. (1990) 'Racism, Cultural Relativism and Child Protection.' In Violence Against Children Study Group *Taking Child Abuse Seriously.* London and New York: Unwin.

Chasnof, I.J. and Lowder, L. (1999) 'Prenatal alcohol and drugs use and risk for child maltreatment.' In H. Dubowitz (ed.) *Neglected Children: Research, Practice and Policy.* Thousand Oaks, CA: Sage.

Christensen, M.J., Brayden, R.M., Dietrich, M.S., McLaughlin, F.J. and Sherrod, K.B. (1994) 'The prospective assessment of self concept in neglectful and physically abusive low income mothers.' *Child Abuse and Neglect 18,* 3, 225–232.

Cleaver, H. and Freeman, P. (1995) *Parental Perspectives in Cases of Suspected Child Abuse.* London: HMSO.

Cleaver, H., Nicholson, D., Tarr, S. and Cleaver, D. (2007) *Child Protection, Domestic Violence and Parental Substance Misuse: Family Experiences and Effective Practice.* London: Jessica Kingsley Publishers.

Cleaver, H., Unell, I. and Aldgate, J. (2011) *Children's Needs – Parenting Capacity.* London: The Stationery Office.

Cleaver, H. and Walker, S., with Meadows, P. (2004) *Assessing Children's Needs and Circumstances: The Impact of the Assessment Framework.* London: Jessica Kingsley Publishers.

Corby, B. (1987) *Working with Child Abuse.* Milton Keynes: Open University Press.

Corby, B., Millar, M. and Young, I. (1996) 'Parental participation in child protection work: Re-thinking the rhetoric.' *British Journal of Social Work 26,* 4, 475–492.

Corby, B. and Mills, C. (1986) 'Child abuse: Risks and resources.' *British Journal of Social Work 16,* 5, 531–542.

Cosis Brown, H., Fry, E. and Howard, J. (2005) *Support Care: How Family Placements Can Keep Children and Families Together.* Lyme Regis: Russell House Publishing.

Courtney, M.E. (1994) 'Factors associated with the reunification of foster children with their families.' *Social Service Review 68,* 1, 81–108.

Courtney, M.E. (1995) 'Re-entry to foster care of children returned to their families', *Social Service Review.' 69,* 2, 224–241.

Courtney, M.E., Piliavin, I. and Wright, B. (1997) 'Note on research. Transitions from and returns to out of home care.' *Social Service Review 71,* 4, 652–667.

Courtney, M.E. and Wong, Y. I. (1996) 'Comparing the timing of exits from substitute care.' *Children and Youth Services Review 18,* 4/5, 307–334.

Crittenden, P. M. (1992) 'Children's strategies for coping with adverse home environments: An interpretation using attachment theory.' *Child Abuse and Neglect 16,* 3, 329–343.

Crittenden, P. (1999) 'Child Neglect: Causes and Contributors.' In H. Dubowitz (ed.) *Neglected Children: Research, Practice and Policy.* Thousand Oaks, CA: Sage.

Daniel, B. (1998) 'A picture of powerlessness: An exploration of child neglect and ways in which social workers and parents can be empowered towards efficacy.' *International Journal of Child and Family Welfare 3,* 3, 269–285.

Daniel, B., Taylor, J. and Scott, J. (2011) *Noticing and Helping the Neglected Child: Evidence-based Practice for Assessment and Intervention.* London: Jessica Kingsley Publishers.

Daro, D. (1988) *Confronting Child Abuse.* New York, NY: Free Press.

Davies, C. and Ward, H. (2011) *Safeguarding Children Across Services: Messages from Research.* London: Jessica Kingsley Publishers.

Davis, I.P., English, D.J. and Landsverk, J. (1993) *Going Home – and Returning to Care: A Study of Foster Care Reunification.* San Diego, CA: San Diego State University, College of Health and Human Services, School of Social Work and the Child and Family Research Group.

Davis, I.P., Landsverk, J.A. and Newton, R.R. (1997) 'Duration of Foster Care for Children Reunified Within the First Year of Care.' In J.D. Berrick, R.P. Barth and N. Gilbert (eds) *Child.* New York, NY: Columbia University Press.

De Bellis, M.D. (2005) 'The psychobiology of neglect.' *Child Maltreatment 10,* 2, 150–172.

DePanfilis, D. (1999) 'Intervening with Families when Children are Neglected.' In H. Dubowitz (ed.) *Neglected Children: Research, Practice and Policy.* Thousand Oaks, CA: Sage.

DePanfilis, D. (2006) *Child Neglect: A Guide for Prevention, Assessment, and Intervention.* Washington, DC: U.S. Department of Health and Human Services, Administration on Children and Families, Administration for Children, Youth, and Families, Children's Bureau, Office on Child Abuse and Neglect.

DePanfilis, D. and Dubowitz, H. (2005) 'Family connections: A program for preventing child neglect.' *Child Maltreatment 10,* 2, 108–123.

Department for Children, Schools and Families (2010a) *IRO Handbook: Statutory Guidance for Independent Reviewing Officers and Local Authorities on their Functions in Relation to Case Management and Review for Looked After Children.* London: DCSF Publications.

Department for Children, Schools and Families (2010b) *Working Together to Safeguard Children.* London: The Stationery Office.

Department for Education (2010a) *Children in Need in England including their Characteristics and Further Information on Children who were the Subject of a Child Protection Plan (Children in Need Census Final), Year ending 31 March 2010.* OSR28/2010, Statistical Release. London: Department for Education.

Department for Education (2010b) *The Children Act 1989 Guidance and Regulations, Vol. 2 Care Planning, Placement and Case Review.* London: Department for Education.

Department for Education and Skills (2007) *Care Matters: Time for Change.* Cm 7137. London: The Stationery Office.

Department of Health (1995) *Child Protection: Messages from Research.* London: HMSO.

Department of Health (2000) *Assessing Children in Need and their Families: Practice Guidance.* London: The Stationery Office.

Department of Health (2002) *Referrals, Assessments and Children and Young People on Child Protection Registers: Year ending 31 March 2002.* London: Department of Health.

Department of Health, Department for Education and Employment and the Home Office (2000) *Framework for the Assessment of Children in Need and their Families.* London: The Stationery Office.

Dickens J. (2007) 'Child neglect and the law: Catapults, thresholds and delay.' *Child Abuse Review 16,* 2, 77–92.

Dickens, J., Howell, D., Thoburn, J. and Schofield, G. (2007) 'Children starting to be looked after by local authorities in England: An analysis of inter-authority variation and case-centred decision making.' *British Journal of Social Work 37,* 4, 597–617.

Dingwall, R., Eekelaar, J. and Murray, T. (1983) *The Protection of Children: State Intervention and Family Life.* Oxford: Blackwell.

Dore, M. and Alexander, L. B. (1996) 'Preserving families at risk of child abuse and neglect: The role of the helping alliance.' *Child Abuse and Neglect 20,* 4, 349–361.

Drotar, D., Eckerle, D., Satola, H., Palotta, J. and Wyatt, B. (1990) 'Maternal interactional behaviour with non-organic failure-to-thrive infants: A case comparison study.' *Child Abuse and Neglect 14,* 1, 41–51.

Dubowitz, H. (1994) 'Neglecting the neglect of neglect.' *Journal of Interpersonal Violence 9,* 4, 556–560.

Dubowitz, H., Black, M.M., Kerr, M.A., Starr, R.H., Jr. and Harrington, D. (2000) 'Fathers and child neglect.' *Archives of Pediatrics and Adolescent Medicine 154,* 2, 135–141.

Dubowitz, H., Black, M., Starr, R.H. and Zuravin, S. (1993) 'A conceptual definition of child neglect.' *Criminal Justice and Behavior 20,* 1, 8–26.

Dubowitz, H., Newton, R.R., Litrownik, A.J., Lewis, T. *et al.* (2005) 'Examination of a conceptual model of child neglect.' *Child Maltreatment 10,* 2, 173–189.

Dutt, R. and Phillips, M. (1996) 'Race, Culture and the Prevention of Child Abuse,' in *Childhood matters: report of the National Commission of Inquiry into the Prevention of Child Abuse Volume 2: background papers.* London: The Stationery Office.

Dutt, R. and Phillips, M. (2000) 'Assessing Black Children in Need and their Families.' In Department of Health *Framework for the Assessment of Children in Need and their Families.* London: The Stationery Office.

Eckenrode, J., Laird, M. and Doris, J. (1993) 'Academic performance and disciplinary problems among abused and neglected children.' *Developmental Psychology 29,* 1, 53–62.

Egeland, B., Sroufe, L.A., and Erickson, M.F. (1983). 'The development consequences of different patterns of maltreatment.' *Child Abuse and Neglect 7,* 4, 465–469.

Emerson, E., Malam, S., Davies, I. and Spencer, K. (2005) *Adults with Learning Difficulties in England.* London: Department of Health. Available at www.dh.gov.uk/en/Publicationsandstatistics/Publications/PublicationsStatistics/DH_4120033, accessed on 26 March 2012.

Erickson, M.F., Egeland, B. and Pianta, R. (1989) 'The Effects of Maltreatment on the Development of Young Children.' In D. Cicchetti and V. Carlson (eds) *Child Maltreatment: Theory and Research on the Causes and Consequences of Child Abuse and Neglect.* New York, NY: Cambridge University Press.

Ethier, L.S., Couture, G., Lacharite, C. and Gagnier, J-P. (2000) 'Impact of a multidimensional intervention programme applied to families at risk for child neglect.' *Child Abuse Review 9,* 1, 19–36.

Ethier, C.S., Lacharite, C. and Couture, G. (1995) 'Childhood adversity, parental stress and depression of negligent mothers.' *Child Abuse and Neglect 19,* 5, 619–632.

Family Justice Review (2011) *Family Justice Review, Final Report.* London: Ministry of Justice, Department for Education and Welsh Government.

Farmer, E. (1992) 'Restoring children on court orders to their families: Lessons for practice.' *Adoption and Fostering 16,* 1, 7–15.

Farmer, E. (1993) 'The Impact of Child Protection Interventions: The Experiences of Parents and Children.' In L. Waterhouse (ed.) *Child Abuse and Child Abusers: Protection and Prevention.* Research Highlights in Social Work No. 24. London: Jessica Kingsley Publishers.

Farmer, E. (1999) 'Holes in the safety net: The strengths and weaknesses of child protection procedures.' *Child and Family Social Work 4,* 4, 293–302.

Farmer, E. (2009) 'Reunification with Birth Families.' In G. Schofield and J. Simmonds (eds) *The Child Placement Handbook: Research, Policy and Practice.* London: BAAF.

Farmer, E. and Moyers, S. (2008) *Kinship Care: Fostering Effective Family and Friends Placements.* London: Jessica Kingsley Publishers.

Farmer, E., Moyers, S. and Lipscombe, J. (2004) *Fostering Adolescents.* London: Jessica Kingsley Publishers.

Farmer, E. and Owen, M. (1995) *Child Protection Practice: Private Risks and Public Remedies.* London: HMSO.

Farmer, E. and Owen, M. (1998) 'Gender and the child protection process.' *British Journal of Social Work 28,* 4, 545–564.

Farmer, E. and Parker, R. (1991) *Trials and Tribulations: Returning Children from Local Authority Care to their Families.* London: HMSO.

Farmer, E., Sturgess, W., O'Neill, T. and Wijedasa D. (2011) *Achieving Successful Returns from Care: What Makes Reunification Work?* London: BAAF.

Ferguson, H. (2005) 'Working with violence, the emotions and the psycho-social dynamics of child protection: Reflections on the Victoria Climbié case.' *Social Work Education 24,* 7, 781–795.

Festinger, T. (1994) *Returning to Care: Discharge and Re-entry into Foster Care.* Washington, DC: Child Welfare League of America.

Forrester, D. (2000) 'Parental substance misuse and child protection in a British sample: A survey of children on the child protection register in an inner London district office.' *Child Abuse Review 9,* 4, 235–246.

Forrester, D. and Harwin, J. (2004) 'Social Work and Parental Substance Misuse.' In R. Phillips (ed.) *Children Exposed to Parental Substance Misuse: Implications for Family Placement.* London: BAAF.

Forrester, D. and Harwin, J. (2006) 'Parental substance misuse and child care social work: Findings from the first stage of a study of 100 families.' *Child and Family Social Work 11,* 4, 325–335.

G v. NCC (2009) 1 FLR 774.

Gardner, R. (2008) *Developing an Effective Response to Neglect and Emotional Harm to Children.* Norwich: University of East Anglia and NSPCC.

Gaudin, J.M. (1993) *Child Neglect: A Guide for Intervention.* Washington, DC: National Center on Child Abuse and Neglect, US Department of Health and Human Services.

Gaudin, J.M. (1999) 'Child Neglect: Short-Term and Long-Term Outcomes.' In H. Dubowitz (ed.) *Neglected Children: Research, Practice and Policy.* Thousand Oaks, CA: Sage.

George, C. and Main, M. (1979) 'Social interactions of young, abused children: Approach, avoidance and aggression.' *Child Development 50,* 306–318.

Gibbons, J., Conroy, S. and Bell, C. (1995) *Operating the Child Protection System.* London: HMSO.

Glisson, C., Bailey, J.W. and Post, J.A. (2000) 'Predicting the time children spend in state custody.' *Social Service Review 74,* 2, 253–280.

Goerge, R. (1990) 'The reunification process in substitute care.' *Social Services Review 64,* 3, 422–457.

Gossop, M., Marsden, J. and Stewart, D. (2001) *NTORS After Five Years. The National Treatment Outcome Study: Changes in Substance Use, Health and Criminal Behaviour During the Five Years After Intake.* London: National Addiction Centre.

Greenfields, M. and Statham, J. (2004) *Support Foster Care: Developing a Short-Break Service for Children in Need.* Understanding Children's Social Care 8, London: Thomas Coram Unit.

Grogan-Taylor, A. (2001) 'The effect of initial placement into kinship care on reunification from foster care: A bivariate probit analysis.' *Journal of Social Service Research 27,* 4, 1–31.

Hallett, C. (1995) *Inter-Agency Coordination in Child Protection.* London: HMSO.

Hallett, C. and Stevenson, O. (1980) *Child Abuse: Aspects of Interprofessional Co-operation.* London: Allen and Unwin.

Haringey Local Safeguarding Children Board (2008) *Serious Case Review 'Child A'. Executive Summary.* London: Haringey Children's Services Department.

Haringey Local Safeguarding Children Board (2009) *Serious Case Review: Baby Peter. Executive Summary.* London: Haringey Children's Services Department.

Harran, E. (2002) 'Barriers to effective child protection in a multicultural society.' *Child Abuse Review 11,* 6, 411–414.

Harris, M.A. and Courtney, M.E. (2003) 'The interaction of race, ethnicity and family structure with respect to the timing of family reunification.' *Children and Youth Services Review 25,* 5/6, 409–429.

Hartley, R. (1989) 'A programme blueprint for neglectful families.' *Protecting Children 6,* 3, 3–7.

Harwin, J. and Forrester, D. (2002) *'Parental Substance Misuse and Child Welfare: A Study of Social Work with Families in which Parents Misuse Drugs and Alcohol.'* London: First stage report for the Nuffield Foundation (unpublished).

Harwin, J., Owen, M., Locke, R. and Forrester, D. (2003) *Making Care Orders Work: A Study of Care Plans and their Implementation.* London: The Stationery Office.

Harwin J., Ryan M., Tunnard J., Pokhrel S. *et al.* (2011) *The Family Drug and Alcohol Court (FDAC) Evaluation Project, Final Report.* London: Brunel University and the Nuffield Foundation.

Henry, L. (2008) 'Protecting Children and Protecting Family Privacy: A Study of Child Neglect.' PhD thesis. University of Bristol.

Herrenkohl, R.C., Herrenkohl, E.C., Egolf, B.P. and Wu, P. (1991) 'The Developmental Consequences of Child Abuse: The Lehigh longitudinal study.' In R.H. Starr and D.A. Wolfe (eds) *The Effects of Child Abuse and Neglect.* New York, NY: Guilford Press.

Hess, P.M., Folaron, G. and Jefferson, A.B. (1992) 'Effectiveness of family reunification services: An innovative evaluative model.' *Social Work 37,* 4, 304–311.

Hester, M., Pearson, C., Harwin, N. and Abrahams, H. (2007) *Making an Impact: Children and Domestic Violence, A Reader.* Second Edition. London: Jessica Kingsley Publishers.

Hildyard, K.L. and Wolfe, D.A. (2002) 'Child neglect: Developmental issues and outcomes.' *Child Abuse and Neglect 26,* 6/7, 679–695.

Hindley, N., Ramchandani, P.G. and Jones, D.P.H. (2006) 'Risk factors for recurrence of maltreatment: A systematic review.' *Archives of Disease in Childhood 91*, 9, 744–752.

H.M. Government (2010) *Drug Strategy 2010: Reducing Demand, Restricting Supply, Building Recovery: Supporting People to Live a Drug Free Life.* London: Home Office.

Horwath, J. (2002) 'Maintaining a focus on the child: First impressions of the framework for the assessment of children in need and their families in cases of child neglect.' *Child Abuse Review 11*, 4, 195–213.

Horwath, J. (2005a) 'Is This Child Neglect? The Influence of Differences in Perceptions of Child Neglect on Social Work Practice.' In J. Taylor and B. Daniel (eds) *Child Neglect: Practice Issues for Health and Social Care.* London: Jessica Kingsley Publishers.

Horwath, J. (2005b) 'Identifying and assessing cases of child neglect: Learning from the Irish experience.' *Child and Family Social Work 10*, 2, 99–110.

Horwath, J. (2007a) *Child Neglect: Identification and Assessment.* Basingstoke: Palgrave Macmillan.

Horwath, J. (2007b) 'The missing assessment domain: Personal, professional and organizational factors influencing professional judgements when identifying and referring neglect.' *British Journal of Social Work 37*, 8, 1285–1303.

Horwath, J. and Bishop, B. (2001) *Child Neglect: Is My View Your View?* Dunshaughlin: North Eastern Health Board and University of Sheffield.

Howe, D. (2009) 'Removal of children at interim hearings: Is the test now set too high?' *Family Law 39*, 4, 320–325.

Howe, D., Brandon, M., Hinings, D. and Schofield, G. (1999) *Attachment Theory, Child Maltreatment and Family Support: A Practice and Assessment Model.* Basingstoke: Macmillan.

Howe, D., Dooley, T. and Hinings, D. (2000) 'Assessment and decision-making in a case of child neglect and abuse using an attachment perspective.' *Child and Family Social Work 5*, 2, 142–155.

Howlin, P. and Clements, J. (1994) 'Is it possible to assess the impact of abuse on children with pervasive developmental disorders?' *Journal of Autism and Developmental Disorders 25*, 337–354.

Hunt, J. and Macleod, A. (1999) *The Best-Laid Plans: Outcomes in Judicial Decisions in Child Protection Proceedings.* London: The Stationery Office.

Hunt, J., Macleod, A. and Thomas, C. (1999) *The Last Resort: Child Protection, the Courts and the 1989 Children Act.* London: The Stationery Office.

Iwaniec, D. (1995) *The Emotionally Abused and Neglected Child.* Chichester: John Wiley.

Iwaniec, D., Donaldson, T. and Allweis, M. (2004) 'The plight of neglected children: Social work and judicial decision making and management of neglect cases.' *Child and Family Law Quarterly 16*, 4, 423–436.

Iwaniec, D. and McSherry, D. (2002) *Understanding Child Neglect: Contemporary Issues and Dilemmas.* Occasional Paper No. 2. Belfast: Centre for Child Care Research.

Jinseok, K. (2009) 'Type-specific intergenerational transmission of neglectful and physically abusive parenting behaviour among young people.' *Children and Youth Services Review 31*, 7, 761–767.

Jones, D.P.H. (1996) 'Editorial: The helping alliance in work with families where children have been abused or neglected.' *Child Abuse and Neglect 20*, 4, 345–347.

Jones, J. and Gupta, A. (1998) 'The Context of decision-making in cases of child neglect.' *Child Abuse Review 7*, 2, 97–110.

Jones, L. (1998) 'The social and family correlates of successful reunification of children in foster care.' *Children and Youth Services Review 20*, 4, 305–323.

Jowitt, S. (2003) *Child Neglect: Contemporary Themes and Issues.* London: Bridge Publishing House.

Kelleher, K., Chaffin, M., Hollenberg, J., and Fischer, E. (1994). 'Alcohol and drug disorders among physically abusive and neglectful parents in a community-based sample.' *American Journal of Public Health 84*, 10, 1586–1590.

Kendall-Tackett, K. and Eckenrode, J. (1996) 'The effects of neglect on academic achievement and disciplinary problems: a developmental perspective.' *Child Abuse and Neglect 20*, 3, 161–169.

Kennedy, M. (1995) 'Perceptions of Abused Disabled Children.' In K. Wilson and A. James (eds) *The Child Protection Handbook.* London: Baillière Tindall.

Knutson, J.F., DeGarmo, D., Koeppl, G. and Reid, J.B. (2005) 'Care neglect, supervisory neglect, and harsh parenting in the development of children's aggression: A replication and extension.' *Child Maltreatment 10*, 2, 92–107.

Korbin, J. (1991) 'Cross-cultural perspectives and research directions for the twenty-first century.' *Child Abuse and Neglect 15*, Suppl. 1, 67–77.

Korbin, J. and Spilsbury, J. (1999) 'Cultural Competence and Child Neglect.' In H. Dubowitz (ed.) *Neglected Children: Research, Practice and Policy.* Thousand Oaks, CA: Sage.

Kotch, J.B., Browne, D.C., Ringwalt, C.L. and Stewart, P.W. (1995) 'Risk of child abuse and neglect in a cohort of low-income children.' *Child Abuse and Neglect 19*, 9, 1115–1130.

Kotch, J.B., Lewis, T., Hussey, J.M., English, D. *et al.* (2008) 'The importance of early neglect for childhood aggression.' *Pediatrics 121*, 4, 725–731.

Kroll, B. and Taylor, A. (2003) *Parental Substance Misuse and Child Welfare.* London: Jessica Kingsley Publishers.

Kurtz, P., Guadin, J., Wordaski, J. and Howing. P. (1993) 'Maltreatment and the school-age child: School performance consequences.' *Child Abuse and Neglect 17*, 5, 581–589.

Laming (2003) *The Victoria Climbié Inquiry: Report of an Inquiry by Lord Laming.* Cm 5730. London: The Stationery Office.

Laming (2009) *The Protection of Children in England: A Progress Report.* London: The Stationery Office.

Lewandowski, C.A., and Pierce, L. (2002) 'Assessing the effect of family-centered out-of home care on reunification outcomes.' *Research on Social Work Practice 12*, 2, 205–221.

London Borough of Brent (1985) *A Child in Trust.* The Report of the Panel of Inquiry into the Circumstances Surrounding the Death of Jasmine Beckford. London: London Borough of Brent.

London Borough of Greenwich (1987) *A Child in Mind: The Protection of Children in a Responsible Society.* The Report of the Commission of Inquiry into the Circumstances Surrounding the Death of Kimberley Carlile. London: London Borough of Greenwich.

London Borough of Lambeth (1987) *Whose Child?* The Report of the Panel Appointed to Inquire into the Death of Tyra Henry. London: London Borough of Lambeth.

Lynksey, M.T., Fergusson, D.M. and Horwood, J.L. (1994) 'The effects of parental alcohol problems on the rates of adolescent psychiatric disorders.' *Addiction* 89, 10, 1277–1286.

Macdonald, G. (2005) 'Intervening with Neglect.' In J. Taylor and B. Daniel (eds) *Child Neglect: Practice Issues for Health and Social Care.* London: Jessica Kingsley Publishers.

Maluccio, A.N. and Ainsworth, F. (2003) 'Drug use by parents: A challenge for family reunification practice.' *Children and Youth Services Review 25*, 7, 511–533.

Margolin, L. (1990) 'Fatal child neglect.' *Child Welfare 69*, 4, 309–319.

Masson, J. (2002) 'Police protection protecting whom?' *Journal of Social Welfare and Family Law 24*, 2, 157–174.

Masson, J., McGovern, D., Pick, K. and Winn Oakley, M. (2007) *Protecting Powers: Emergency Intervention for Children's Protection.* Chichester: Wiley.

Masson, J.M., Bailey-Harris, R. and Probert, R. (2008a) *Cretney's Principles of Family Law, 8th Edition.* London: Sweet and Maxwell.

Masson, J., Pearce, J. and Bader, K. with Joyner, O. *et al.* (2008b) *Care Profiling Study.* Ministry of Justice Research Series, 4/08. London: Ministry of Justice.

McConnell, D. and Llewellyn, G. (2002) 'Stereotypes, parents with intellectual disability and child protection.' *Journal of Social Welfare and Family Law 24*, 3, 297–317.

McGee, R.A., Wolfe, D.A., Yuen, S.A., Wilson, S.K. and Carnochan, J. (1995) 'The measurement of maltreatment: A comparison of approaches.' *Child Abuse and Neglect 19*, 2, 233–49.

McGlone, F., Park, A. and Roberts, C. (1996) 'Relative Values: Kinship and Friendship.' In R. Jowell, J. Curtice, A. Park, L. Brook and K. Thomson (eds) *British Social Attitudes: 13th Report*, 53–72. Dartmouth: Dartmouth Publishing Co.

McGuigan, W.M. and Pratt, C.C. (2001) 'The predictive impact of domestic violence on three types of child maltreatment.' *Child Abuse and Neglect 25*, 7, 869–883.

McSherry, D. (2004) 'Which came first, the chicken or the egg? Examining the relationship between child neglect and poverty.' *British Journal of Social Work 34*, 5, 727–733.

Miller, L.B. and Fisher, T. (1992) 'Some obstacles to the effective investigation and registration of children at risk. Issues gleaned from a worker's perspective.' *Journal of Social Work Practice 6*, 2, 129–140.

Minty, B. (2005) 'The Nature of Emotional Child Neglect and Abuse.' In J. Taylor and B. Daniel (eds) *Practice Issues for Health and Social Care*. London: Jessica Kingsley Publishers.

Minty, B. and Pattinson, G. (1994) 'The nature of child neglect.' *British Journal of Social Work 24*, 6, 733–747.

Moore, J. (1985) *The ABC of Child Abuse*. Aldershot: Gower.

Morris, J. (1998a) *Still Missing? Vol. 1: The Experiences of Disabled Children Living Away From Their Families*. London: The Who Cares? Trust.

Morris, J. (1998b) *Still Missing? Vol. 2: Disabled Children and the Children Act*. London: The Who Cares? Trust.

Moyers, S., Farmer, E. and Lipscombe, J. (2006) 'Contact with family members and its impact on adolescents and their foster placements.' *British Journal of Social Work 36*, 4, 541–559.

Munro, E. (1996) 'Avoidable and unavoidable mistakes in child protection work.' *British Journal of Social Work 26*, 6, 793–808.

Munro, E. (1998) 'Improving social workers' knowledge base in child protection work.' *British Journal of Social Work 28*, 1, 89–105.

Munro, E. (1999) 'Common errors of reasoning in child protection work.' *Child Abuse and Neglect 23*, 8, 745–758.

Munro, E. (2005a) 'A systems approach to investigating child abuse deaths.' *British Journal of Social Work 35*, 4, 531–546.

Munro, E. (2005b) 'What tools do we need to improve identification of child abuse?' *Child Abuse Review 14*, 6, 374–388.

Munro, E. (2011) *The Munro Review of Child Protection: Final Report: A Child-Centred System*. Cm 8062. London: The Stationery Office.

Nottinghamshire Safeguarding Children Board (2009) *Serious Case Review Executive Summary Relating to Sarah*. Nottingham: Nottinghamshire Safeguarding Children Board.

NSPCC (2003) *It Doesn't Happen to Disabled Children*. Report of the National Working Group on Child Protection and Disability. London: NSPCC.

O'Hagan, K. and Dillenburger, K. (1995) *The Abuse of Women within Childcare Work*. Buckingham: Open University Press.

Olds, D.L. (2006) 'The nurse-family partnership: An evidence-based preventive intervention.' *Infant Mental Health Journal 27*, 1, 5–25.

Packman, J. and Hall, C. (1998) *From Care to Accommodation: Support, Protection and Control in Child Care Services*. London: The Stationery Office.

Parker, R., 'A Brief History of Child Protection' in Farmer and Owen (1995) *Child Protection Practice: Private Risks and Public Remedies*. London: HMSO.

Parton, N. and Mathews, R. (2001) 'New directions in child protection and family support in Western Australia: A policy initiative to re-focus child welfare practice.' *Child and Family Social Work 6*, 2, 97–113.

Paul, A. and Cawson, P. (2002) 'Safeguarding disabled children in residential settings: What we know and what we don't know.' *Child Abuse Review 11*, 5, 262–281.

Paul, A., Cawson, P. and Paton, J. (2004) *Safeguarding Disabled Children in Residential Special Schools.* London: NSPCC.

Pearce, J.F., Masson, J.M. and Bader, K.F. (2011) *Just Following Instructions? The Representation of Parents in Care Proceedings.* Bristol: School of Law, University of Bristol.

Perez, C.M., and Widom, C.S. (1994). 'Childhood victimization and long term intellectual and academic outcomes.' *Child Abuse and Neglect 18*, 8, 617–633.

Perry, B. (2000) 'The neuroarcheology of childhood maltreatment: The neurodevelopmental costs of adverse childhood events.' In B. Geffner (ed.) *The Cost of Child Maltreatment: Who Pays? We All Do.* New York: Haworth Press.

Platt, D. (2007) 'Congruence and co-operation in social workers' assessments of children in need.' *Child and Family Social Work 12*, 4, 326–335.

Polansky, N.A., Guadin J.M., Ammons P. W. and Davis K.B. (1985) 'The psychological effect of the neglectful mother.' *Child Abuse and Neglect 9*, 265–275.

Pollak, S.D., Cicchetti, D., Hornung, K. and Reed, A. (2000) 'Recognizing emotion in faces: Developmental effects of child abuse and neglect.' *Developmental Psychology 36*, 679–688.

Prime Minister's Strategy Unit (2004) *Alcohol Harm Reduction Strategy for England.* London: Cabinet Office. Available at www.cabinetoffice.gov.uk/strategy/work_areas/alcohol_misuse. aspx, accessed on 27 March 2012.

Quinton, D. (2004) *Supporting Parents: Messages from Research.* London: Jessica Kingsley Publishers.

Quinton, D., Rushton, A., Dance, C. and Mayes, D. (1998) *Joining New Families: A Study of Adoption and Fostering in Middle Childhood.* Chichester: Wiley.

Radford, L., Corral, S., Bradley, C., Fisher, H. *et al.* (2011) *Child Abuse and Neglect in the UK Today.* London: NSPCC.

Radford, L. and Hester, M. (2006) *Mothering Through Domestic Violence.* London: Jessica Kingsley Publishers.

Re E (Care Proceedings: Social Work Practice) (2000) 2 FLR 254 (per Bracewell J), at 256.

Re K and H (2007) 1 FLR 2043, para 16.

Re L (2007) EWHC 3505 (per Ryder J).

Re L-A (2009) EWCA Civ 822.

Reder, P. and Duncan, S. (1999) *Lost Innocents: A Follow-up Study of Fatal Child Abuse.* London: Routledge.

Reder, P., Duncan, S. and Gray, M. (1993) *Beyond Blame: Child Abuse Tragedies Revisited.* London: Routledge.

Rees, G., Stein, M., Hicks, L. and Gorin, S. (2011) *Adolescent Neglect: Research, Policy and Practice.* London: Jessica Kingsley Publishers.

Rixon, A. and Turney, D. (2007) 'Safeguarding.' In M. Robb (ed.) *Youth in Context: Frameworks, Settings and Encounters.* London: Open University Press/Sage.

Rose, W. and Barnes, J. (2008) *Improving Safeguarding Practice: Study of Serious Case Reviews 2001–2003.* London: Department for Children, Schools and Families.

Ryan, M. (2000) *Working with Fathers.* Abingdon: Radcliffe Medical Press Ltd (for the Department of Health).

Ryan, M., Harwin, J. and Chamberlain, C. (2006) *Report on The Feasibility of Establishing a Family Drug and Alcohol Court at Wells St Family Proceedings Court.* Prepared for LB Islington, Westminster, CAFCASS, Wells St Inner London FPC and Brunel University.

Sanders, R., Colton, M. and Roberts, S. (1999) 'Child abuse fatalities and cases of extreme concern: Lessons from reviews.' *Child Abuse and Neglect 23*, 3, 257–268.

Schofield, G., Thoburn, J., Howell, D. and Dickens, J. (2007) 'The search for stability and permanence: Modelling the pathways of long-stay looked after children.' *British Journal of Social Work 37*, 4, 619–642.

Schuerman, J.R., Rzepnicki, T.L. and Johnson, P.R. (1994) *Outcomes in Evaluation of the 'Family First' Reunification Program of the Department of Children and Family Services.* Final Report. Chicago, IL: Chapin Hall Center for Children at the University of Chicago.

Scourfield, J. (2006) 'The challenge of engaging fathers in the child protection process.' *Critical Social Policy 26*, 2, 440–449.

Secker, J. (1993) *From Theory to Practice in Social Work.* Aldershot: Avebury.

Secretary of State for Social Services (1974) *Report of the Committee of Inquiry into the Care and Supervision Provided in Relation to Maria Colwell.* London: HMSO.

Selwyn, J., Sturgess, W., Quinton, D. and Baxter, C. (2006) *Costs and Outcomes of Non-Infant Adoptions.* London: BAAF.

Sheldon, B. (1987) 'The Psychology of Incompetence.' In Department of Social Policy and Social Science, Royal Holloway and Bedford New College (eds) *After Beckford? Essays on Themes Related to Child Abuse.* Egham: Department of Social Policy and Social Science, Royal Holloway and Bedford New College.

Sheppard, M. (1997) 'Double jeopardy: The link between child abuse and maternal depression in child and family social work.' *Child and Family Social Work 2*, 2, 91–107.

Shipman, K., Edwards, A., Brown, A., Swisher, L. and Jennings, E. (2005) 'Managing emotion in a maltreating context: A pilot study examining child neglect.' *Child Abuse and Neglect 29*, 9, 1015–1029.

Sinclair, I., Baker, C., Lee, J. and Gibbs, I. (2008) *The Pursuit of Permanence: A Study of the English Care System.* London: Jessica Kingsley Publishers.

Sinclair, R. and Bullock, R. (2002) *Learning from Past Experience: A Review of Serious Case Reviews.* London: Department of Health.

Smith, C.A., Ireland, T.O. and Thornberry, T.P. (2005) 'Adolescent maltreatment and its impact on young adult antisocial behavior.' *Child Abuse and Neglect 29*, 10, 1099–1119.

Smith, G. (1995) *The Protectors' Handbook. Reducing the Risk of Child Sexual Abuse and Helping Children Recover.* London: The Women's Press.

Smith, J. (1992) *Report of the Scotforth House Inquiry.* Lancaster: Lancaster County Council.

Sobsey, D. and Doe, T. (1991) 'Patterns of sexual abuse and assault.' *Sexuality and Disability 9*, 3, 243–259.

Srivastava, P., Stewart, J. and Ayres, P. (2005) 'Common Operational Approach Using the 'Graded Care Profile' in Cases of Neglect.' In J. Taylor and B. Daniel (eds) *Child Neglect: Practice Issues for Health and Social Care.* London: Jessica Kingsley Publishers.

Stanley, J. and Goddard, C. (2002) *In the Firing Line: Violence and Power in Child Protection Work.* New York, NY: Wiley.

Stevenson, O. (2005) 'Working Together in Cases of Neglect: Key Issues.' In J. Taylor and B. Daniel (eds) *Child Neglect: Practice Issues for Health and Social Care.* London: Jessica Kingsley Publishers.

Stevenson, O. (2007) *Neglected Children and Their Families (Second edition).* Oxford: Blackwell.

Stone, W. (1998) *Child Neglect: Practitioners' Perspectives.* London: NSPCC.

Stuart, M. and Baines, C. (2004a) *Progress on Safeguards for Children Living Away from Home.* York: Joseph Rowntree Foundation.

Stuart, M. and Baines, C. (2004b) *Safeguards for Vulnerable Children: Three Studies on Abusers, Disabled Children and Children in Prison.* York: Joseph Rowntree Foundation.

Sullivan, M.W., Bennett, D.S., Carpenter, K. and Lewis. M. (2008) 'Emotion knowledge in young neglected children.' *Child Maltreatment 13*, 3, 301–306.

Sullivan, P., Vernon, M. and Scanlon, J. (1987) 'Sexual abuse of deaf youth.' *American Annals of the Deaf 132*, 4, 256–262.

Sullivan, P.M. and Knutson, J.F. (2000) 'Maltreatment and disabilities: A population-based epidemiological study.' *Child Abuse and Neglect 24*, 10, 1257–1273.

Sullivan, S. (2000) *Child Neglect: Current Definitions and Models. A Review of the Literature.* Ottawa: Family Violence Prevention Unit.

Tanner, K. and Turney, D. (2003) 'What do we know about child neglect? A critical review of the literature and its application to social work practice.' *Child and Family Social Work 8*, 1, 25–34.

Tarleton, B., Ward, L. and Horwath, J. (2006) *Finding the Right Support: A Review of Issues and Positive Practice to Support Parents with Learning Difficulties and their Children.* London: Baring Foundation. Available at www.bristol.ac.uk/norahfry/research/completed-projects/rightsupport.pdf, accessed on 28 March 2012.

Terling, T. (1999) 'The efficacy of family reunification practices: Re-entry rates and correlates of re-entry for abused and neglected children reunited with their families.' *Child Abuse and Neglect 23*, 12, 1359–1370.

Thoburn, J. and Lewis, A. (1996) 'Significant harm and children's experiences of domestic violence.' *Child and Family Social Work 1*, 1, 33–42.

Thoburn, J., Wilding, J. and Watson, J. (2000) *Family Support in Cases of Emotional Maltreatment and Neglect.* Norwich: The Stationery Office.

Thornberry, T.P., Ireland, T.O. and Smith, C.A. (2001) 'The importance of timing: The varying impact of childhood and adolescent maltreatment on multiple problem outcomes.' *Development and Psychopathology 13*, 957–979.

Thorpe, D. (1994) *Evaluating Child Protection.* Milton Keynes: Open University Press.

Triseliotis, J., Borland, M., Hill, M. and Lambert, L. (1995) *Teenagers and the Social Work Services.* London: HMSO.

Trotter, C. (2002) 'Worker skill and client outcome in child protection.' *Child Abuse Review 11*, 1, 38–50.

Tunnard, J. (2002a) *Parental Drug Misuse: A Review of Impact and Intervention Studies.* Totnes: Research in Practice.

Tunnard, J. (2002b) *Parental Problem Drinking and its Impact on Children.* Dartington: Research in Practice.

Tunstill, J., Blewett, J. and Meadows, P. (2009) *Evaluating the Delivery by Action for Children of Targeted Family Support.* London: Synergy Research and Consulting Ltd.

Turnell, A. and Edwards, S. (1997) 'Aspiring to partnership: The Signs of Safety approach to child protection.' *Child Abuse Review 6*, 3, 179–190.

Turney, D., Platt, D., Selwyn, J. and Farmer, E. (2011) *Improving Child and Family Assessment: Turning Research into Practice.* London: Jessica Kingsley Publishers.

Tymchuk, A. (1992) 'Predicting adequacy of parenting by people with mental retardation.' *Child Abuse and Neglect 16*, 2, 165–178.

Tymchuk, A. and Andron, L. (1990) 'Mothers with mental retardation who do or do not abuse or neglect their children.' *Child Abuse and Neglect 14*, 3, 313–323.

Utting, W., Baines, C., Stuart, M., Rowlands, J. and Vialva, R. (1997) *People Like Us: The Report of the Review of the Safeguards for Children Living Away From Home.* London: The Stationery Office.

Velleman, R. (1993) *Alcohol and the Family.* London: Institute of Alcohol Studies.

Velleman, R. (2002) 'The Children of Problem Drinking Parents: An Executive Summary.' *Executive Summary Series; Centre for Research on Drugs and Health Behaviour, Executive Summary 70*, 1–5.

Velleman, R. and Orford, J. (1999) *Risk and Resilience: Adults Who Were the Children of Problem Drinkers.* Amsterdam: OPA.

Wade, J., Biehal, N., Farrelly, N. and Sinclair, I. (2011) *Caring for Abused and Neglected Children: Making the Right Decision for Reunification or Long-Term Care.* London: Jessica Kingsley Publishers.

Walker, M. and Glasgow, M. (2005) 'Parental Substance Misuse and the Implications for Children: Lessons from Research and Practice in One Centre.' In J. Taylor and B. Daniel (eds) *Child Neglect: Practice Issues for Health and Social Care.* London: Jessica Kingsley Publishers.

Ward, H. (ed.) (1995) *Looking After Children: Research into Practice.* The Second Report to the Department of Health on Assessing Outcomes in Child Care. London: HMSO.

Ward, H., Brown, R., Westlake, D. (2011) *Safeguarding Babies and Very Young Children from Abuse and Neglect.* London: Jessica Kingsley Publishers.

Ward, H., Munro, E.R. and Dearden, C. (2006) *Babies and Young Children in Care: Pathways, Decision-Making and Practice.* London: Jessica Kingsley Publishers.

Ward, H., Munro, E.R., Dearden, C. and Nicholson, D. (2003) *Outcomes for Looked After Children: Life Pathways and Decision-Making for Very Young Children in Care or Accommodation.* Loughborough University: Centre for Child and Family Research.

Wells, K. and Guo, S. (1999) 'Reunification and re-entry of foster children.' *Children and Youth Services Review 21,* 4, 273–294.

Westcott, H. (1993) *Abuse of Children and Adults with Disabilities.* London: NSPCC.

Westcott, H. and Cross, M. (1996) *This Far and No Further: Towards Ending the Abuse of Disabled Children.* Birmingham: Venture Press.

Who Cares? Trust, The (2006) *The Journey Home: How Children's Services Can Support the Reunification of Children with their Families.* London: The Who Cares? Trust.

Wilding, J. and Thoburn. J. (1997) 'Family support plans for neglected and emotionally maltreated children.' *Child Abuse Review 6,* 5, 343–356.

Subject Index

Note: page numbers in italics refer to figures, tables and boxes.

abuse and neglect, final three-year period *141*
AD and OD v. United Kingdom 110
adolescents
    behavioural difficulties 96
    child protection plans 76
    see also children; young people
adversities
    final three-year period 143–5, *145*
    number of 44–5, *45*, 181–2
    and well-being 176, 179, 194–5
age of child
    and appropriateness of support 57
    and number of types of support 53
    and severity of neglect 43
    and stability 171, 174, 175, 193, 194
    summary of findings 195–6
    and support for parents 49
    and well-being 176, 194–5
agencies, cooperation 56
aggression 46
aims, follow-up study 24–5
alcohol misuse 83
    evaluation of support 50
    failure to address 69
    help for 47, 200–1
    parents 16
    treatment 128–9
    and well-being 195
Alcoholics Anonymous 129
anti-social behaviour 39
assessments 185
    lack of 66
    position of local authority 65
    problematic 81–2
    quality of 19
    social work assessments 64
    specialist assessments 64–5
    timing 63–4
    types 63
attachments, development of 13
audits 205
avoidance 88–9

behavioural difficulties 95–6
    failure to address 69–70
    and stability 171, 193

and well-being 176, 178, 179, 195
black and minority ethnic (BME) children
    stability and well-being *168*
    well-being 179
black and minority ethnic (BME) families 17–18
    see also ethnicity

CAMHS 116
Care Matters: Time for Change 198
care orders 189, 207–8
    and case management 100
    final three-year period 143
    unsafe returns 79–80
Care Planning, Placement and Case Review Regulations 198–9
care proceedings 77–84, 188–9
    delay 79
    final three-year period 143
    insufficient evidence 78, 101
    lack of 77
    lack of action following unsuccessful returns 84–5
    problematic assessments 81–2
    unsafe returns 79–80
    use of 207–8
care system
    children's early experiences 34
    containing children 96
    experiences of 17–18
care, views of children/young people 134
carers, children's relationships with 145
case closure, inappropriate 93, 187, 208
case file sample, characteristics *32*
case files, reviews and summaries 27–8
case management 18–20
    adequacy of follow-up 66–9
    assessments 63–6, 185
    care proceedings 77–84
    case planning 85–6
    change of social worker 94–5
    criticism in case files 105–10
    dealing with neglect 185–7
    disagreement with decision to return children 108
    disagreements and criticisms 109
    drift 95

effectiveness 189–1
engagement with parents and children 185
errors 201–3
and ethnicity 92–3, 186, 196–7
expectations of parental standards 186
failure to contain children 95–6
failure to safeguard 70–3
findings 184–7
five year outcomes 208–9
focus of concern 60–1
inappropriate case closure 93, 187, 208
interim care orders 78
intervention triggers 61–3
knowledge of cases 186
lack of action following unsuccessful returns 84–5
lack of response to referrals 109–10
overall criticism 105–6
overview 60
parents given too many chances 186
passive 100–4, 190
passive then proactive 98–9, 189–90
planning and safety 208
plans for permanence 85
practice monitoring 206–7
proactive 104–5, 190–1
proactive then passive 99–100, 190
problems not addressed 69–70
repeated attempts to return home 72
responding to referrals 184
and stability 171–2, 193
supervision orders 82–3, 84
threatening behaviour 103–4
thresholds for intervention 203–4
unallocated cases 93–4
unsafe returns 79–80
variability of safeguarding 72
and well-being 176–7, 179
case planning 85–6, 189
cases
    Abdullah and Falzah *41*
    Adam 104–5
    Ailsa 68
    Alan 61–2, 72

Author Index